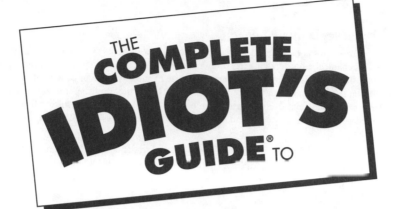

# Spies and Espionage

*by Rodney Carlisle, Ph.D.*

International Standard Book Number: 0-02-864418-2
Library of Congress Catalog Card Number: 2002117446

05   04   03      8   7   6   5   4   3   2   1

Interpretation of the printing code: The rightmost number of the first series of numbers is the year of the book's printing; the rightmost number of the second series of numbers is the number of the book's printing. For example, a printing code of 03-1 shows that the first printing occurred in 2003.

*Printed in the United States of America*

**Publisher:** *Marie Butler-Knight*
**Product Manager:** *Phil Kitchel*
**Senior Managing Editor:** *Jennifer Chisholm*
**Senior Acquisitions Editor:** *Randy Ladenheim-Gil*
**Development Editor:** *Michael Thomas*
**Production Editor:** *Billy Fields*
**Copy Editor:** *Cari Luna*
**Illustrator:** *Chris Eliopoulos*
**Cover/Book Designer:** *Trina Wurst*
**Indexer:** *Brad Herriman*
**Layout/Proofreading:** *Mary Hunt, Ayanna Lacey*

# Contents at a Glance

# Contents

# Foreword

"The King has note of all that they intend,
By interception which they dream not of"
William Shakespeare
Henry V Act II Scene 2

A key ingredient for effective decision-making by top officials of any country is fore-knowledge of external threats. It is vital to the protection of the national interests of the nation. Almost all nations, large or small, rich or poor, employ some system for obtaining and analyzing information about the world around them. To have as accurate and complete as possible an understanding of intentions, capabilities, and personalities of one's adversaries lies at the heart of intelligence. In one sense, intelligence is the information gathered and analyzed about world or battlefield conditions. It is often considered the first line of defense of a nation's efforts to protect itself in an uncertain world.

Intelligence is usually thought of in three major categories: (1) the collection and analysis of information; (2) covert action activities (activities designed to effect the affairs of other countries); and (3) counterintelligence (thwarting enemy intelligence activities).

Intelligence gathering is as old as civilization. Deciding what information to collect is an essential part of the intelligence process. Once it is determined what information is needed, the next step is to decide what method to use to collect it. Much of the data can be obtained through open (publicly available) sources. Some data, however, is concealed or protected by governments in order to keep their capabilities and intentions secret. To acquire this information requires secret methods—espionage.

For the actual collection of information intelligence services depend on three primary sources, the first overt and the second two covert. Most of the information governmental officials and intelligence agencies gather is publicly available. It includes diplomatic reports, government studies, newspaper and journal accounts, TV broadcasts, and library information. It is often referred to as open source collection. Covert or clandestine collection consists of human intelligence (HUMINT) and technical intelligence (TECHINT). HUMINT consists of classical espionage activities such as using spies, agents, and "sources." TECHINT relies on technological means for collection of the data—satellites, reconnaissance aircraft, wiretaps, and other visual and auditory devices. These systems may be used to photograph military bases or missile sites or to intercept communications or signals. The development of sophisticated overhead reconnaissance systems by the United States in the 1950s and 1960s revolutionized intelligence collection capabilities. These systems enabled the United States to monitor Soviet Union bomber and missile capabilities and developments.

Once the information is collected it needs to be analyzed. Although espionage activities and covert action operations garner most of the attention of the media and the general public, the main purpose of intelligence is to provide policymakers with up-to-date information derived from all sources of intelligence. The raw intelligence from all sources is processed into finished usable intelligence for policymakers. This is the key to accurate, objective, informative intelligence. Of course, policymakers often choose to ignore or disregard available finished intelligence reports. Further, for intelligence to be effective, it must reach decision makers in good time for them to act on it. Intelligence as foreknowledge has always had particular relevance in military matters. It can give a military commander a decisive advantage.

Intertwined with intelligence collection and analysis activities are often covert action operations and counterintelligence. Covert operations, also known as "special activities," include any operation designed to influence a foreign government, person, or event. This is done to promote a sponsoring government's foreign policy goals or objectives and is usually designed so as to keep the sponsoring government's role a secret. There are various types of covert action activities: propaganda, often called "psychological warfare"; secret financial and economic aid to friendly politicians or governments; and paramilitary or political actions designed to overthrow or support a regime, an individual, or an organization. A good example here is the U. S. government's secret invasion plans for Cuba at the Bay of Pigs in 1961.

Counterintelligence (CI) is often the overlooked aspect of the intelligence effort. Its purpose is to discover hostile foreign intelligence operations aimed at a country and to destroy their effectiveness; to guard against espionage, spying, and sabotage; and to protect the nation against infiltration by foreign agents. Offensively, it attempts to control and manipulate enemy intelligence operations. During World War II and the cold war, the United States became the primary target of espionage activities by the Soviet Union and its allies. To thwart these hostile activities and protect vital U. S. secrets, the U. S. government turned primarily to the Federal Bureau of Investigation (FBI). The FBI had the main responsibility for the collection and analysis of information relating to suspected subversives and monitoring the activities of suspected or confirmed foreign intelligence agents operating within the United States.

Intelligence services and their systems, by necessity, operate primarily in secret. Their activities are rarely publicized. Usually a country has to be defeated in war and its archives revealed before we get a true look at its activities. With the end of the cold war, however, there has been a proliferation of literature about foreign intelligence services and their operations. It is now possible to study their activities in some detail and to judge their impact on world conflicts and events.

Intelligence has had an enormous impact on international relations and world events. Yet, it is little understood or analyzed. The public view of intelligence and the role it plays in shaping foreign policy is often greatly distorted. TV, movies, novels, and newspapers and magazines all portray a selective, often twisted and misunderstood image of intelligence. For many, the fictional James Bond, high-tech espionage gadgets, secret operations, and Tom Clancy accounts characterize the world of intelligence. This widely held view is unfortunate. The role of espionage and intelligence in the formulating and conducting of foreign policy is complex and difficult to discern and understand. The basic operational concepts and terms used in espionage and intelligence issues are often confusing and difficult to get a handle on. The uniqueness, complexity, and value of intelligence often elude the general public.

Professor Rodney Carlisle has produced a remarkable reference tool for helping to understand the complex world of espionage and intelligence. Assembled entirely from the public record, this volume provides the reader or researcher clear and concise definitions and terms used in the intelligence field and offers a brief historical background on the use of espionage and intelligence in the modern period. He provides information on a host of modern day intelligence operations, espionage and counterespionage events, technological collection developments and cryptologic efforts. He offers insights into the role intelligence played and how world powers viewed and used intelligence. The world of intelligence, often confusing and secretive and often described as "a wilderness of mirrors," becomes much clearer with Professor Carlisle's important primer.

Gerald K. Haines
Former Chief Historian
Central Intelligence Agency

# Introduction

Spies and espionage are as old as human history, with references in the Bible and in Ancient Greek and Roman history to the adventures of spies and infiltrators, the military deceptions, secret messages, and traitors who passed intelligence to the enemy. Legends and myths of heroes and heroines of espionage from the American Revolution and the Civil War make for fascinating reading.

Before the twentieth century, such tales were highlights and sidelights to history, anecdotes and episodes that added color and human interest to the rise and fall of empires, but only rarely influenced the outcome of great events.

With our focus on spies and espionage, we leave a lot out. In the first place, the concentration in this book is on the twentieth century, and on spies and counter spies in Britain, the United States and Russia, with just an occasional glance at other countries. So if you want to learn about the intelligence operations of countries like Japan, China, India, or Pakistan, or ancient Babylon and Early Modern Europe, this is not the place. Since we focus on spies and espionage, we look at sources, agents, and their controllers, not on the back room operations of intelligence analysis that are so important to the correct usage of the raw data gathered in the field. We consider a few cases of good and bad analysis, but we're mostly concerned with the men and women who collected the information.

Espionage stories involve closely held secrets, loyalty and betrayal, adventure and mystery—all elements that have deep appeal to human nature. Such suspense-filled tales seem to waft, like exotic tropical breezes, through the sometimes dusty and dry pages of real history. But in the twentieth century, the outcome of many great world events hinged on moments of treason and betrayal, courage and corruption, that characterize the craft of intelligence.

In Room 40 of the British Admiralty building, code-breakers deciphered the Zimmermann Note, which probably pushed the United States over the final brink into World War I in 1917. When Germany prepared to attack the Soviet Union in June 1941, Stalin was warned by a network of spies, but failed to heed the warnings. When Japan attacked the United States in 1941, Congress searched for an intelligence scapegoat to blame for leaving the battleships as sitting ducks. The British and Americans used dozens of deceptions to pass false clues to the Germans in World War II to help conceal invasion routes. Soviet spies penetrated the highest levels of the British and American governments, and several worked to pass secret designs of the atom bomb to Moscow during and after World War II.

During the cold war that lasted from 1947 to 1988, nearly every year saw multiple spy scandals. From the revelations of the work of Klaus Fuchs, Elizabeth Bentley, Alger Hiss, Ruth Kuczynski, John Walker, and Christopher Boyce to the notorious Cambridge Five in Britain and the intelligence sources like Igor Gouzenko and Oleg Penkovsky, it was the spies and traitors whose successes and failures tell the tales of the confrontation between the Soviets and the West. Behind the men and women spies, the deeply cloaked agencies lurked, with master controllers dangling the strings to the figures on the stage. The American CIA and the British MI-5 and MI-6 engaged in a quiet but often deadly war against the Soviet KGB and GRU.

Despite the revelations that came after the cold war ended, giving ever more details about the spies of the prior four decades, it turned out that Russia still sought spies in the heart of America's own intelligence agencies, the CIA and the FBI. Catching them was made even harder by the fact that the traitors, because of their positions, could keep close watch on the investigators who tried to expose them.

Finding your way through all these characters and agencies and crucial influences on world outcomes requires a roadmap, and this book is the right place to start. The work puts the agencies in perspective, constructs the context, and reveals the roles of the important spies, ranging from the slick professionals to the bumbling amateurs.

*The Complete Idiot's Guide to Spies and Espionage* is not an encyclopedia of espionage, but it is a good place to learn the language, discover the patterns, and see the real spies. Some of the adventures of James Bond and even of Maxwell Smart were based on facts, and this book helps you spot the remnants of reality behind the fanciful fictions.

**Part 1, "The Roots of Modern Spying:"** In this part we look briefly at earlier eras of spying, and identify some of the legendary spies of the American Revolution and the Civil War. Then we turn to the period during and after World War I, and tell the stories of Mata Hari, Sidney Reilly, the Fraulein Doktor, and others. In Russia, the Cheka, under Feliks Dhzerzhinsky, sets the precedents for the agencies that will follow. We learn the story of Herbert Yardley, and then look at the major code-cracking work in England and the United States in the first years of World War II.

**Part 2, "Spying in World War II:"** In this part, we learn about the deceptions in World War II, some of the spies and spy rings, and the masterful breaking of the *Enigma Machine* codes that shaped events. CICERO, the actual character behind the classic film *Five Fingers*, spied for Germany in Turkey, while the little-known Allied double agent Juan Pujol was so good at deceiving Hitler that the Germans gave him a medal.

The United States established the Office of Strategic Services under "Wild Bill Donovan," setting precedents for later operations. The Soviet Union built up a network of spies and undercover agents often deeply dedicated to their ideology. Richard Sorge and Ruth Kuczynski were among the best, but some others failed miserably or changed sides.

**Part 3, "Spying During the Early Cold War:"** As the cold war began, Americans discovered that the Soviet Union had planted spies inside the Manhattan Project to learn how the atomic bomb was designed. Meanwhile, Russian moles burrowed their way to the top of the British government. In the United States, President Harry Truman endorsed the establishment of a Central Intelligence Agency. We look at some of the early triumphs and fiascos of the new CIA.

**Part 4, "Espionage in Retreat:"** No sooner had the CIA begun to work around the world to offset Soviet influence than it came under criticism at home. Of course, the Soviet Union planted disinformation about the agency, but some of the CIA's mistakes earned embarrassment. When Gary Powers, flying a U-2 high over Russia, was shot down in 1960, the world was shocked. When a CIA-planned invasion of Cuba at the Bay of Pigs collapsed, President Kennedy took some of the blame. During and after the Vietnam War, a new wave of critics claimed that the intelligence establishment was out of control. U.S. agencies began to rely more on technical and signal intelligence, the gathering of information by satellites and other mechanical means. In the 1980s stories of Americans like John Walker and Christopher Boyce, who sold out to the Soviet Union, rocked the country.

**Part 5, "Retrospects and Prospects:"** After the cold war, both sides revealed batches of old secrets, leading to a fuller understanding of what had gone on over the prior 40 years. But spies kept spying. Two of the most highly placed informants for Russia were Aldrich Ames and Robert Hanssen. In 2001 and 2002, the United States confronted new threats. Then, with the terrorist attacks of September 11, American intelligence agencies faced new challenges. Some of the intelligence crises in the War on Terror were similar to earlier ones, of sorting through masses of data, coordinating information, "connecting the dots." Some of the retrospective lessons of twentieth century espionage would apply in the new world of the twenty-first century, but different intelligence challenges required new methods. Here we try to use the lessons of the past to peer through the dark glass that is the future.

# Extras

To help find your way through the mass of information, this book has a few little extras. In addition to the main story, illustrated with photographs from public and private espionage collections, there are some special tools. Definitions, life-story sketches, and technical details all have their own boxes.

### Techint

Lots of intelligence was gathered by technical means, that is, machinery, satellites, communications tapping, and other gadgets. Some of this *techint* gets defined in these boxes.

### Spy Bios

In addition to the longer stories of spies in the main text, included here are thumbnail views of some of them, ranging from the famous to the little known.

### Spy Words

The world of espionage developed its own jargon, and when a term is introduced, these boxes give a few words of definition. These definitions, together with a few dozen others, are rounded up in a glossary at the back of the book. Look out for microdots and SMERSH!

### Tradecraft

The techniques of espionage, ranging from how to make contact between an agent and control, to how to organize espionage cells, is called *tradecraft*, and these boxes provide some keys to the methods.

# Sorting Out Fact and Fiction

Since the facts of espionage involve all the elements of good mystery stories, like danger, risk, secrets only gradually revealed, bloodshed, and sometimes sex and romance, the real events often sound just like a fictional movie or novel. Furthermore, because espionage is by its nature a secret operation, getting the facts is often difficult, since methods and sources remain concealed for years or decades or forever. The story told one year may turn out, a few years later, to have been a planted rumor, superceded by a new account.

This book has relied on well-substantiated and balanced information, and has avoided the wilder speculation of conspiracy theories that thriller writers put together. The facts are interesting enough. The book tells the stories and talks about the cases that have been well substantiated, not the guesswork about what might have happened or who might have been behind a mystery yet unsolved.

The information presented in this book is all derived from *open literature*. Included in the text are references to key books, such as memoirs, biographies of spies, and some really great summaries of espionage operations. A list of about a hundred is gathered in the bibliography at the end of the book. Most of the books in the list make for fascinating nonfiction reading and are worth tracking down in a library or bookstore.

Nothing in this work is drawn from a document that is now classified. Some information however, came from secret document collections, like the *Venona Files* or the *Mitrokhin Archive* opened up after the cold war (see Chapter 19). Some of the open literature books and articles used have included information that the U.S. government will neither confirm nor deny.

I received support and help in the project from several sources. Elizabeth Knappman of New England Publishing Associates assisted in planning the work. Jeffery Dorwart, a colleague at Rutgers who has studied Naval Intelligence, encouraged me to teach a course in Modern Espionage and offered lots of ideas and concepts that I have boldly borrowed. The hundreds of students who passed through the course over the years raised some very thought-provoking questions. My beautiful and brilliant wife, Loretta, has reminded me to give recognition to the important women spies along with the men. Suggestions from Gerald K. Haines were very helpful. Michael Thomas, editor at Alpha Books, also made suggestions that helped a great deal. I thank them all.

Rodney Carlisle, Ph.D.
History Associates Incorporated, Rockville, Maryland
Professor Emeritus, Rutgers University

## Trademarks

All terms mentioned in this book that are known to be or are suspected of being trademarks or service marks have been appropriately capitalized. Alpha Books and Penguin Putnam Inc. cannot attest to the accuracy of this information. Use of a term in this book should not be regarded as affecting the validity of any trademark or service mark.

# Part 1

# The Roots of Modern Spying

Spies and secret codes are so much in the news these days that they must be something new, right? Wrong. The history of espionage and writing in codes can be traced through the centuries, alongside the history of warfare. Spies began to develop professional skills and more sophisticated systems of ciphers as early as the 1500s.

Here we look briefly at earlier eras of spying, and identify some of the legendary spies of the American Revolution and the Civil War. Through and after World War I, we look at spies like Mata Hari, Sidney Reilly, and Herbert Yardley. Then we look at the major code-cracking work in England and the United States in the first years of World War II.

# Spies and Espionage Before the Twentieth Century

## In This Chapter

- ◆ History undercover
- ◆ Civilian spies in early U.S. wars
- ◆ Beginnings of spy agencies
- ◆ Dawn of a new age

Although intelligence gathering was always crucial in time of war, and especially important on the battlefield or in a naval engagement, the activities of civilian spies rarely were well documented. Legends and tales of a few spies, both men and women, have come down through the ages, but it is not until the late nineteenth century that permanent intelligence agencies began to be established.

In this chapter, we'll take a quick look at the history of spies and espionage before the twentieth century. We review the highlights of a few of the famous tales of individual spies in the American Revolution (1775–1781) and the American Civil War (1861–1865). Then we look at the hesitant efforts of the U.S. government to move into establishing permanent means of gathering foreign intelligence, even in peacetime. Finally, we note some of the issues in intelligence that emerged at the dawn of the twentieth century.

# Problems in Spy History

Before the twentieth century, espionage tended to become important during periods of war or civil war. Governments did not maintain permanent peacetime espionage agencies. Instead, they relied on shifting arrangements of key advisors to the monarch or prime minister, paid informants, the reports of diplomats, and now and then, highly placed traitors.

The early history of spies, codes, decryption, betrayal, and deception by clandestine methods goes hand in hand with military and diplomatic history. As a history topic, the subject is a difficult one, since by its nature, *espionage* was rarely a matter of public record. If a civilian spy or traitor was detected and brought to trial, the case might draw some public attention. Yet the details were scarce in such cases, because the errors of the spy or the methods used to apprehend a traitor were best kept secret in case they might be used again in a later case. Successful espionage required that records be suppressed, and since historians prefer to write history from documents rather than folktales, the literature of early espionage is quite uneven.

**Spy Words**

**Espionage** is the act of spying. The word refers to a wide range of secret activities, including gathering secret intelligence through such means as interviews and the use of paid informers or traitors.

The history of *cryptography* has been somewhat easier to reconstruct from the survival of a number of manuals and treatises on the topic. Such works, lovingly collected from rare book dealers and auctions, show the evolution of ciphers. A noteworthy study that explores the use of ciphers and codes over the centuries is David Kahn's *The Codebreakers*.

**Spy Words**

**Cryptography** represents all the methods of concealing a message through the use of codes (with secret meanings for particular words) and systems of ciphers, which transpose individual letters into other letters or numbers. A cryptographer puts messages into secret codes and ciphers, and a cryptanalyst tries to break the codes and ciphers of the other side.

In a few cases, after a war was concluded, episodes of successful wartime espionage might be recounted in memoirs to capitalize on a career or to round out official histories by honoring previously unsung heroes. Such accounts could rarely be verified from source documents, and later writers usually have had to rely on secondhand accounts rather than released original documents. Episodes and anecdotes, often no more than legendary tales, repeated from text to text, leave the modern reader with lists of some civilian heroes and heroines, but little detail as to their methods, accomplishments, and their real importance to the outcome of battle.

Some close studies of battles show the role of tactical intelligence, secret communication, and good or bad methods of protecting information from the enemy. Often a study of a battle will show how the outcome was shaped by a good general, working with his staff. Such officers sometimes made crucial estimates of the enemy's troop disposition, movement, supplies and fighting capacity that illustrate, in retrospect, the function of intelligence and counterintelligence in warfare.

## A Glance Backward

Tales of codes, ciphers, spying, and traitors are found throughout history. In ages of conspiracy and war, the passing of secret messages was a matter of life and death. In the religious civil and international wars in Europe in the sixteenth century, enciphered messages and their decoding often played a part in matters of state. Mary Queen of Scots, for example, plotted to overthrow Elizabeth I, but her encoded messages arranging the assassination were uncovered and deciphered, leading to her own execution in 1587.

| Spy Bios |
| --- |
| John Dee was a secret agent for Elizabeth I, and a scientist, astrologer, and geographer. He often signed his documents *007*. Dee provided research for Sir Edward Dyer, an active go-between at the Elizabethan court. In 1597, Dyer was acting on behalf of the Privy Council in negotiations with the merchants of the Hanseatic League, a group of city-states mostly on the Baltic Sea. Dyer needed background on the rights of maritime trade, and Dee directed Dyer to sources he had written on the topic in 1576. Dee was a forerunner of later intelligence analysts who worked quietly at gathering and collating information and digesting it into briefing papers for statesmen. |

Nicholas Faunt, a secretary to Sir Francis Walsingham, secretary of state to Elizabeth, left a set of instructions on the gathering of intelligence that have provided a look into the espionage of the era. Faunt detailed how scholarly research into various types of documents could be used to glean intelligence. He distinguished between the value of documents such as opinions, advertisements, briefs, projects, and plots. Faunt spelled out the mutual relationship between what a modern age would call intelligence analysts and action officers.

Although spying was not organized into formal agencies at the period, Elizabeth's courtiers developed many of the techniques and patterns of later generations of spies.

Elizabethan officials kept men planted in the major cities of Europe, and paid them to send in regular intelligence reports. The networks were made up of people with official positions abroad, such as merchants' agents, as well as amateurs including young men simply acting as tourists, but sending back reports of foreign intelligence.

As espionage evolved and the exchange of key intelligence by courier expanded, it became ever more essential to develop methods of concealing the meaning of a written message in case it was captured. At almost the same time that Dyer, Walsingham, and Dee operated in Britain, in France, Henry of Navarre employed the mathematician François Viète to decode secret messages sent by King Philip of Spain to his French Catholic allies.

Intelligence gathering in the Age of Nelson, when Britain was almost constantly at war with France (1793–1815), was hardly more organized. However, in that period the collection of intelligence was primarily the task of diplomats, who performed on-scene observation, read the local press, and recruited agents when they had a chance. The British government supplemented this information with a system of opening the mails and diplomatic pouches and reading and decrypting the messages found in code operated through the post office. In the capitals of other governments, such as Vienna, the offices that engaged in rapid opening and decrypting of messages came to be known as *Black Chambers*.

### Spy Words

In the eighteenth century, a number of countries operated **Black Chambers,** but the most famous was the *Geheime Kabinets-Kanslei* of Vienna. Every morning the bags of mail to be delivered to embassies were brought to the chamber, where their seals were melted, the letters opened, and important sections copied, some by reading out loud and using shorthand for the copy. After copying, the letters were resealed with forged seals and were sent on their way within two or three hours. Regular mail was also examined, as was all the outgoing mail from the embassies. Anything in code was especially noted, and code-breakers received bonuses for cracking a new code.

During the naval wars between Britain and France, British naval officers developed an early form of breaking signal codes or *signals intelligence*. Raiding parties made quick sorties ashore to retrieve codebooks at shore-side fortifications and at semaphore stations. Then, with personnel planted ashore or with observation from sea, British naval officers could obtain valuable information about French fleet units. Another technique was to get recognition codes from captured or sunk vessels and provide the signals to British ships so that they could masquerade as French ships—a classic deception.

A problem noted by Admiral Lord Nelson and his contemporaries was that most intelligence was out-of-date by the time it was received. Although there were no intelligence staff officers attached to naval captains or admirals, some, like Nelson himself, were quite adept at collecting intelligence and including it in their planning.

**Spy Words**

Signals intelligence is a modern term that refers to information gathered from breaking or analyzing secret radio and telephonic communications used by a foreign power or illegal group.

# Some Spies of the American Revolution

Americans tend to forget that the American Revolution was also a domestic civil war, in which loyalists who favored remaining part of the British realm fought against patriots, who stood for independence. In almost every community, there were civilians committed to both sides. Thus when New York or Boston were controlled by the British and their loyalist allies, local patriots tried to smuggle details to their comrades beyond the cities.

Meanwhile, loyalists scattered through regions controlled by the patriots collecting information on troop movements and supplies, and establishing networks to get the information to the British. As in past eras, sending such messages required clandestine methods, codes, trusted couriers, and carefully arranged points in a network to hand off the messages in a relay system to the American or British general who could use them.

## Patriot Games: The Culper Ring

Perhaps the most famous American Revolution spy network was established at the order of George Washington in 1778. Benjamin Tallmadge set up the network in New York City, occupied by British forces. Tallmadge was extremely cautious, not even informing Washington of who the participants in his net were. There was no one named Culper, but SAMUEL CULPER was the code name for the group that included Robert Townsend, Aaron Woodhull, Austin Roe, Caleb Brewster, and at least one woman, Anna Strong.

Townsend went by the code name Culper Junior. He was a society reporter for a New York City newspaper and ran a small dry goods store. Through his reporting, he picked up details of troop information and made contacts with British officers. He could use the contacts for his store with customers and with other merchants and suppliers to relay information. Austin Roe would visit the shop from patriot-held Long Island, and leave a set of inquiries. Then Townsend would write a report that answered the questions and smuggle it out in goods carried by Roe. Roe used what later agents would call a *dead drop*, in a pasture where he tended his own cattle. Later, Woodhull (Culper Senior) would pick up the letter, add some details, and look for a signal from Anna Strong; Strong used clothes on a clothesline to indicate that Brewster, who served as a courier, was available to ferry the report across the bay to Fairfield, Connecticut. There the message would be carried by Tallmadge himself to Washington's headquarters in New Windsor, New York.

The elaborate scheme was almost fatal. One of the letters was intercepted by British troops, but fortunately all of the informants and couriers were identified only by code names. Later, Tallmadge used invisible ink.

### Spy Words

A **dead drop** or "drop box" is a location known to a spy and his contact, for leaving messages to be picked up. Since the exact location, which might be in a public park or in a public building, is known only to the spy and his contact, secret communications can be dropped off and picked up without either party being observed.

### Tradecraft

According to legend, Anna Strong used her clothesline to signal a courier that Caleb Brewster was available with a small boat to carry clandestine messages. She would hang out a black petticoat when Brewster's boat was in, and the number of handkerchiefs indicated at which particular bay or dock he could be found. The signal could be seen from across the bay. Culper Senior would wait until dark, then bring the encoded message to the proper cove to link up with Brewster. Later generations of spies would use similar innocent-appearing signals, sometimes chalking or taping a post, or placing a thumbtack on a certain pole in a public place.

## And the Tories

Benjamin Thompson, a noted colonial American scientist, was openly pro-British, and he had been run out of town in New Hampshire for sending British deserters back to British-controlled Boston for court-martial. Thompson settled in Woburn, Massachusetts, where he began to make secret reports to General Thomas Gage and later to General William Howe in Boston. Thompson reported on political details, such as the resolution by the Continental Congress to raise 30,000 men. When Howe evacuated Boston, Thompson sailed to England to help the British effort more directly, but he vanished after that, presumably lost at sea.

Benedict Arnold, the patriot general who switched sides to become a loyalist, was also involved, as might be expected, in a series of deceptions and secret messages that fall in the area of intelligence work. Arnold was disgruntled that he had not been promoted, and when Philadelphians accused him of profiteering, he decided to volunteer his services to the British.

In order to arrange his switching sides, Arnold met with Major John André. André proposed that Arnold remain nominally in the service of the patriot cause, but work as a double agent. Using both ciphers and codes, André explained the plot to a loyalist, Joseph Stanbury, who was to relay the plan to the British authorities. André was full of ideas on how to communicate secretly, including suggestions that Benedict Arnold's wife, Peggy Shippen, should write innocuous social letters with invisible writing in the spaces between the visible lines.

 **Tradecraft**

Using a copy of Blackstone's *Commentaries on the Laws of England*, André enciphered words by representing each word with three numbers: page in the book, number of the line on the page, and number of the word in the line. Without knowing the key book, the code would be impenetrable even if the message, written in invisible ink, were developed, since each word would be represented with numbers such as 187-8-8 (for "obliged") or 148-8-28 (for "intelligence") that would only make sense if you had the key. Often the invisible inks in those times were simple transparent dilute acids such as lemon juice that would emerge on the page when heated.

André was captured in September 1779, and the treachery of Arnold was revealed. Benedict Arnold was then openly appointed as a general in the British forces and led a couple of attacks in Virginia on behalf of the British. He evacuated with the British to Britain, where he died in 1801, never having received any significant or really important command in the British service.

The André letters and their layers of encipherment and encoding suggest some of the patterns of espionage, treason, and cryptography that would later lie behind the day-to-day headlines of the twentieth century.

# Heroes and Heroines in the Civil War

Civilian spies on both sides of the American Civil War were the stuff of legends. As in the Revolution, because both sides spoke the same language, and because civilians, both black and white, could readily pass as innocent bystanders to the action, several tales of spies survived the war.

Often spying was conducted by those least noticed because of the values of the time, including African Americans and white women. The principle that the preconceptions of the enemy provide the best shelter for espionage activities was played out over and over in the course of this war. Who would suspect a black servant, presumed to be ignorant by the racist standards of the day, of carefully eavesdropping and writing down the details of policy meetings? Who would imagine a white socialite, presumed to be wrapped up in questions of romance by the gentlemen officers she met at cotillions, would be spying for the other side?

In fact, both categories proved a rich source of volunteer civilian spies. The stories of such episodes became well remembered because they carried the implied morale: simple-minded prejudice can be more dangerous to the bigot than to the target of the bigotry.

## African American Agents for the Union

A major source of information for the Union during the Civil War came from debriefing runaway slaves and fugitives from the Confederacy. However, other African Americans provided assistance, often facilitated because the Confederates held them in low regard. Two black American servants in the household of Confederate President Jefferson Davis in Richmond were probably the most highly placed Union agents during the war.

Several African American spies for the Union cause:

♦ W. H. Ringgold. Ringgold was a free black man who had been impressed into service on a riverboat on the York River in Virginia. After six months' service, he was released, and made his way North. In Baltimore, he sought out Union officers and then provided detailed information on Confederate defenses on the York River, used in the peninsular campaigns of General George McClellan in 1862.

♦ William Jackson. Jackson was a slave hired out by the year, who served as coachman to Jefferson Davis. He carried reports of overheard conversations to Union lines near Fredericksburg, where they were telegraphed to the War Department in Washington.

◆ Mary Bowser. Mary Bowser had been a slave in the Van Lew family. Elizabeth Van Lew, who feigned eccentricity, headed a spy network in Richmond, and obtained a position for Bowser in the Davis household. Although she pretended to be ignorant, Mary Bowser was highly perceptive, and could read and write. She had a photographic memory and memorized documents, later reporting every word of them. Her contributions were recognized in 1995 (yes, 1995, not 1895!) with her induction into the U.S. Army Intelligence Hall of Fame at Fort Huachuca, Arizona.

◆ Dabney. A runaway slave, Dabney crossed Union lines with his wife and found work at the headquarters of General Hooker, near Fredericksburg, Virginia. Dabney's wife returned to work on the Confederate side of the lines. Soon Dabney began providing details of Confederate troop movements. His wife signaled him by hanging out laundry in a particular sequence, giving messages as to which commands had moved and in what direction. The story had such an appeal it was repeated over and over and became part of the legends associated with intelligence during the Civil War. Interestingly, the clothesline signaling system resembled that employed by Anna Strong in the Culper Ring some 80 years previously.

◆ Harriet Tubman. Tubman ran her own espionage and underground railroad escape networks. She had escaped slavery in Maryland and then organized escape routes for slaves prior to the war. In 1863, she began organizing short-term spying expeditions behind the lines in South Carolina. Disguised as a field hand or poor farm wife, she would observe details of troop movements and supply points. She reported to Colonel James Montgomery, who commanded a black unit, the Second South Carolina Volunteers. David Hunter, the general in command of all the Union forces in the area, asked Tubman to guide a raiding party. She led a group on June 2, 1863, past Confederate picket lines. The raid destroyed several million dollars of Confederate supplies, and led to freeing more than 800 slaves. When she died in 1913, she was given a full military funeral.

## White Women: Overlooked but Vigilant

Elizabeth Van Lew, known as Crazy Bet because of her eccentricities, not only convinced the Jefferson Davis household to take on Mary Bowser as a servant, but conducted considerable intelligence gathering on her own for the Union cause. Visiting Union prisoners of war to take food and medicine, she routinely questioned them about troop dispositions and fortifications they had observed and then routed her information to Generals Benjamin Butler and Ulysses Grant through a courier system that she established. Grant later rewarded her with the position of postmistress of Richmond, a job she held from 1869 to 1877.

Literally dozens of women spied for the Confederacy during the Civil War. A few became famous later, but many kept their stories quiet. However, two Southern women—Rose O'Neal Greenhow and Isabelle "Belle" Boyd—became famous in Britain for their exploits in the Confederate cause.

Rose O'Neal Greenhow was born in Montgomery County in Maryland, and had emerged as a leader in Washington high society. She passed a message to General Pierre Beauregard that helped him in his victory at the Battle of Manassas (known in the North as Bull Run). Jefferson Davis himself credited the victory to Greenhow. Apprehended in Washington, she was kept under house arrest, and then held in prison, but she continued to smuggle out encoded messages. Finally she was exiled to Richmond. She then toured Britain and France as a propagandist for the Confederates, and published her memoirs in Britain. Attempting to return to the Confederacy on a blockade-runner, her ship ran aground and she was lost. According to legend, the weight of gold from royalties on her book helped sink her off Wilmington, North Carolina, a tale that most authors would doubt. Her body was recovered and buried with military honors by the Confederates in October 1864.

Belle Boyd was born in Martinsburg, in what was then Virginia, now West Virginia. She entered Washington society at the age of 16, known for her beauty. When the war broke out she moved back to Martinsburg, and after Union forces occupied the town, she began feeding information gathered from the troops across the lines to Confederate officers. Her information was said to have aided Stonewall Jackson in driving Union troops from the Shenandoah Valley. After serving as a courier and scout, she was captured and then paroled. Like Greenhow, she went on a mission to England, with letters from Jefferson Davis. A Union Navy vessel seized her ship, and then the Union officer, Lt. Samuel Harding, smitten with her charm, released her and the Confederate master of the captured ship, who then sailed on to England with her. Lt. Harding was court-martialed, discharged, and then he sailed to Britain and married Belle Boyd. Like Greenhow, she wrote an account of her life. She went on stage where she recounted her life story and lived until 1900.

Since the accounts of both the Greenhow and Boyd exploits smacked of romantic novels of the era, some scholars have discounted their accuracy. Nevertheless, generations of readers have enjoyed the gothic qualities of stories like that of Belle Boyd, Crazy Bet Van Lew, and Rose O'Neal Greenhow and accept the colorful tales as truth stranger than fiction. Maybe so. Whether the details of the memoirs and legends were true, the stories certainly illustrate the point that the best cover for a spy is the prejudice of the intelligence target.

## Civil War Spies: Not All Were Amateurs

Not all intelligence gathering was done by the amateurs, heroes, and heroines of legend. In both Richmond and Washington, the war departments organized intelligence units. Jefferson Davis established a Signal Bureau that carried on correspondence in cipher with Confederate agents in key locations behind Union lines. Other Confederate officers for intelligence worked out of the president's office, out of the secretaries of war, and from the office of the provost marshal. Soon, the lack of coordination damaged the effort. Furthermore, without a concerted counterespionage system in the Confederacy, Union spies easily penetrated the seceding states.

The border between the Union and Confederacy was so porous it was relatively simple to run courier networks in both directions. Regular crossing points, such as that on the Potomac near the point where Highway 301 now crosses the river south of Washington, became so well known that they became semiformal ferry points for the exchange of postal mail. It was across that particular route that John Wilkes Booth fled after shooting Abraham Lincoln.

The Union, too, relied on a variety of offices. The Secret Service was established as a presidential bodyguard. The State Department and the War Department jostled for control of intelligence. The Pinkerton private detective agency was recruited to provide information. In both the North and the South, newspapers provided a ready source of information, since plans, schemes for deception, troop movements, and other vital information were often freely printed.

Numerous legends surround particular news stories read by a particular general that resulted in outwitting the enemy, on both sides. The legends appeal, because like the stories of black and female spies, they carry an instructive moral for later generations of spies: If information is crucial, be sure it doesn't leak to the press.

At the conclusion of the war, many records of espionage were destroyed. So what has survived has tended to be the stories of those who wrote their own memoirs, or who received official recognition. The memoirists probably sought to sensationalize their own importance, and those who were officially thanked may not have been the most important of the spies, but rather those whose cover was exposed and who had become notorious. For all of these reasons, it's a lot easier to accept the legends and enjoy them than to uncover the historical reality and to try to assess the specific effect of espionage on the outcome of events.

# Organizing Intelligence

Military officers study the history of battles to learn lessons that might be applied in future conflicts. The role of espionage and intelligence during the Civil War, even when filtered through the romanticized memoirs and cherished legends of the conflict, suggested several needs: better security, some systematizing of information, and a closer eye on presumably innocent civilian observers. But in the years immediately after the Civil War, both the Army and Navy tended to be more concerned with the issues of limited funding and lack of preparedness for war than with setting up intelligence bureaus. The first permanent intelligence agency in the United States was formed in the Navy in 1882, as part of a larger reform of the Navy.

## Navy Needs

Officers in the Navy understood that their careers and the defense of the United States depended on the ships and weapons of the fleet. Even more than the Army, the Navy was a technological service, concerned that its equipment be a match for that of any potential enemy. The development of iron-clad vessels in Europe in the decade before the American Civil War, and then the clash of the USS *Monitor* with the CSS *Virginia* (the refitted *Merrimac*) brought home the question of technology for the post Civil War generation of naval officers. In the 15 years following the Civil War, naval officers nervously followed developments in Europe and South America, recognizing that American ships were outclassed by those of countries like Italy and Chile. By 1881, they convinced Congress to fund the modernization of the fleet with the construction of a new Navy, consisting of steel ships, powered by steam, and carrying new ordnance of rifled cannon, rather than the smoothbores of the Civil War era.

But modernization required technical information. Numerous officers recognized that it would be important to create an agency within the Navy to make sure that such information was current, competitive with that of other nations, and well utilized.

## Office of Naval Intelligence

The Secretary of the Navy established an Office of Naval Intelligence (ONI) in 1882. At first staffed with only a few officers and focused on technical information, the office expanded its role and mission, step by step, into that resembling a true intelligence agency. Following a method employed at the State Department to record information, ONI set up card files, detailing data on foreign shipbuilding, armor, weapons, mines, and signals systems. Getting the information at first simply required that officers visiting foreign ports send in reports on what they observed. The information mounted to a flood, including published materials, manuals, reports, plans, specifications, and other information.

The gathering methods were not so different from those employed in Elizabethan England. But there was an important exception. The ONI, unlike the officers of the British Privy Council, was a permanent institution, regularly funded, and capable of expansion and mission evolution. By the 1890s, ONI had a regular supply of information coming not only from officers in the fleet, but from naval attachés working in American embassies and ministries abroad. Instructions to the attachés spelled out exactly the kinds of information required and increasingly, the agents began to gather not only public documents, but also data copied or stolen by paid informants. Before the turn of the century, the rudiments of an American intelligence collection system were in place.

# Twentieth Century: A Glance Forward

In the brief Spanish American War, fought between April and August 1898, the United States emerged victorious, largely because the new reform-era ships of the U.S. Navy outclassed and outgunned the antiquated vessels of Spain. As a result of the war, the United States liberated Cuba from Spain, acquired from Spain the territories of Puerto Rico, Guam, and the Philippines, and at the same time established control over Hawaii. Suddenly, the United States was a world power, with holdings that placed new demands on the Navy and on the nation's need for international intelligence.

With its interest in the rapidly modernizing technology of warfare and closely following political developments, ONI was quick to learn of certain ominous threats on the horizon at the opening of the twentieth century. In the decade 1900–1910, it became clear that the wars of the future would be far different in their methods, in their level of devastation, and in their consequences.

## Impending Clash of Titans

ONI files began to bulge with reports on the naval arms race emerging between Germany and Great Britain. Ships were being built on a new scale, with weapons that could fire exploding shells more than five miles. Even more dangerous than the arms race itself were certain geo-political developments that presaged a changing world.

Germany, a latecomer to the race for colonies, was expanding its overseas holdings and both Germany and Britain sought influence in South America. Americans were building a canal across the Isthmus of Panama to aid in the defense of both coasts of the United States and to enable naval ships to reach both Caribbean and Pacific holdings. Japan, Americans were surprised to learn in 1905, defeated Russia in a brief war, creating a new major power in the Pacific. Rumors of Japanese and German snooping around Panama made for troubling reading.

## New Technologies

Future wars would be different because of three major developments in technology, closely followed by ONI. In 1895, the United States purchased its first submarine from John Holland. In 1901, Guglielmo Marconi demonstrated that wireless radio could be used to communicate across a distance of 2,000 miles. And in 1903, the Wright brothers demonstrated that manned heavier-than-air flight was possible. Submarines, radio, and aircraft would change the nature of warfare. It was quite possible, the visionaries of ONI noted, that each of these systems would create new opportunities and new problems for the gathering of intelligence. As you'll see when you read the rest of this book, they were right.

## The Least You Need to Know

- Before the end of the nineteenth century, intelligence was collected and used primarily during wartime.

- American civilians on both sides of the American Revolution and the Civil War became active spies, using encoded messages and secret networks.

- Although military commanders often used intelligence wisely, governments and military commands tended to be poor at counterespionage.

- The most famous tales of spies from the Civil War involve African Americans and white women whose espionage often went unsuspected because of the prejudices and preconceptions of the enemy.

- The first permanent American intelligence agency was the Office of Naval Intelligence (ONI), established in 1882.

# Chapter 2

# World War I Myths and Realities

## In This Chapter

- ◆ Central Powers, Allies, and neutrals
- ◆ Sidney Reilly, Feliks Dzherzhinsky, Mata Hari
- ◆ Cryptography and cryptanalysis
- ◆ Cheka and Black Chambers

In this chapter, we look at some of the legends and some of the actual cases of espionage that took place in "The Great War." To set the stage, we review the parties to the conflict and the chronology of events. From the American perspective, the United States tried to stay neutral, regarding the conflict as a European matter. We look at how both European sides used secret agents and espionage to try to affect the American position.

Britain, Russia, and the United States each set up some long-lasting organizations and began to work with techniques that would characterize modern espionage, especially secret messages and photographic reconnaissance. So we range from the romantic (and sometimes unbelievable) adventures of Mata Hari and Sidney Reilly, to the hard realities of code-cracking and photo interpretation.

# World War I: Allies, Central Powers, Neutrals

Sometimes in the public memory, the First World War (1914–1918), gets mixed up with the Second World War (1939–1945). Some of the same countries fought in both wars, but the line-up of countries on each side was quite a bit different.

In World War I, the Austrian-Hungarian Empire and its ally, Germany, represented the "Central Powers." They went to war against Serbia after a Serbian nationalist group assassinated the Crown Prince of Austria-Hungary on June 28, 1914, while he was on a visit to Bosnia. Within days, Russia came to the aid of Serbia, and then France came to the aid of Russia. When Germany struck through Belgium against France, Britain went to war, as a protector of Belgium.

Britain made offers to Italy and Japan to agree to transfer to them territories belonging to or occupied by Austria-Hungary and Germany, and they joined on the British side. So the Allies eventually consisted of Russia, France, Britain, Italy, and Japan. The Ottoman Empire, based in Turkey, but controlling much of the Middle East, joined on the side of the Central Powers.

What a tangle! The Americans looked at these events and felt glad that an ocean kept the war away from them. America remained neutral for about two and a half years (August 1914–April 1917), under the leadership of President Woodrow Wilson (1913–1921).

## The Eastern and Western Fronts

In Europe, the Central Powers had increasing success against Russia on the eastern front. But the western front soon bogged down into a stalemate. Because of changes in weapons, defenses, and transportation, the two sides found themselves engaged in a desperate conflict in a nearly continuous battlefield running from the Atlantic coast in northern France all the way southeast to neutral Switzerland.

Lines of trenches faced each other, with each side hoping to launch an attack to break through the barbed wire and machine-gun emplacements of the enemy's defenses. Artillery barrages, drawn-out battles, and bayonet charges took lives by the tens of thousands. Information, or *intelligence*, about the other side's planning, as in every war, was crucially important.

If the Germans planned to assemble troops at a particular point to attempt a push through, the Allies could rush troops to that spot on the line by railroad, truck, horse-drawn carriage, or even taxicab to bolster the defense; or if need be, make a strategic retreat to save lives. The traditional means of gathering intelligence remained important, and all sides developed new methods.

**Spy Words**

Intelligence refers to all the information that can be used in military or diplomatic planning. As a joke, veteran soldiers often claim that "military intelligence" is an oxymoron. But in fact, since ancient times, the side that is best in gathering detailed information about troop dispositions, plans, communications, and "order of battle" (that is, the units and organization of the other side), is always in a better position to win than the side with poorer information. Modern agencies make a distinction between tactical intelligence, used in battle, and national or strategic intelligence, used to make policy decisions at the level of the head of government.

The traditional means of gathering tactical intelligence included questioning captured prisoners and scrutinizing captured or intercepted documents and maps. Another method was to develop agents behind the enemy lines who would relay information through (or around) the lines. The Germans recruited a few agents who worked in France, including the most notorious female spy of all time, Mata Hari.

Aerial surveillance became a new part of the intelligence toolkit, allowing observation from the air of troop movements, train routes, congestion of trucks, and other hints of an impending attack across the battle line.

### Techint

During the Civil War (1861–1865) traditional intelligence methods had been supplemented with observation from balloons. With the development of aircraft from 1904 to 1908, pilots could easily look down at the enemy's troop movements. Within weeks of the start of World War I, British pilots reported German troop movements in Belgium, allowing a timely British retreat. At the Battle of Verdun, an eight-month slaughter of tens of thousands on both sides in 1916, the French set up film-developing stations to analyze aerial photographs within one hour of their exposure, sometimes turning out 5,000 prints a day. In 1917–1918, the British took more than 500,000 photographs from the air, and pieced hundreds of them together to make a map of the whole front.

## War at Sea

Some changes in technology began to affect war at sea. Although Germany had built a few "dreadnaughts" or battleships before the war, they knew that the British Royal Navy was superior in numbers. But the development of the diesel engine–powered submarine that ran on electric batteries and motors when submerged gave the Germans a new type of ship. The submarine *U-9* was able to sneak into a British harbor and in one raid, launch torpedoes that sank three major warships on September 22, 1914.

Submarines and warships could communicate with the home base and with each other by the newly developed "wireless telegraphy" developed in 1900, by Italian physicist Guglielmo Marconi. Unlike point-to-point communication lines such as telephone and telegraph, radio was "broadcast," meaning that both sides could pick up the messages with receiving equipment. That change suddenly made new methods to encode and rapidly decode messages crucial.

## Neutral to Belligerent

Two countries, Japan and Italy, joined the Allied side early in the war: Japan declared war on Germany less than two weeks after Britain did so, in August 1914; Italy declared war on Austria in May 1915. But Americans, protected by two oceans, thought they would be able to remain officially neutral.

**Spy Words**

Clandestine activity is a broad term that covers spying, sabotage, and the planting of false or skewed information or propaganda.

Since the British were able to blockade Germany by stopping and inspecting cargo ships with their own naval vessels, American trade to Germany just about dried up within a few months. At the same time, American companies shipped food, horses, automobile parts, fuel, and other commodities to Britain and France. Through 1915 and 1916, Germany saw America increasingly supplying its enemies, and both Britain and Germany began various types of *clandestine activity* in the United States.

Early in 1917, Germany decided that it could risk war with the United States by sinking U.S. merchant ships carrying cargo to Britain. The Germans calculated that it would take at least a year before the Americans could mount an effective force and get it to Europe. In that time, they believed, they could starve Britain into negotiating a peace, simply by cutting off U.S. shipping. They would warn the Americans not to send ships to Britain, and if the Americans did so, German subs would sink them. Perhaps the Americans would stay neutral and simply stop shipping.

Like many wartime plans, the calculation was brutal and risky, and at first it appeared it would work. American companies stopped sending ships and cargoes. Soon, a few U.S. ships were torpedoed at sea. Meanwhile, the British did what they could to convince Americans that joining the Allies was in their best interests.

## From Belligerent to Neutral

Getting the United States into the war was all the more important to the British, because Russia began to drop out of the war. Russia had been the weak link in the alliance against the Central Powers almost from the beginning. In the first of two revolutions, in February 1917, the Russian tsar was overthrown and replaced with a weak democratic government under Alexander Kerensky that could not stop desertions of the troops from the front with Germany.

In April, the Germans smuggled Vladimir Ilyich Lenin by train into Russia. Lenin was the leader of a revolutionary branch of the Russian Social Democratic Party, and he and others succeeded in overthrowing the Kerensky regime in the Communist Revolution of November 1917. Within days, the new government offered an armistice to the Central Powers. Russia dropped out of the war entirely just a few months after the Americans came in.

The British worked with a number of secret agents in Russia, trying to get those who resisted the communist regime to marshal their forces to overthrow Lenin. The adventures of these agents created some of the classic romantic tales of spycraft in the twentieth century.

# Legends and Cases

Since espionage by agents involved clandestine work, and since few facts about actual cases and individuals ever come to light, it was only natural that the stories that did surface were often surrounded by exaggeration and legend. In a number of cases, some bare facts behind the myths are known to history. Fiction writers, or the spies themselves turned writer, sometimes embellished the tales. As a result, later generations have to glean the facts from very scattered sources.

## Mata Hari and the Fraulein Doktor

One of the greatest spy myths of World War I was the story of Mata Hari, supposedly a beautiful exotic dancer who, for payments from the Germans, coaxed information from French officers after plying them with her charms. According to legend, she was a Eurasian girl, born in the Dutch East Indies to a Javanese temple dancer, and fathered by a Dutch sailor-adventurer. While a young girl she had learned the temple dances of Java and brought them to the West, adopting the stage name Mata Hari, after one of her dances, meaning "Eye of Dawn" in Javanese.

In fact, her real name was Magareta Zelle, born in 1876 in Holland, to a proper, middle-class family. At the age of 18, she married a sea captain by the name of MacLeod, who took her on a voyage to the East Indies. The marriage fell apart, but in Java she learned something of the local style of dancing. Returning to Europe, she got a divorce and became a nightclub dancer. The former Mrs. MacLeod performed an exotic dance that was pretty risqué for those days, involving a striptease with several layers of veils.

At the age of about 38, she was performing in Paris when the war broke out. By this time, she was supplementing her dance income with cash payments for sexual favors from those who could afford her price. The Germans recruited her to spy for them, and she spent some time in a German spy school operated in German-occupied Belgium by Elsbeth Schragmueller, a young German woman who had just completed a doctorate in economics.

Schragmueller had come to the attention of German intelligence officers with her command of several languages, and showed proficiency not only in translating intercepted enemy documents, but also in interpreting them. Known as the "Fraulein Doktor," Schragmueller soon trained recruits in intelligence work, including Mata Hari, who after a few weeks of study was sent back to Paris.

Mata Hari was not entirely successful, and after several blunders on her part, the French authorities arrested her. The evidence against her was that she had received 30,000 marks from a German officer. In U.S. dollars, that was about $5,000. She claimed it was for the "price of my favors," but the all-male French court, well aware that the going price was only a fraction of that amount, found her guilty. She was executed October 15, 1917 by a firing squad. She declined the blindfold.

The legends of Fraulein Doktor and Mata Hari lived on, with numerous fictional accounts, movies, and thrilling tales over the next two decades. In every treatment, both women became more beautiful and their characters more extreme. In 1932, Schragmueller denied she was a drug addict, but legends grew that she had been a beautiful, cigar-smoking lesbian.

## Sidney Reilly

The adventures of Sidney Reilly also became the source of adventure yarns. Reilly, during the days of the Russian Revolution, tried to develop counterrevolutionary actions in Russia. His widow published a supposedly autobiographical account entitled *Reilly, Britain's Master Spy*, in 1933.

Reilly was born in 1874. By his own popularly accepted account, he was the son of an Irish merchant sea captain and a Russian mother. By another account, he was the product of a liaison between his Catholic mother and a Jewish physician.

The story he gave suggested that he was educated in St. Petersburg, and then worked as an agent for a French shipping company in Port Arthur, in the Russian Far East. In 1904, he returned to St. Petersburg and took a job with a company of naval contractors, and helped in negotiations to repatriate Russian prisoners captured by the Japanese in the Russo-Japanese War (1904–1905).

Before World War I broke out, Reilly was already well known in Russia as a leading businessman, fluent in Russian, English, and German. In 1909, he was selected to head a club of airplane enthusiasts in Russia. In 1914, he continued his commercial work for a period, placing orders in Japan and in the United States for equipment for Russia. With the Russian revolutions of 1917, Reilly was stranded without employment. He offered his services to the British, and over the next two years, penetrated into Germany and smuggled out information to the British. That is his version.

Robin Bruce Lockhart, the son of Bruce Lockhart who worked in British Intelligence during and after World War I, later tried to establish the real story behind the Reilly legend.

The account developed by Robin Lockhart, in *Reilly: Ace of Spies* (Penguin, 1984), showed Reilly (until then going by the name Georgi Rosenblum, adopting the surname of his natural father) as a British agent as early as 1899. Lockhart claimed Rosenblum built a reputation as a businessman under the name of Sidney Reilly in the period 1899–1914 as part of his *cover*.

**Spy Words**

The term **cover** has almost become part of everyday usage through the popularity of spy fiction and thrillers. It refers to a false identity adopted by an agent.

Reilly's own narrative and that of his wife focused on his efforts in the period 1918–1925 to develop resistance to the communist regime in Russia. Reilly worked with British funds for a period, trying to organize anticommunist groups in Russia. He was betrayed several times, the last when he smuggled himself into Russia from Finland to meet with members of a resistance group in 1925. It turned out that the resistance group, The Trust, was a false front established by the Soviet secret police, the Cheka, for the purpose of rounding up dissidents. Reilly was imprisoned (or possibly killed on the night of his entry into Russia) and never heard from again, although rumors that he was alive persisted for years.

## Dzherzhinksy and the Cheka

Feliks Dzherzhinksy (1877–1926) was a colleague of Lenin and one of the masterminds behind the communist coup in November 1917. Dzherzhinksy made sure that all the telephone, telegraph, and messenger services were in the hands of Lenin's Bolshevik supporters when Alexander Kerensky was overthrown, allowing no information to go through unless it came from a Bolshevik source.

---

**Spy Bios**

Feliks Dzherzhinksy was born to a well-off family in Poland. In 1897, he joined the Social Revolutionary Party, and began work as a courier between the underground cells of the party in Russia and overseas groups. He was arrested by the Tsar's secret police and sentenced to a labor camp in Siberia. In 1903, he joined Lenin's wing of the social democrats, the Bolsheviks. Lenin admired Dzherzhinksy's ruthless qualities and began to trust him with special jobs. Dzherzhinksy was at Lenin's side in the November 1917 revolution, and headed the Cheka, the early secret police of the new communist state. He died in 1926 from tuberculosis.

---

Soon after taking power, Lenin called on Dzherzhinksy to establish a secret police. Dzherzhinksy formed the Cheka by rounding up former tsarist secret policemen and threatening them with death unless they worked with the new regime. On that base, he built the organization that evolved into the *KGB*.

**Spy Words**

The secret police in the Soviet Union underwent numerous reorganizations, so it was known by different acronyms over the decades after the Russian revolution of 1917. Here's a quick rundown:

1917-1922: Cheka

1923: GPU *Gosudarstvennoe Politicheskoe Upravlenie* (State Political Administration)

1923-1934: OGPU *Obedinennoe Gosudarstvennoe Politicheskoe Upravlenie* (Unified State Political Administration)

1934–1938: NKVD *Norodnyi Komissariat Vnutrennikh Del* (People's Commissariat for Internal Affairs)

1938–1943: NKGB *Norodnyi Komissariat Gosudarstvennoe Bezopasnosti* (People's Commissariat for State Security)

1946–1954: MGB *Ministerstvó Gosudarstvennoe Bezopasnosti* (Ministry of State Security)

1954–1991: KGB *Komitet Gosudarstvennoe Bezopasnosti* (Committee for State Security)

1991–present: SVR *Sluzhba Vneshnei Razvedki* (Foreign Intelligence Service [of Russia])

There were a couple of other bureaucratic shifts in the 1930s and the early 1940s. Histories of the "committee for state security" tend to simplify things by referring to the "KGB" even when the earlier agency had another set of initials.

In December 1917, Dzherzhinksy had only about 24 men, no money, and no experience. Within weeks, he had recruited several thousand agents who operated under fear for their lives. He moved the Cheka to headquarters in Moscow, in a building that remained the center for the KGB for decades, on Lubyanka Street. Soon the building was simply called "Lubyanka," the place where arrested individuals vanished forever. By 1918, Dzherzhinksy had almost 100,000 agents, and he began overseas operations. In that year, working from information from a communist French agent, the Cheka arrested the chief American agent in Russia, Xenophon Kalmatiano, a Greek American, along with British agents.

In the "Red Terror" of 1918, Dzherzhinksy rounded up some 500 former officials of the tsarist regime after a foiled assassination attempt on Lenin. They were all executed. Dzherzhinksy arrested thousands of other Russians, and began to use the Cheka to clamp down on anyone he suspected wanted to infringe on his turf. Dzherzhinksy established the false organization known as "The Trust" that recruited Russian anticommunist refugees overseas. It was The Trust that fooled Reilly into coming back, only to be eliminated.

## From Author to Spy and Back

Somerset Maugham (1874–1965) was already a well-known and established British author when he visited Russia in 1917. Living in Switzerland, where he hoped the air would help his tuberculosis, Maugham was recruited by British Military Intelligence 1c, (MI 1c), the office that evolved into MI-6 in later years. This office dealt with overseas military intelligence, and Maugham's job was to watch German agents in Switzerland. Maugham later wrote a fictional account of his work in Switzerland in a series of spy stories, *Ashenden*.

In Russia Maugham witnessed the arrival of Lenin and the rapid collapse of the Kerensky regime. He reported back that only a large amount of money or a massive invasion with troops, or both, could stop the Russian revolution. But the Allies were engaged at the moment in fighting the Central Powers, and Maugham's advice at first fell on deaf ears.

Disillusioned with espionage, and his tuberculosis unimproved, Maugham returned to Switzerland, retired from the spy business, and

> ### Spy Bios
>
> Somerset Maugham was born in Paris, and studied medicine at St. Thomas Medical School in London. He wrote a number of major works, including *Of Human Bondage* (1915), *The Moon and Sixpence* (1919), and *Cakes and Ale* (1930). He produced the *Ashenden* series on espionage in 1928. He died at his villa in the south of France in 1965.

worked on his fiction. He was lucky he got out before Dzherzhinksy organized his round-up of foreign agents. While Maugham worked his Swiss experience into some of his fiction, he never wrote about his time as a British agent in Russia.

# Operations in the United States

During the period of neutrality, Germany became increasingly convinced that American trade with Allies had to be stopped or cut back. Their first efforts involved sabotage, some of it spectacular. Meanwhile, the British leaked specific pieces of information they had decoded to the American authorities, in hopes of convincing the United States to join the Allies.

## German Sabotage

On July 30, 1916, a munitions factory located on Black Tom Island in New Jersey blew up. A huge explosion shook New York City; windows were shattered in downtown Manhattan and in towns a dozen miles from the blast in New Jersey, and the noise was heard as far away as Maryland. Only a few people were lost in the explosion that occurred in the middle of the night, but the property damage was estimated at $22 million. The explosion centered on a pier loaded with 1,000 tons of munitions destined for France, Britain, and Russia.

### Spy Words

The word **sabotage** came into European languages as a result of radical labor agitators and anarchists who believed that an effective way to protest working conditions and low wages was to destroy the factory machinery. In the Flemish section of Belgium and France, workers wore "sabots" or wooden shoes, which when tossed into the works of a textile factory would bring the machinery to a halt. In warfare, sabotage, using explosives in the enemy's home country, could be directed at weapons factories and transport facilities. Since the United States supplied so many goods to Germany's enemies while remaining neutral, Germany sent several "saboteurs" to disrupt American production.

The Black Tom explosion was an apparent act of *sabotage* by German agents. The year before, Captain Franz von Rintelen had arrived in New York on a Swiss passport. He was fluent in English and easily moved undiscovered in New York. He contacted German sailors and officers who had been stranded in New York with their ships, and he got a group of them to use a workshop aboard one ship as a miniature bomb factory. The factory soon turned out a series of pipe bombs smuggled into coal-bunkers of ships bound for Britain. Rintelen later claimed that he enlisted Irish long-shoremen to help in planting the bombs.

*The July 20, 1916, explosion of ammunition at Black Tom Island in New York Harbor left these scenes of wreckage the next morning.*

*(Courtesy of the Library of Congress)*

The fires in the coal supplies damaged the ships and when the holds were flooded to douse the flames, the munition cargoes were ruined. Rintelen was captured when the British stopped a Dutch ship, tipped to his presence by a decoded message. He was arrested, and later sent to the United States for trial. Oddly, he could only be tried for inciting dockworkers to strike. Rintelen later published his memoirs in Britain as *The Dark Invader: Wartime Reminiscences of a German Naval Intelligence Officer.*

Saboteurs got credit for fires and bombs at other American factories, and one estimate claimed that about 43 factories were damaged or destroyed and about 48 ships suffered from the German bombs. The total value of all the damage, including the Black Tom explosion, was put at $150 million. The details of exactly who was involved in the Black Tom explosion were never uncovered.

Probably the sabotage did more to convince Americans that they should be fighting on the Allied side than it did to damage the supply of goods to the Allies, and in this sense, the whole effort backfired on the German agents. However, there is some evidence that the Black Tom explosion put a severe crimp in the munitions supply of the Russians just when they needed it, and it may have contributed to some German victories on the eastern front.

## British Use of the Zimmerman Note

When the Germans decided in February 1917, to unleash unrestricted submarine warfare against all merchant ships, neutral or belligerent, headed for Britain, it was not at all clear how the United States would react. Possibly, as the Germans hoped, American businesses would simply stop shipping goods. On the other hand, the United States might go to war over it. But the sentiment for neutrality and peace in the United States remained strong.

The British decided to provide a nudge. In British Naval Intelligence, their "Room 40," a decoding office, had intercepted and deciphered many German messages. William "Blinker" Hall, the head of the office (so named because he couldn't stop blinking), had at hand the ideal decoded information. A month before the Germans announced their unrestricted submarine warfare policy, Nigel de Grey, a young decoder, walked into his office. Hall later recounted the tale in his own memoirs.

De Grey said, "D'you want to bring America into the war?"

Calmly, Hall responded, "Yes, my boy. Why?"

De Grey answered: "I've got something here which—well it's a rather astonishing message which might do the trick *if* we could use it. It isn't very clear, I'm afraid, but I'm sure I've got the most important points right. It's from the German Foreign Office to Bernstorff." Count von Bernstorff was the German ambassador in the United States.

The "astonishing message" was later described by more than one historian as the single intelligence coup with the most profound consequences in World War I. It had been sent by the head of the German Foreign Ministry, Arthur Zimmerman. Decoded by the British, the message announced the plan to start unrestricted submarine warfare. It also instructed Bernstorff to pass on to the Mexican ambassador an offer to recognize the transfer back to Mexico of U.S. territory at the end of the war, if Mexico would join with Germany in war against the United States. That territory comprised most of the western United States, including Texas, New Mexico, Arizona, California, Nevada, and Utah. The note also suggested that Mexico could help convince Japan to settle on a separate peace.

The question confronting the British was how to use the telegram, especially without revealing that they had cracked the diplomatic code in which it was sent. Revealing that they had cracked the code would prompt the Germans to create a new one. Blinker Hall considered not using it at all, but simply waiting to see whether the unrestricted submarine attacks would bring the United States into the war.

Surprisingly, the Germans made it easy for Room 40 to conceal how they learned of the message. The Germans sent the message by three different routes, including not only the wireless telegraph, but also via cable sent from Sweden to the United States. Using a bit of deception, the British claimed they had uncovered the message in Mexico, and also provided enough information so that the Americans could decode the message from their own cable sources.

It was not at all clear that Wilson would regard attacks on U.S. shipping as an act of war. When he read the Zimmerman telegram, decoded and translated, he was shocked. When it was released to the press, the American public and Congress were outraged, and the arguments for neutrality were severely weakened.

While the United States might have gone to war as the sinking of U.S. ships began to increase, the telegram certainly helped tip the balance. The United States declared war on Germany on April 6, 1917, after overwhelming votes in favor of war in both the Senate and the House of Representatives. Mexico, of course, never took up the German offer.

# The American Black Chamber

By contrast to notorious spies like Sidney Reilly, "Fraulein Doktor" Schragmueller, Feliks Dzherzhinksy, and Mata Hari, the Americans engaged in intelligence work in World War I appeared less colorful. However, America produced a pioneer in code-breaking, Herbert O. Yardley, who was himself a bit of a character. Like Admiral Blinker Hall in Britain, he later wrote about his experiences, contributing to his place in history.

**Spy Words** _____

Yardley called his memoir of his work in setting up a decoding system for the U.S. government, *The American Black Chamber*. In earlier years, many European governments had established "Black Chambers" for the decoding of messages, and the so-called "Room 40" in British Naval Intelligence was just such a Black Chamber. When Yardley published his story in 1931, it created quite a sensation, and became something of a bestseller. He sold over 17,000 copies in the United States, another 5,400 in Britain, and not surprisingly, over 33,000 copies in Japanese translation. The Japanese were shocked to find that their diplomatic messages had been read by the Americans for several years.

Yardley was no self-effacing bureaucrat, stuck behind a desk all his life. He was a hard-drinking, poker-playing bachelor who enjoyed a range of lady friends. In later years he supported himself by offering his freelance decoding expertise as a kind of international mercenary, serving for a while with the Chinese government in the war against Japan. He also assisted the Canadians in establishing their "Examination Unit." After the British and Americans forced the Canadians to drop Yardley, he returned to the United States to do other government work during World War II, and later he wrote a popular book, *The Education of a Poker Player*.

# Herbert O. Yardley

Yardley was born in 1890 in Worthington, Indiana, and his early life was fairly typically midwestern middle-class. He attended public school, was editor of his school paper and captain of the football team. He learned to be a telegraph operator from his father, and he worked at that job for railroads. He picked up poker at a local saloon, and loved the game. His friends thought him brilliant, and he sought a wider world in 1913, moving to Washington where he took a job as a telegrapher and code clerk for the U.S. State Department at $900 per year.

When the war started in Europe, his imagination was fired by the opportunity to crack coded messages. In fact, he impressed his superiors by breaking the State Department's own code, which he thought ridiculously simple. When the United States entered the war, he received a commission as a lieutenant in the Army and helped organize the Army's Cipher Bureau, the eighth section of Military Intelligence, or MI-8.

MI-8 began cracking codes, finding formulas for reading invisible ink and tracking down specialists who could read outdated and mysterious German shorthand messages. Through his methods, a number of German agents were apprehended, including a Madame Maria de Victorica, who had a plan to import explosives for sabotage in the United States and had worked on a plan to damage the Panama Canal.

| Spy Bios |
| --- |

Madame Maria de Victorica was an agent for Germany. Her father, Baron Hans von Kretschman, was a general, her mother, Countess Jennie von Gustedt, a diplomat. An accomplished linguist, she entered the German Secret Service in 1910. She married an Argentine citizen by the name of Manuel Gustave Victorica, himself arrested by French authorities in 1917. The British tried to track her down as early as 1914, but an exchange of secret-ink messages allowed American authorities to find her. She had developed a plot to import explosives to the United States concealed in holy figures. She was arrested April 27, 1918, tried and convicted of espionage against the United States. She died in prison in 1920.

Yardley went to Europe and helped during the peace negotiations. Both Yardley and his superiors in military intelligence believed a peacetime organization should be established for both *cryptography* and *cryptanalysis*.

### Spy Words

The American MI-8 and the British Room 40 engaged in both making codes, **cryptography,** and in cracking the codes of other countries, **cryptanalysis.** Cryptanalysis involved several steps. Messages would be changed into ciphers, in which each letter of the sent message was represented by a substituted letter. To make the message more secure, a completely different alphabet-substitution would be used for letters in the first position, in the second, in the third, and so on, often with five or more completely different substitution alphabets employed. Herbert Yardley, like Blinker Hall in Britain, set up teams of brilliant and intuitive specialists who were able to break many ciphers and codes.

## Yardley in the 1920s

By the end of World War I, the American MI-8 had read almost 11,000 messages in 579 different cryptographic systems. After the war, Yardley received funding from both the Army and the State Department to continue operations, and he set up a facility in New York City. Lodged in an ordinary looking brownstone building, the Cipher Bureau continued operations for a decade.

### Tradecraft

One of the simplest forms of encoding messages is the substitution method, in which every letter is represented throughout the message by the same substituted letter. When the message is printed with the spacing between words that occurs in plain text, such substitution cryptograms are very easy to decipher, and are often printed in newspapers on the puzzle pages. The following cryptogram is just such a "puzzler." If you need help in deciphering it, you can find a clue in this key: Throughout the message, the letter "e" is represented by the first letter in the first bulleted word in the "In This Chapter" box at the beginning of Chapter 5.

TZ TE FGDIM ZKIZ I YDA ZKIZ FKIWRDE HTZK DIFK QDEEIRD

BMUJTNDE QUMD EDFOMTZA ZKIW UWD ZKIZ TE OEDN UJDM IWN UJDM

PUM EDJDMIG QDEEIRDE. —NIJTN YIKW: ZKD FUNDCMDIYDME

One of the greatest successes of the Cipher Bureau came in 1922, during the Washington Naval Conference. At that meeting, the United States, France, Italy, and Japan all agreed to limit their heavy warships to a certain ratio. For every five heavy ships built by the British and the Americans, the Japanese would agree to build only three. This ratio, known as the 5:5:3 ratio, rankled the Japanese. Yardley's Cipher Bureau discovered, prior to the negotiations, that although the Japanese would ask for a more generous proportion in the shipbuilding ratio, they would accept the 5:5:3 numbers. With the decoded instructions and information from other sources, the American negotiators held out and achieved the limitation.

In November 1928, republican Herbert Hoover was elected president and he selected Henry L. Stimson for secretary of state. When Stimson learned that the State Department was supporting a cipher bureau that took the secret messages of countries like Japan and Britain and decoded them, he was shocked. He cut off the funds, and later remarked that his reason was straightforward: "Gentlemen do not read each other's mail."

Without funding, the Cipher Bureau closed, and Yardley decided to publish his memoirs. After his book came out, word spread that the American authorities tried to suppress it. Yet Yardley had violated no law in writing his memoirs. For quite a while it was hard to find a copy of the book, until popular reprints in the 1980s. A later revelation in the 1960s showed that Yardley received a payment of $7,000 from the Japanese for some cryptographic secrets in 1930, a crime for which he was never prosecuted. Despite his contributions to American cryptography, he remained quite a controversial figure long after his death in 1958.

*Herbert O. Yardley, shown here with his best-selling memoir that revealed U.S. cryptographic methods.*

*(Courtesy of the National Security Agency)*

## Origins of Real Agencies and Romantic Legends

Despite the disbanding of the Cipher Bureau, the Army continued to maintain a decoding effort, which later grew into the National Security Agency (NSA). In Britain, Room 40 became the origin of the Government Code and Cipher School (GC&CS), later moved to a country manor, Bletchley Park (discussed in more detail in Chapter 3). As we have seen, Dzherzhinksy's Cheka was eventually transformed into the notorious KGB.

The cast of characters, partly because some of them chose to write their own memoirs, and partly because fiction writers used them as raw material for spy stories and movies, were often remembered in a distorted way. But behind the tales of beautiful female spies, secret ink, sabotage with hidden explosives, and intercepted radio messages, there were quite a few based in fact. Successful U.S. signals intelligence work with materials from Japan and Mexico, for instance, helped establish the value of cryptanalysis for policy makers.

## The Least You Need to Know

- Although later writers romanticized their stories, there were some flamboyant agents in World War I including Mata Hari, Doktor Schragmueller, Madame Victorica, Sidney Reilly, Bruce Lockhart, and Somerset Maugham.

- World War I saw the introduction of aircraft photo surveillance to identify troop concentrations and movements.

- In Britain, Sir William "Blinker" Hall established the code-breaking facility, Room 40, that broke the Zimmerman Telegram, playing a crucial part in convincing Americans to go to war on the Allied side.

- In the United States, Herbert O. Yardley established the first real cryptanalysis and cryptography center in MI-8, and later in *The American Black Chamber*.

- In Russia, Feliks Dzherzhinksy set up the secret police that later became one of the world's premier espionage organizations, the KGB.

# Pearl Harbor and Midway

## In This Chapter

- ◆ Code-cracking in the United States after Yardley
- ◆ Tracking subversion
- ◆ Pearl Harbor: Who knew what when
- ◆ Naval intelligence and Midway
- ◆ JN25 and "Purple"
- ◆ The lesson of Pearl

In this chapter, we look at the evolution of American intelligence efforts in the 1930s, as cryptography continued within the Army and Navy after the closure of Yardley's Black Chamber. The FBI tracked the activities of foreign agents from both Germany and the Soviet Union, while other uncoordinated intelligence agencies tried, sometimes amateurishly, to track foreign agents in the United States.

We look at the controversies surrounding Pearl Harbor. Did President Franklin Roosevelt have advance knowledge of the attack? Was all available information provided to U.S. commanders in Hawaii and the Philippines to help them be prepared for attack? We also look at the first U.S.

intelligence successes of World War II, when U.S. Navy code-crackers anticipated the Japanese attack at Midway. The attack on Pearl Harbor would serve as a warning that the American intelligence system needed fixing, and we look at how later advocates of a stronger intelligence establishment looked to the lessons learned from Pearl Harbor to address those issues.

# U.S. Intelligence Between the Wars

During the 1930s, as the United States dealt with the Great Depression and focused on such issues as banking, labor relations, farm policy, and unemployment, American intelligence agencies worked in some isolation from each other, and generally operated in secret. The separate agencies that took on the issue of internal security in the United States watched the growth in membership numbers in the *Communist Party of the United States of America (CPUSA)* with concern.

 **Spy Words**

The **Communist Party of the United States of America (CPUSA)** had its beginnings in the early 1920s, as some members and branches of the existing socialist parties in the United States came together to form a party along the lines of that established by Lenin in Russia. The Communist Party of the Soviet Union provided financial support only to those overseas communist parties that adopted the policy of the Comintern, pledging support to the system in the Soviet Union. Although the CPUSA was divided by factions and quite weak, it did begin to recruit a few American agents for Soviet espionage in the early 1930s. While American government officials suspected that such activities were afoot, they had no idea of the success of Soviet recruitment.

Among the early Soviet recruits were Martha Dodd, daughter of the U.S. ambassador to Germany, who was given the code name "Liza," and U.S. Congressman Samuel Dickstein, who demanded such high payments that the Soviets gave him the code name "Crook." Details of these and other Soviet spies were not revealed until decades later, when some of the archives of the KGB were made available to researchers.

America's oldest intelligence agency, the Office of Naval Intelligence (ONI), continued to work on war plans, gathering information through its network of naval attachés at U.S. embassies abroad. Ambassadors and U.S. consuls in foreign cities sent back reports through the State Department that varied a great deal in quality and detail.

President Franklin Roosevelt, inaugurated in March 1933, often worked through overlapping networks, sometimes consulting with existing agencies, but also calling on an informal network of friends and acquaintances. The Justice Department's Bureau of Investigation, known after 1930 as the Federal Bureau of Investigation, gathered intelligence in Latin America, and was formally given responsibility for issues of national security in 1939.

## William Friedman and Signals Intelligence

After Herbert Yardley was told to shut down the Black Chamber in 1929, and after he published his notorious memoir, the American public might have been justified in believing that the U.S. cryptographic enterprise had come to an end. But that was not the case. Army cryptographic work continued, to be headed by a far less flamboyant character than Yardley, William Frederick Friedman.

Friedman was born in 1891 in Russia, the son of a Rumanian interpreter who worked for the Russian post office. The family immigrated to the United States when William (originally named "Wolfe") was one year old, and settled in Pittsburgh, Pennsylvania. William graduated at the head of his high school class and enrolled at Michigan Agricultural College in 1910, and he then transferred to Cornell in 1911.

One of his first jobs out of college was to work as a geneticist for an eccentric textile merchant and gentleman farmer, George Fabyan. One of Fabyan's many interests was to demonstrate that Francis Bacon was the real author of Shakespeare's plays, and he hired a number of bright young college graduates to work on the problems of cipher that he hoped would prove the Bacon case. Friedman met Elizabeth Smith, another worker at the Fabyan estate, Riverbank, and they married in 1917. William and Elizebeth Friedman together developed a passion for cryptography and became "the most famous husband and wife team in the history of cryptology," according to the leading historian of the subject, David Kahn.

The staff at Riverbank helped train Army cryptographers in World War I, and after the war William and Elizebeth went to work for the War Department. Friedman had prepared several monographs on the subject of cryptography while at Riverbank, and he continued to produce technical studies on the subject for the War Department's Signal Corps.

In 1922, Friedman became Chief Cryptanalyst of the Army Signal Corps. During the period 1922–1929, Friedman was in charge of creating codes and ciphers. With the closing of the Black Chamber in 1929, the Signal Corps consolidated the code-making and -cracking efforts into one office under Friedman.

*William Friedman, by contrast to Herbert Yardley, was a quiet and self-effacing expert in cyptography.*

*(Courtesy of the National Security Agency)*

Accordingly, the Signals Intelligence Service was established, and Friedman hired three junior staff members: Frank Rowlett, Solomon Kullback, and Abraham Sinkov. The latter two had just completed doctoral degrees in mathematics. The recruitment of Rowlett, Kullback, and Sinkov, and the devoted work of the brilliant Friedmans, represented a transition from the amateur to the professional in this aspect of U. S. intelligence work.

---

### Spy Bios

William Friedman (1891–1969) led the transition from paper and pencil cryptography to machine analysis, and is credited with establishing the forerunner of the Army Security Agency that later evolved into the National Security Agency (NSA). He authored a number of specialized publications, including *The Index of Coincidence*, *The Elements of Cryptanalysis*, and *Military Cryptanalysis, Parts I–IV*. Even after retirement, he served as a consultant to NSA. He won several awards, including the Presidential Medal for Merit (1946) and the Presidential National Security Medal (1955). Congress awarded him $100,000 for the inventions and patents in the field of cryptology that he created and that remained government property.

---

## Navy

Meanwhile, the U.S. Navy also developed its capabilities. In 1924, Lieutenant Laurance Frye Safford (1893–1973) set up a radio intelligence activity in the Code and

Signal Section, hiring a select team of bright young people to work on code-cracking. He established a training course, and one of his first trainees was Ensign Joseph N. Wenger. After a couple of tours of duty at sea, and a stint running an interception station at the U.S. consulate in Shanghai, Safford began building up the Navy's capability in cryptography in an office designated OP-20-G from 1936. Safford, like Friedman, was later awarded $100,000 by Congress for the inventions and patents he turned over to the government.

---

**Spy Dios**

Joseph N. Wenger (1901–1970) attended the U.S. Naval Academy and graduated in 1923. He worked under Laurence Safford in OP-20-G in the 1920s. He was a radio intelligence officer for the Asiatic Fleet, 1932–1934, and took charge of the research section of OP-20-G in 1935. During World War II, he headed up the Navy's cryptographic effort. When NSA was established in 1952, he became deputy director. In 1956, he coordinated U.S. and NATO communications electronics programs. After retirement in 1958 with the rank of Admiral, he served on the NSA Scientific Advisory Board.

---

During the 1930s, the Office of Naval Intelligence (ONI) conducted its own surveillance of *subversive activities* within the United States, with some ONI agents reporting directly to Roosevelt.

**Spy Words** _____

**Subversive activities** are any activities deemed by the government as tending to "subvert" the American way of life. The American intelligence agencies, including the FBI, the Army's G-2, and the Office of Naval Intelligence, learned of Soviet activities in recruitment of agents but had little understanding of the nature or extent of the Soviet work. Most FBI and military officers engaged in counterespionage work in the period tended to regard all activities by the CPUSA, even those that were open and political, as subversive.

## G-2

In the Army's table of organization, "G-2" referred to General Staff-2, or intelligence gathering. G-2 during World War I and the early 1920s had done quite a bit of domestic intelligence gathering in the United States against organizations that were actually subversive, and others that were simply viewed as subversive. Targets of investigation included the early Communist Party organizations, the Industrial Workers of the World (I.W.W.), other labor unions, and pro-German groups. During the 1920s, some Army intelligence officers who were in the reserves continued to supply such information through a special intelligence section of the Quartermaster Reserve Corps. These informal efforts continued without official sanction.

In 1931, Army Chief of Staff General Douglas MacArthur gave permission to G-2 to report on various communist groups, and authorized Corps Area commanders in the United States to report on subversive activities in their areas. When the World War I veterans began to organize spontaneous marches on Washington, the so-called "Bonus Marchers," in 1932, MacArthur stepped up surveillance. However, when MacArthur used Army troops to disperse the marchers, he was widely criticized. Henceforth, G-2 domestic activities were conducted very quietly. Army Intelligence chief Ralph Van Deman had retired in 1929, but he continued to keep up an informal network that reported to G-2 in Washington.

President Roosevelt appointed General Marlin Craig as Army Chief of Staff in 1935, and Craig increased domestic surveillance through the next few years, mostly focused on labor union groups and Communist Party organizations.

## Cracking the Bootlegger Codes

After working in Signals Intelligence with her husband in 1921–1922, Elizebeth Friedman (1892–1980) worked for the U.S. Navy in 1923, and later was employed by the U.S. Treasury Bureaus of Prohibition and Customs. She spent most of her professional code-breaking career working against liquor smugglers and drug runners.

In 1928–1930, while working for the Customs Investigative services, Elizebeth Friedman worked on cases of Gulf of Mexico and Pacific Coast smugglers, and in 1933, she appeared as the star witness for the Coast Guard against "Consolidated Exporters Company," the largest bootlegging ring. Her evidence led to the indictment of 35 smugglers for conspiracy to violate the National Prohibition Act. In 1937, she cooperated with the Canadian government, helping to crack a code in Chinese that led to the breakup of an opium smuggling ring.

## The Federal Bureau of Investigation

In August 1936, President Roosevelt called J. Edgar Hoover, the head of the FBI, to the White House. Roosevelt and Secretary of State Cordell Hull approved a general survey by the FBI of subversive activities in the United States, and Hoover followed up on September 5, with a secret order to all his agents to begin to supply information on subversive organizations. The investigations bore fruit when, in February 1938, the Justice Department got indictments against 18 Germans in New York for violating the Espionage Act. Only two were convicted.

# The Intelligence Dilemma

In the 1920s and 1930s, the Army, Navy, and the FBI all confronted a basic dilemma. Since the CPUSA operated as a legitimate and legal political party, the act of governmental surveillance appeared to be an infringement on the civil liberties of the party members. To use a government agency to spy on a political party violated basic American rights.

But the CPUSA also used its funds and contacts to build a clandestine network of informants who would report to the Soviet Union. It was far easier for the U.S. agencies to detect and report on the well-publicized and often open "above-ground" and legitimate political activity of the party than it was to track down the agents, most of whom went undiscovered for decades. It was difficult to prove that the Communist Party leadership helped recruit people to get them to commit industrial and governmental espionage for the Soviet Union. It was not until after World War II that a few of the networks and individuals were exposed by defections, code-breaking, and some confessions.

Despite the extensive reports on "subversive" behavior filed by G-2, by ONI, and by the FBI, most of what the agencies uncovered was completely legal behavior such as political organization, propaganda, and speech-making. When ONI and G-2 discovered efforts by the party to recruit sailors or soldiers on military bases, the security agencies believed they had found a major subversive activity. By denouncing such activities (especially when they were perfectly legal), the agencies sometimes won sympathy for the party from those who saw the government engaged in attempted suppression of political rights.

The American intelligence "experts" were often out of their depth. A 1933 rumor that Japanese agents tried to organize African Americans in a group known as the "Fellowship of God and the Brotherhood of Man" was simultaneously investigated by G-2, the Immigration Service, the Secret Service, the Department of Justice, the Kansas City Detective Squad, and the Navy. Finally, the FBI concluded that the organization was simply a scam to raise money.

## Amateur Sleuths

Loosely organized volunteers, often revealing their own prejudices against minorities or political liberals, would report on suspicious activities to G-2, resulting in a flood of information about such organizations as the American Civil Liberties Union, the Federal Council of Churches, and the Civilian Conservation Corps.

Probably the net effect of such scattershot reporting on everyone who did not share the political views of the volunteers only tended to obscure any evidence of real subversion. In retrospect, such reports are reminiscent of the Aesop fable of the boy who cried wolf—when a wolf really showed up, too many false alarms had destroyed his credibility.

## State Department Sources

American foreign service officers had little training or experience in evaluating intelligence information. In May and June 1940, for example, Ambassador Edwin C. Wilson, stationed in Montevideo, Uruguay, reported that there was about to be a Nazi coup in that country. He urged Roosevelt to send a fleet of up to 50 warships to cruise off the coast of South America and to station a powerful squadron off Montevideo. Roosevelt responded by sending two cruisers, *Quincy* and *Wichita*.

Nothing came of Wilson's alarm. On June 13, 1940, local authorities broke up the Uruguayan Nazi Party, arresting a few leaders. Even after the Uruguayan authorities released them, Wilson continued to report that the Nazi threat was imminent.

The U.S. Navy's intelligence officer stationed as a naval attaché to the U.S. embassy in London, Captain Alan G. Kirk, also feared that a German takeover in Latin America was a threat in June of 1940. Rumors of plans to sabotage the Panama Canal by either German or Japanese agents continually surfaced. Although Germany did in fact have plans for expansion in South America, it was difficult for U.S. leadership to assess the immediacy of the threat.

The Army and the Navy each had separate systems of alert status, and each sent different levels of alerts to Hawaii and Panama through 1940 and 1941. Local officers later reported that they had trouble sorting out whether an alert was a drill, or "the real thing."

## Coordination

After World War II broke out in Europe, Americans again preferred to stay neutral as they had during World War I, and during the period of U.S. neutrality, September 1939–December 1941, the United States had limited information about developments inside the Axis powers: Germany, Italy, and the Japanese Empire. ONI and State Department representatives provided a constant flow of reports, usually based on rumor or public information. There was little effort to coordinate the data, or to integrate the material coming in from the flow of decrypted messages from several sources.

Domestic information, like international information, was a hodgepodge of rumor and fact. With at least three agencies conducting overlapping surveillance of subversive and espionage activities in the United States, Roosevelt sought some form of cooperation on that front. He asked Under Secretary of State George Messersmith to work out a system, and Messersmith called representatives of the agencies together.

Finally, on June 5, 1940, ONI, G-2, and the FBI decided on an agreement dividing internal security. The FBI remained in charge of most civilian investigations, but G-2 retained responsibility for civilian investigations in the Panama Canal Zone, in the Philippines, and on military reservations. Even so, G-2 and ONI continued to investigate cases in defense plants with major Army or Navy contracts.

Despite some cooperation, the three agencies continued to squabble over jurisdiction. In general, all three agencies remained highly suspicious of any union activity, regarding any strike or slowdown on the part of organized labor as evidence of subversion. Pacifists, socialists, African American, and Jewish groups continued to receive close scrutiny.

## Soviet Espionage in the United States—1930s

The United States officially recognized the Soviet Union in 1933, and soon the GPU (forerunner of the KGB) was able to operate through the diplomatic mission established in Washington and the consulates in New York and San Francisco. Even so, Lubyanka warned Peter Gutzeit, the GPU station chief in New York, to be careful. Moscow repeatedly sent instructions to concentrate on three areas of interest: scientific and industrial secrets that might help the Soviet Union; policy documents relating to German and Japanese threats to the Soviet Union; and anti-Soviet Russian emigrés, either organized as "Trotskyites" (supposed followers of Leon Trotsky), representing independent communist groups, or pro-tsarist groups. Among the recruits who later became notorious when the espionage rings were exposed were Elizabeth Bentley, Julius Rosenberg, and Alger Hiss, discussed in more detail in Chapters 8 and 10.

As the threat from Germany increased, and when the Civil War in Spain (1936–1939) pitted fascist-supported rebel forces against communist-supported loyalist forces, Moscow began to increase its demand for more technical information from the agents in the United States. In particular, the agents were asked to find information about airplanes, naval ships, tanks, chemistry useful in war, chemical warfare, and night-vision equipment.

In 1938, the NKVD (then the initials of the Soviet Intelligence Agency) assigned a young American agent, Harry Gold, to try to get information from an engineer at the National Aeronautics Center at Wright Field in Dayton, Ohio. Harry Gold would play an important role during World War II Soviet espionage against the U.S. atomic bomb project, the Manhattan Engineer District. (See Chapter 8.)

---

**Spy Bios**

Elizabeth Bentley was born January 1, 1908, in New Milford, Connecticut, a descendant of Mayflower immigrants. She attended Vassar College and graduate school in 1932–1933 at Columbia University. In 1936, she began spying for the GRU. In 1938, she met and fell in love with Jacob Golos, a Soviet agent in the United States.

Golos was something of a maverick, and his superiors even suspected him of Trotskyite sympathies. Yet Golos successfully operated as a talent-spotter and recruiter for the Soviets among the American Communist Party. After the death of Golos in November 1943, Bentley became disillusioned, and in November 1945, she "defected" to the FBI. Her information helped the bureau break up several fairly high-level spy rings in Washington and apprehend a total of 41 agents. After testifying before congressional committees, she became known in the press as the "Red Spy Queen."

---

# Pearl Harbor

On December 7, 1941, at 7:55 in the morning local time, the Japanese began bombing the U.S. Naval Base at Pearl Harbor. American forces, although warned to be on a generally increased alert, did not expect an attack, especially one more than 4,000 miles from the nearest Japanese fleet base. The surprise attack stunned America, and after reacting the next day with a declaration of war against Japan, Congress and the American people wondered how it could have happened that the United States was so ill prepared.

## "Back Door to War" Theorists

Conspiracy theories abounded. It was clear that Roosevelt had taken a tougher stand against both Japan and Germany than that favored by the American general public. In a series of steps, the United States had provided aid to Britain, most famously trading 50 U.S. destroyers for 99-year leases on airbases in British possessions in the Western Hemisphere in September 1940. In March 1941, the United States enacted the Lend-Lease Act that allowed $7 billion in aid through leased materials to the Allies in its first year.

Other steps by the U.S. government put pressure on the Japanese, including a ban on export of scrap iron and steel (essential war resources for the Japanese) in September 1940, and a freeze on all Japanese assets in the United States in July 1941. As the

Japanese expanded their control in China, and then in French Indochina (the territory that included Vietnam), the United States protested vigorously. The freeze on assets brought Japanese purchases of all kinds from the United States to a halt. It was no secret that Roosevelt believed that the interests of the United States lay with the Allies and not with the Axis.

Although the Pearl Harbor attack tended to unify Americans in demanding full-scale war, some of those who had argued for neutrality wondered if Roosevelt had concealed knowledge of the impending Japanese attack to ensure a devastating blow that would require the United States to go to war. At first only an ugly rumor, the question persisted and became one of the great intelligence history debates of the twentieth century.

## Who Knew What When?

Some of those who later argued that Roosevelt must have known about the Japanese intentions pointed to the fact that American code-breakers had broken the Japanese diplomatic code long before the attack.

Close study of the information received by Admiral Harold Stark, General William Short, and Admiral Husband Kimmel in later years showed that the chiefs of staff in Washington thought a lot more intelligence was going to the Hawaiian commanders than in fact they were receiving. For example, General Marshall in Washington assumed they were getting full Magic decrypts, when in fact they got only occasional summaries.

### Tradecraft

American cryptographers called all the material from various Japanese codes that they cracked, "Magic." Very few people within the U.S. government were allowed to know of Magic, in order to protect the secret that a particular code had been broken. The Army and the Navy sent transcriptions of Magic material to the State Department and to the White House by courier, but neither Secretary of State Cordell Hull nor President Roosevelt was allowed to keep the copies. The courier would wait while the material was read, and then take it back. Rarely was Magic material analyzed, but simply summarized. After July 1940, the high level "Purple" diplomatic code was cracked, and it was part of the Magic material. However, the Japanese navy code designated "JN25" was not cracked prior to Pearl Harbor. High-ranking American Army and Navy officers, including General George Marshall and Admiral Stark, often made statements in the record that showed that at the time, they were unclear about the distinction between Magic, Purple, and the naval codes.

Brigadier General Sherman Miles, acting chief of G-2, advised Roosevelt in July 1940, that Japan and Germany were extensively exchanging messages in an unbroken Japanese code, and that something important must be afoot. Sure enough, in September 1940, Germany, Italy, and Japan announced the "Tripartite Pact" that formed the World War II Axis alliance. A few weeks after the pact was announced, William Friedman cracked the Japanese high-level diplomatic code, named by the Americans "Purple."

By May 1941, the Navy discovered that the Germans had informed the Japanese that the United States had broken Purple, and both the Army and Navy began to curtail the flow of all Magic information to Roosevelt, offering only summaries. Even so, by the summer of 1941, the Magic source was the only good information available to Roosevelt about Japanese intentions.

## Purple Cracking Compromised

On July 16, 1941, there was a drastic change in the Japanese cabinet, with the Japanese foreign minister Yosuke Matsuoka replaced by Teijiro Toyoda, and Japan then took over all of French Indochina by July 24. Apparently Toyoda took more seriously the German warning that their codes had been compromised, and began to severely limit the content of coded radio messages sent to Japanese overseas embassies, such as the one in Berlin. After July 1941, American code-breakers no longer had access to high-level, secret policy decisions made in Tokyo.

Another cabinet shift in Japan in October placed the more militaristic General Hideki Tojo as prime minister, and Shigenori Togo as foreign minister. Like his predecessor Toyoda, Togo tended not to send any messages by "Purple" that would embarrass the Japanese government.

Even so, Cordell Hull and Franklin Roosevelt were aware in November from Magic transcripts that if negotiations to reach a settlement with Japan were not reached by November 25, 1941, the Japanese were prepared to take some form of drastic action. In an official intelligence estimate of November 27, about 10 days before the attack, General George C. Marshall and Admiral Harold Stark warned that if the final negotiations broke down, Japan would immediately attack somewhere in the Far East, listing possible targets as Burma, Thailand, Malaya, the Dutch East Indies, the Philippines, the Soviet Union, or China. The records of these days indicate that although the U.S. intelligence establishment relied on Magic transcriptions, the U.S. officers could get no precise understanding of Japanese plans.

## Intelligence Failure or Cover-Up?

The U.S. intelligence community relied on the Magic intercepts, even after they learned that the Japanese knew that "Purple" had been cracked. Relying on one source, especially one that had been compromised, and not coordinating information with other sources, looks in retrospect like a shortsighted and ineffectual policy.

Apparently no one bothered to tell either Hull or Roosevelt that the Japanese knew that Purple had been cracked. In November 1941, Hull and Roosevelt had every reason to believe that the appraisals and the Magic documents they saw told the full story. From these details, it seems FDR and Cordell Hull were as surprised as anyone when Pearl Harbor was attacked.

Rumors that Hull and Roosevelt knew of the impending attack started almost at once, and Hull vigorously denied them. After the end of the war, in November 1945, a joint committee of Congress on the Investigation of the Pearl Harbor Attack called Hull as a witness. Indignantly, he presented a statement about 100 pages long. When asked specifically whether he had foreknowledge of the attack, he stated loudly, "I stood under that infamous charge for months." Everyone knew, he said, that the claims were lies. The committee exonerated Hull, but of course, the concept lingered on. Evidence points to bad intelligence policy, not to duplicity.

## Conspiracy Theories Live On

In later years, researchers continued to search for evidence of a conspiracy. James Rusbridger, in *Betrayal at Pearl Harbor*, suggested that the British had cracked enough of the Japanese naval codes to be able to predict the Pearl Harbor attack. He claimed that Winston Churchill withheld the facts from Roosevelt. But there is no solid evidence that the British had such information, and no evidence that the Japanese sent any messages that would have given away their plans. Despite the unfounded nature of the allegations, they kept surfacing for decades, probably because of the lasting appeal of conspiracy theories.

# Midway

Although Pearl Harbor may have represented a great intelligence failure, the naval base at Pearl Harbor and OP-20-G in Washington also produced one of the great American intelligence triumphs of the war, only a few weeks after the attack. In a basement in an administration building at the Pearl Harbor Navy Yard was a secret room, the Combat Intelligence Unit, a radio intelligence outfit that served the Navy's whole Pacific fleet. Although the Japanese navy (JN) high-level codes had not been fully broken, the Combat Intelligence Unit used other techniques: interception, direction finding, and traffic analysis.

---

**Techint**

When a coded radio message was overheard, there were other techniques besides decoding it that would help reveal information. If the same message was received at several different points, the location of the broadcast station could be detected by *direction finding*. High-frequency direction finding (HF/DF or "Huff-Duff") often could be used to spot the location of a particular ship or submarine. *Interception* and transcription of the message might not reveal too much except a jumble of Morse-code numbers and letters. However, a pattern might be determined if the same call signals, signature lines, or specific code words were repeated. *Traffic analysis*—a quantification of the location and intensity of radio transmissions—might reveal a build-up of forces, even when the content of the messages was not known.

---

## Combat Intelligence Unit

At the Combat Intelligence Unit at Pearl Harbor, a staff of about 30 naval personnel, headed by Lieutenant Commander Joseph John Rochefort, struggled with the flow of unbroken Japanese naval radio messages. There were only two or three cryptanalysts on the staff, and most of the rest were trainees, clerks, aides, and translators. On December 10, three days after the raid on Pearl Harbor, the unit was given the job of beginning an attack on the high-level Japanese naval code known to the Americans as "JN25." Although parts of the code had been broken, only fragments of messages could be read.

*Laurance Safford established the Navy's Code and Signal Section that later cracked Japanese naval codes.*

*(Courtesy of the National Security Agency)*

With the outbreak of the war, the small unit began adding personnel, some from damaged ships, so that by May 1942, the staff had ballooned to 120, working 24 hours a day. Some of the key members of the team had studied the texts and reports of Friedman and had worked under Safford at the Navy's Code and Signal section of Naval Intelligence.

# JN25

The Americans called the new code introduced by the Japanese navy in 1939 "JN25" because it was the twenty-fifth Japanese naval code the U.S. Navy's OP-20-G tried to crack. JN25 went through several editions, as the Japanese would grow uneasy that it might be deciphered. The first version of JN25 had been partially broken in 1939, under the leadership of Agnes May (Meyer) Driscoll, who had worked briefly with the Friedmans at Fabyan's Riverbank Laboratories. Captain Laurance Safford credited her as the nation's foremost expert on the Japanese naval codes. The Japanese introduced a new version on December 1, 1940, and the American teams followed the changes closely. They worked hard to crack messages in what they called JN25B, making slow progress.

By December 1941, before Pearl Harbor, Op-20-G could only read about 10 percent of the JN25B messages. However, by April 1942, the U.S. Navy's cryptanalysts had broken enough of JN25B that they could anticipate an effort by the Japanese to attack Port Moresby in Northern Australia. Admiral Chester Nimitz sent the carriers *Lexington* and *Yorktown* to intercept the invasion fleet. The result was the Battle of Coral Sea, in which the Japanese carrier *Shoho* was sunk. The United States lost *Lexington*, and *Yorktown* was badly damaged. Although the U.S. losses were severe, the Japanese turned back from their invasion attack, representing a long-range or strategic victory of sorts for the Allied side.

# Finding "AF"

In May 1942, the Japanese planned an attack somewhere in the North Pacific Ocean against American facilities. With much of the JN25B code broken, the American cryptanalysts discovered that the target was at a location the Japanese designated as "AF." Earlier, the cryptanalysts had learned that the Japanese had a grid map of the Pacific, and that A sector and F sector intersected at Midway Island, so they were almost sure that Midway was the target of the intended Japanese attack.

However, to make certain, Rochefort conceived a deception. He had the U.S. garrison at Midway send a message in plain text stating that its desalination (fresh-water) plant had broken down. A few days later, the Japanese, who had picked up the message, included in their planning messages a notation that "AF" was running out of fresh water. The confirmation was in.

*Joseph J. Rochefort's traffic analysis led to anticipating the Japanese attack on Midway.*

*(Courtesy of the National Security Agency)*

By the end of May, Admiral Nimitz had excellent information about the impending attack, knowing the ships that would be involved and the location. The U.S. code-breakers had trouble deciphering the exact date and time of the planned attack, as the Japanese had an extraordinarily complicated way of encoding such information. American cryptanalysts struggled over this last obstacle and finally cracked the complex arrangement, predicting the attack to begin June 2, in a diversion against the Aleutian Islands, and June 3, against Midway.

## The Carrier Battle

Nimitz positioned three carriers, *Hornet*, *Enterprise*, and the freshly patched-up *Yorktown* (that the Japanese believed had been destroyed at Coral Sea) to be able to attack the Japanese force by surprise. By luck, the Japanese put in place a new version of JN25 the day of the battle; had they used it a few weeks earlier, the Americans would never have been able to predict the time and place of the attack.

In a series of raids, aircraft from the U.S. carriers caught the Japanese planes on their carrier decks, loaded with fuel and bombs. The Japanese lost the carriers *Kaga*, *Akagi*, *Soryu*, and *Hiryu*, and the Americans lost *Yorktown*.

The battle, even more than Coral Sea, was a turning point in the Pacific naval war. Nimitz himself believed it was a "victory of intelligence," and gave full credit in his memoirs to the cryptanalysts in the Navy for their work.

The little code shop in the basement of the admin building at Pearl Harbor continued to thrive. Renamed Fleet Radio Unit, Pacific Fleet, or "FRUPAC," it had over 1,000 personnel by the end of the war.

# Pearl Harbor as "Lesson"

In the years after World War II, when the cold war began, the decision was taken to form the Central Intelligence Agency (see Chapter 11). At that time, the failure to fully report on the quality of intelligence and the failure to coordinate among agencies that had led to the Pearl Harbor surprise became an argument for consolidation and coordination of intelligence.

Often in the world of military planning, the lessons of the previous war are carefully studied and applied to the next. Although using history in this fashion seems wise, it often seems that each war is fought using the tools, weapons, ideas, and organizations that should have been in place in the prior war. These observations apply just as well to intelligence as a "weapon" as they do to guns and bombs.

In a world of nuclear weaponry a surprise attack could be far more devastating than the Pearl Harbor raid. To avoid the mistakes of 1941, it was hoped, a new agency would provide U.S. leadership with good, timely, complete intelligence. Before that 1947 decision was taken, however, the United States, Britain, and Russia fought World War II, during which espionage and intelligence work played many crucial roles.

## The Least You Need to Know

- While the Soviet Union was beginning to recruit American Communist Party members and sympathizers to spy on the government and on defense industries after 1930, U.S. counterespionage efforts remained uncoordinated and amateurish.

- American cryptanalysts called decoded Japanese diplomatic messages "Magic" and provided material to the president and the secretary of state.

- The Japanese knew that their high-level diplomatic codes had been cracked and were careful not to reveal the Pearl Harbor attack plan in such messages, leaving President Roosevelt and Secretary of State Hull unaware.

◆ U.S. Navy cryptanalysts were able to predict the time and location of the Japanese-planned attack on Midway and their information contributed to the Japanese defeat there.

◆ The failures of intelligence coordination revealed by Pearl Harbor provided lessons for the next generation of American intelligence planners.

# Chapter 4

# Enigma and Ultra

## In This Chapter

- ◆ The Enigma machine
- ◆ Room 40 to GC&CS
- ◆ Bletchley Park
- ◆ Controlling Ultra Secrets
- ◆ A man called Lucy

In this chapter, we look at the development and use of a code-making and -deciphering machine, known as Enigma, that the German armed forces used to send messages to and from headquarters. We explore how the British broke the system and how they concealed all evidence of their ability to read the German messages during World War II. The information was so valuable that the British wanted to share it with their Allies, and they created several brilliant methods to control and distribute the information so the Germans would never realize their code had been broken.

## The Enigma Machine

The German military came to rely on the Enigma machine and the British came to rely on the information they derived from breaking Enigma-coded messages. The role of the information derived from the code-breaking in some of the most decisive battles of World War II remained largely untold until 1974, when British Group Captain Fred W. Winterbotham published the first account, *The Ultra Secret*. His memoir and later studies required that the historical understanding of the way World War II was fought had to be seriously revised.

## Enigma Origins

During and after World War I, code-makers and -breakers like Herbert Yardley and William Friedman in the United States, and Blinker Hall in Britain recognized the need to develop a mechanical or electro-mechanical method to encipher and decipher messages. In 1919, Dutch inventor Hugo Koch patented an enciphering machine, and in 1923, German engineer Arthur Scherbius set up Cipher Machines Company, which made the first machine to which he gave the brand name Enigma. Intended for private companies to protect their business correspondence, the machine did not find a market and Dr. Scherbius went bankrupt.

| Techint |
| --- |
| At almost the same time that Arthur Scherbius developed the Enigma machine, an American, Edward Hugh Hebern, set up a company to make a similar device. His Hebern Electric Code machine was very interesting to the U.S. Navy. Like Scherbius's Cipher Machines Company, Hebern's company went bankrupt. However, he kept working and provided several machines to the Navy. Lieutenant Safford worked with Hebern, and later, the Hebern ideas were incorporated in some Navy machines. Although the Navy paid for some of Hebern's enciphering machines, he felt he had been cheated out of fair payment for the use of his ideas in other machines built by other companies. Despite a lengthy patent claim, he died in 1952 without getting what he felt was his just reward. |

Even though an encoding machine held great potential for all military services, the Germans were the first to make use of it. Germany had pledged to disarm under the Versailles Treaty that ended World War I, but through the 1920s, Germany secretly began to rebuild its armed forces. Although officially allowed to maintain an army of 100,000 men, Germany began training troops and sailors in Russia, Spain, and elsewhere.

In 1926, the German Navy introduced a Scherbius-designed Enigma machine that they used until 1934, when they replaced it with an improved "Enigma-M" design. The German army adopted an Enigma machine in 1928, and the German air force, the Luftwaffe, began using still another Enigma design. The commercial Enigma machine had been withdrawn from the market, but the name survived as the design evolved.

Although the British at first ignored these developments, the U.S. Signals Intelligence Office, working through G2, acquired an Enigma machine in 1928. Friedman studied the machine, but could not conceive of a way to consistently break the messages.

## How Enigma Worked

The machine looked like a sort of old-fashioned typewriter or cash register, with a keyboard set on a boxy frame. Inside, however, it was ingenious. When the operator typed a letter on the keyboard, a light would come on under another letter on a display. As each letter was typed, a different letter was displayed. The route from the keyboard to the display through electrical wiring was tortuous, changed each time by a series of drums, a reflector, and three rotors. Each time a key was pushed, the wheels would turn, yielding a different code for each position in a message.

*This Enigma machine is in the collection of the National Cryptologic Museum, at Fort Meade, Maryland.*

*(Courtesy of National Security Agency.)*

The rotors each had a different arrangement of letters, and by having a set of spare rotors available, the operator could increase the potential alternatives. In addition, rotors could be inserted in a different order, and a set of plug wires could also add to the potential number of variations. The messages could be deciphered only if an operator with an identical machine used a set of identical wheel settings and plug arrangements. Typing in the enciphered message would yield a clearly deciphered text. By adding more rotors, the machines could develop millions of alternate alphabets. The German military were convinced that they had an unbreakable system. They had good reason. With a three-rotor Enigma, the number of possible permutations was estimated at 3 times $10^{18}$ (that is, 3 followed by 18 zeros).

## The Polish Contribution

The story of how the British cracked the Enigma codes began in Poland. After World War I, Poland recognized that it had two potential enemies. To the west lay defeated Germany, seething with anger at the humiliation of Versailles. To the east lay the Soviet Union, with a stated goal of spreading revolutionary communism. Caught between the two massive and potentially aggressive nations, Poland needed military, strategic, and diplomatic intelligence to survive. Experienced Polish code-breakers closely monitored the radio traffic of both countries.

Polish code-breakers suddenly encountered a problem in 1926, as some of the German messages became indecipherable. The Poles rightly assumed the Germans had adopted a mechanical encoding device. The Poles had already purchased a commercial Serbius machine, but the Germans had added plugs and jacks, as well as other modifications.

## The French Connection

After the war, several legends emerged as to how the Poles made progress against the German Enigma. In one story, a Polish worker smuggled a modified German machine out of a German factory in parts. In a more reliable version, a French Intelligence staff officer, Captain Gustave Bertrand, began working in clandestine meetings with the Poles, relaying information from a German officer by the name of Asché. Although Bertrand probably exaggerated his own role in his memoirs, he did assist the Poles and the British in breaking the Enigma systems.

Asché's information, although sketchy, may have given the Poles enough data to figure out the changes in wiring plugs that the Germans used. Using old signals they had recorded, and a set of plug instructions, the Poles began to understand the German practices in establishing the wheel and plug settings of Enigma.

With this information, they were able to build machines similar to the German devices, and by the time Germany invaded in September 1939, the Poles had built 15 duplicates of the German machines. In addition, they had developed an early computing machine to assist in the deciphering. They called their machine a *bomba* or *bombe*.

<table>
<tr><td>

**Techint**

The bomba was named not for an explosive bomb, but for an elaborate cylinder-shaped dessert dish that it resembled. The first bomba had parts of six Enigma machines wired into it. The first Polish bombas could decipher messages from the three-rotor Enigma machines used by the Germans until 1939. However, when the Germans added new rotors, the Pole's bombas were foiled. Later, when the British used similar electro-mechanical decoding machines, they adopted the French name, "bombe."

</td></tr>
</table>

Between 1934 and 1939, the Poles regularly read the German cipher messages by radio, all of which were encoded by a three-rotor Enigma machine. The Poles recognized from the messages that their country was a target for German aggression, and opened discussions about intelligence matters with both the British and French. In January 1939, at a secret rendezvous in a Paris restaurant, the French Captain Bertrand met with Colonel Gwido Langer and Major Maksymilian Ciezkim, the heads of the Polish effort, and with Commander Alistair Denniston, head of the British Government Code and Cipher School. At this meeting, the Poles did not present all the details of Enigma they had learned, but as war approached, the Poles decided to share more tricks of the trade.

**Tradecraft**

While the Poles decoded Enigma messages before World War II, they closely guarded the fact that the information had been broken. They adopted the code word *Wicher* (meaning "Gale") for the body of messages broken, and limited the spread of *Wicher* information strictly to those with a "need-to-know."

# From Poland, with Love

On July 25, 1939, the Poles met with representatives of both the French and British, and handed over complete models of the Enigma machine, plans and drawings for their bombas, and other cryptoanalytical devices. They moved the material by French diplomatic bag, getting a treasure-trove of information and machinery to Britain.

Meanwhile, the British had been struggling with the Enigma-encoded messages at the Government Code and Cipher School, but they had made some progress in understanding the principles at work. After the war started, the Polish Colonel Gwido Langer and some of his team fled, first to Paris, and then to London, bringing more copies of the Enigma machine as well as their findings and their skills to help in the British effort.

# GC&CS

The British Government Code and Cipher School had been established after World War I, headed for years by Blinker Hall and Alistair Denniston. The abbreviation "GC&CS" was the occasion for typically disparaging British humor, with the claim that it stood for "Girl's Club and Choral Society." In fact, GC&CS played a central role in the Allied victory in World War II.

## Room 40: Origins of GC&CS

At the end of World War I, the British Foreign Office took over the staff of the Admiralty's Room 40. Located for about 19 years in a London office near Victoria Station, the GC&CS operated under the control of Commander Alistair Denniston, one of the original Room 40 cryptographers. In the summer of 1939, for the sake of safety, Denniston moved the GC&CS to a country estate known as Bletchley Park.

Bletchley Park was an old estate about 40 miles outside London once belonging to the dukes of Buckingham. In the 1870s, a mansion was built on the land, and the Foreign Office added a number of outbuildings, including a cafeteria, and a series of temporary structures known simply by "hut" numbers. Huts 3, 4, 6, and 8 were to be the locales of some of the greatest breakthroughs in cryptography of the war. At its heyday in World War II, Bletchley Park had 7,000 personnel, who took residential quarters in the nearby towns.

## Boffins and Bombes

At the London office and at Bletchley Park, military officers were impressed with the mathematical geniuses employed in designing machines to crack the codes generated by other machines. The "back room boys" or the "boffins," as these intellectuals were called by the officers, included several who would rank as world-class geniuses.

The military men were a bit mystified, not only by the boffins, but also by the work of the bombes, which used electrical relays to click their way through thousands of possible combinations, giving off a sound like knitting needles. Fred Winterbotham himself called the main mechanical computer "The Bronze Goddess," never attempting to understand how it yielded its results. But he trusted the product and understood exactly how it could help win the war.

Many of the "back room boys" of Bletchley Park would later move on to professorships of Classics, to high positions in the British government, on stage, in publishing, and other fields. For example, Peter Calvocoressi, of "Hut 3," later became CEO of

Penguin Books; Alan Price Jones went on to become editor of *The Times Literary Supplement*; others became college presidents, or internationally recognized linguists or mathematicians.

*Enigma codes were cracked using electro-mechanical analog computers first called bombes, like these used by American cryptanalysts.*

*(Courtesy of the National Security Agency)*

Alfred Knox, a veteran of Room 40 who had worked on the Zimmerman telegram, headed the theoretical mathematics section. Knox had spent eight years translating 700 verses of the ancient Greek historian Herodotus, working with a text that required cryptographic skills. Knox was assisted by Alan Turing, later regarded as one of the major minds at the Bletchley Park GC&CS.

### Spy Bios

Alan Turing (1912–1954) was educated at King's College at Cambridge and at the Institute for Advanced Study in Princeton, where he studied under Albert Einstein, earning a doctorate in logic in 1938. He declined a post at Princeton to return to Britain. Turing developed a mathematical theory of computing that formed the basis for later computers. The first bombe at Bletchley was often called the Turing Machine or the Turing Engine, following his principle of a machine to duplicate the operation of another machine. Turing was an odd character, known for an unkempt personal appearance and brilliant insights broken with childlike or eccentric behavior. He would sometimes show up for meetings in London, having run the 40 miles from Bletchley Park on foot, with an alarm clock tied to his waist. Troubled by an arrest for homosexuality in 1952, he committed suicide at age 41.

# U-110

In addition to the brilliant minds at work at GC&CS, and the staff and equipment provided by the Poles, the British had a few lucky breaks in their work on codes. One came in May 1941, when the German submarine *U-110* attacked a British convoy of ships, only to be captured. The convoy's escort commander, Captain Baker Cresswell, organized a boarding party from his ship *Bulldog*.

After removing all the German crew, who had set demolition charges to sink the U-boat, a team led by a 20-year-old second lieutenant, David Balme, went aboard the sub and were able to unscrew from a desk a complete Enigma machine and also retrieve a set of code books showing the settings. Meanwhile, the prisoners and the crews of the convoy sailed out of sight, so only a very limited group had knowledge of the captured material. The machine and the records played a crucial part in cracking the German maritime code, known as "Hydra," used for U-boats, patrol-craft, and minesweepers. The capture of *U-110* was regarded as a major victory at sea, and Balme received a medal for his part in the action.

# U-505

About three years after the British salvaged the Enigma machine from *U-110*, the U.S. Navy captured an entire German submarine. On June 4, 1944, two days before the D-Day invasion of Europe, Captain David Gallery, in charge of a task force consisting of a small carrier and some destroyers, tracked down the German submarine *U-505* off the coast of North Africa. After being damaged from depth charges, the submarine surfaced and the crew abandoned ship. Again, no demolition charges went off, although the crew had removed a valve cover to flood the vessel. American sailors stopped the flooding and immediately salvaged two Enigma machines and several volumes of codebooks with their settings.

The carrier took the submarine in tow and headed for a North African port about 150 miles away. Reporting to headquarters, Captain Gallery received an urgent message. He was to change course and tow the German sub to Bermuda, nearly 2,000 miles away. Rather than risk a report getting back to Germany on the eve of D-Day that the Enigma had been captured, the Office of Naval Intelligence chose the more secure British port of Bermuda.

Among the material salvaged from the sub was a grid map of the North Atlantic, allowing the U.S. Navy to pinpoint the location of all German subs when they reported their position by reference to the encoded charts. Over the next 11 months, many other German U-boats were tracked down and sunk, partly with the help of this information. The Navy learned a great deal about German submarines from the

*U-505*, including the engineering details of a new type of acoustic-homing torpedo, the Model T-5, captured aboard the sub.

All 3,000 men of Gallery's task force were sworn to secrecy, and the capture of *U-505* remained classified until after the war. Years later, the veterans of the action lobbied to save the submarine from destruction, and it was towed by way of the St. Lawrence Seaway and the Great Lakes to Chicago, where it remains on display on dry land.

## Controlling the Information

From the beginning of the war, the British, like the Poles, recognized that the fact that the German Enigma codes were being cracked had to be concealed. Fred Winterbotham, the representative of Air Intelligence at the British Secret Intelligence Service, worked with others in establishing a system similar to the Pole's *Wicher*, dubbing it *Ultra*. Information would be shared to people in the field through small groups known as Special Liaison Units, and severe restrictions would be placed on transmitting decrypted messages. If the Germans ever decoded a British message that included one the Germans had originally sent by Enigma, the Germans would realize that their system had been compromised. So extreme care was taken, successfully through the war, to protect the "Ultra Secret" from such disclosure.

# Ultra Secrets

As a result of the protection surrounding Ultra, the British had detailed information regarding German plans throughout the war. Often, the decoding crews at Bletchley Park knew the instructions sent from Berlin to German field commanders even before the commanders had received their own decrypted messages. When France surrendered to Germany on June 22, 1940, all material related to Enigma and Ultra was carefully hidden and removed from France. The Germans continued to believe that Enigma protected their messages, although from time to time they upgraded the machines with mechanical changes.

## Ultra at Dunkirk

In late April 1940, Ultra signals received at Bletchley Park began to reflect movement orders by the Germans, revealing that the alignment of aircraft and heavy armor would soon produce an attack against Belgium, Holland, and northern France. The information, together with other warnings, such as photoreconnaissance by high-flying British Spitfire aircraft, was forwarded to the French command, but in general the warnings were discounted. The German offensive began May 10.

As the German orders and discussions of how to proceed were transmitted by radio over the next few days, Bletchley Park worked furiously to keep up with the flow of information. Soon the British reading Ultra realized the scale and direction of the German attack would overwhelm the Belgian and French defenders, and that if Britain were to have a force to defend the British Isles, British troops would have to be evacuated.

The planning for the Dunkirk evacuation took shape and succeeded with full knowledge of German plans and troop movements. The fact that German commanders disagreed and debated exactly how to proceed, using Enigma signals, only played into the hands of the teams at Bletchley Park. The British were able to rescue from the Dunkirk beaches the better part of the British Expeditionary Force, together with thousands of French who would fight in later battles against the Germans.

## Ultra in the Battle of Britain

Over the late summer and autumn of 1940, the Luftwaffe began attacking British air defenses with a view to a planned invasion of Britain, code-named "Operation Sea Lion." Later, the German bombing campaign came to be called "the Battle of Britain." Ultra provided exact information about each incoming air raid, even to the number and type of planes, the direction of the attack, and the intended targets. Again and again, British fighter aircraft scrambled off their airfields before being attacked, and each German air raid cost the Germans severe losses of aircraft, pilots, and bomber crews.

When the Luftwaffe changed tactics from attacking airfields and aircraft factories to bombing London itself, the Royal Air Force remained prepared. In the 1970s, when the Ultra Secret was finally revealed, several of those in the know agreed that without the cracked Enigma messages, the Battle of Britain would probably have been lost, opening the way for a successful Operation Sea Lion.

At Bletchley Park, in September 1940, the code-breakers read with relief the secret orders from Hitler calling off Operation Sea Lion, in preparation for his attack on Russia. Even though the invasion was cancelled, the "blitz," as the British called the bombing of London, continued into November.

## The Legend of Coventry

Perhaps out of a desire to dramatize the lengths to which the British would go to defend the very secret of Ultra, early writers on the topic spread a story that Winston Churchill knew in advance of a terrible air raid on the British city of Coventry through Ultra decrypts, yet did nothing to defend the city. The story has no foundation in fact, but it shows up so much in the literature of Ultra that it's worth knowing about.

The dramatic dilemma in the story was that Winston Churchill had a terrible decision to make. If the authorities in Coventry were given explicit warning, the Germans might detect that their Enigma messages had been decoded. According to the legend, to protect the Ultra decodes, Churchill ultimately decided that no evacuation order or special warnings should be sent to Coventry.

Coventry was in fact wrecked by the attack, with the ancient Cathedral burned down, and over 50,000 houses destroyed or damaged. Records showed 554 fatalities, and nearly another 5,000 with wounds and burns. So,according to the tale, Coventry had paid a severe price for keeping the Ultra Secret. In point of fact, the messages detailing the raid were never decoded in time, and Churchill never faced the dilemma that has been retold so many times. Tragic story, but just another morality tale that made a point so well that it did not have to be based on fact.

## Ultra Pays Off at El Alamein

One of the early Allied successes in World War II against Germany came in North Africa. The British, defending Egypt, pushed back the forces of Field Marshall Erwin Rommel, "the Desert Fox," at El Alamein in a series of battles from August to October 1942. British General Bernard Montgomery learned from Ultra of the exact lines of supply by ship to the German forces across the Mediterranean Sea from Italy.

To protect Ultra, elaborate deceptions were undertaken. Before bombing an Italian merchant ship whose departure time and date, port of call, and arrival time were all predicted from Ultra intercepts, a "spotting plane" would often fly over the ship, allowing the captain time to report that he had been detected by a lone British airplane. Then the attack would begin, leaving the Germans with the impression that once again, their supply ships had been detected from the air.

Montgomery had other information as well. He knew exactly how many troops Rommel had, their locations, and their condition. Rommel's forces were defeated in a series of battles around El Alamein on November 4 and 5, 1942. By early 1943, with the help of Ultra, the British forces defeated the German Afrika Corps. German and Italian losses in Africa: 600,000 men, 8,000 airplanes, and 2,500 tanks. The British lost 70,000 men.

# A Man Called Lucy

In the period from September 1, 1939, to June 22, 1941, Germany and the Soviet Union were not at war. The two countries signed a nonaggression pact in August 1939, and together they invaded and divided Poland. While Britain and France declared war on Germany for the invasion of Poland, they did not go to war against the Soviet Union. Long before Germany invaded the Soviet Union in June 1941, British code-breakers learned of the German plans to break their nonaggression pact.

Getting the word to Russia presented a problem, however. The Russians were not allies of the British. Churchill believed that if the Ultra secret were revealed to the Russians, they could not be trusted to conceal it from the Germans. On the other hand, if the Russians understood the German intentions and prepared for the coming invasion, their war effort against the Germans would be more effective and in the long run would serve British interests. So the dilemma for the British was how to get Ultra information to the Russians without letting them know about Ultra. The solution was a man called Lucy.

## The Swiss Connection

During World War II, only a few European countries remained neutral: Sweden, Portugal, and Switzerland. Although each took measures in different ways that tended to assist the Axis powers, they remained officially neutral. In addition, Spain pledged to support the Axis, but held off joining the war. Switzerland continued diplomatic relations with Britain, the United States, the Soviet Union, Germany, and Italy. Since all the major combatants had embassies and consulate offices in Switzerland, it soon became a hotbed of espionage. For Britain, the Swiss connection would provide a way to get Ultra information to the Soviet Union without revealing its source.

The Soviet Union had a network of spies in Europe, known to the Germans as the "Rote Kapelle" or the "Red Orchestra." Part of the reason for the nickname was the fact that the spies reported from their outposts in Belgium, Holland, France, and Switzerland by short-wave radio. The original Red Orchestra was an underground group in Germany. The agents would encrypt their messages, using *one-time pads*, and then send a burst of Morse-code messages at specific times.

A complex schedule of when to send the messages, and a schedule that required the senders to shift from one specified frequency to another, all tended to confuse any attempt to locate the senders or decipher their messages. Like a scheduled symphony orchestra, the spies would go on the air for a few minutes every day.

### Spy Words

A **one-time pad** was a system of encryption that did not rely on a machine like Enigma. Instead, the sender and receiver would have a pad of paper with identical sets of random numbers printed on each sheet. Using the top sheet, the sender would encode his message, with each random number indicating the displacement for each letter in the alphabet. The receiver would have an identical pad to decode the message. After the message was sent, the sheet would be torn off and discarded. In this way, no two messages ever used the same code. In its way, a one-time pad yielded ciphers that were perhaps even more difficult to crack than those of Enigma.

The Swiss Red Orchestra, headed by a man named Alexander Rado, the resident director of the Soviet network there, was particularly effective. Code-named Dora (an obvious anagram of his name), Rado reported back to Moscow "Center" from his location in Geneva with information he picked up from his network. One of his sources was a German resident in Switzerland, Rudolf Rössler (sometimes spelled Roessler). Rössler's code name was "Lucy."

Rado's sources were all *compartmentalized*, so that even he did not know exactly who "Lucy" really was, or where Lucy got his information. The British fed a supply of Ultra information through contacts in Switzerland to Lucy, and Lucy provided them to Rado. Rado in turn sent the material in to the Center. At first, the Center doubted the reliability of the information, but as more and more proved to be good data about German plans, the Center tried to find out exactly who Lucy and Lucy's sources were. They never did.

### Tradecraft

**Compartmentation**, or dividing a network into separate compartments or cells, remains a standard security measure in espionage and counterespionage. The less any individual knows about the rest of the network, the more secure in case one spy is detected and interrogated. Often a director of a network would know his contacts only by a code-name, and would never meet the couriers and contacts who reported to those he did contact. Thus, in Switzerland, Rado did not know the identity of Rössler nor of Rössler's contacts.

Another source was a Britisher living in Switzerland, Alexander Allan Foote. Foote was a double agent, working for both the British and the Russians. Foote was known by his code name, "Jim." Early publications about the Lucy ring, Rado, and Foote depicted Foote as a British communist who simply helped the Soviet Union by spying in Switzerland and France during the war. Later evidence has suggested that Foote had been planted by the British all along and that his real loyalty lay with Britain. In any case, he became a separate route for information from Ultra to Rado to Moscow Center.

Both Lucy (Rössler) and Jim (Foote) provided information to Rado, letting Rado believe it came directly from sources in Germany. In a sort of private code, Rado called information about the German army, the Wehrmacht, "Werther." Information about the Luftwaffe, he called "Olga." And information about the foreign office, the *Augswärtiges Amt*, he called "Anna." The initials made it easy for him to remember this system. Later, as the Germans began to discover that the Swiss Red Orchestra was relaying information from "Werther," they assumed that was a code name for a particularly highly placed traitor in Berlin. But "Werther" was just a name for Wehrmacht information through Ultra from Bletchley Park.

## From Bletchley to Rado to Center

Thousands of valuable pieces of information for the Russians flowed in the channel from Bletchley Park, to Lucy and to Foote, to Rado, and on to Moscow Center. Before Germany invaded in June 1941, details of the German operation Barbarossa invasion plans were relayed. Moscow ignored them, believing that somehow the British were planting false rumors to drive divisions between the Soviet Union and Germany.

However, once the invasion began and the Russians recovered enough to put up defenses, Moscow Center began to look closely at the information flowing out of Switzerland, trusting it more and more. As the Germans attacked through Russia toward Stalingrad, Moscow knew every disposition of troops. Hitler made it all the easier; in this phase of the war, he began to take a personal interest in each decision, making sure that all reports came to him and that his orders were relayed directly to the field. He used the Enigma transmitting system, of course, and Bletchley Park caught the messages, decoded them, and relayed them via Lucy to Rado to Center.

In this way, the Soviet Union received advance information that helped them plan the defense of Stalingrad, and then the counterattack in the winter of 1942–1943 that resulted in the defeat and capture of massive German armies.

## Bletchley and Kursk

As the Russians pushed west, the largest tank battle of the war shaped up at Kursk in 1943. About 6,300 tanks and more than 2,000,000 soldiers fought over an area about 50 miles long and 15 miles wide. Hitler planned an attack that would cut off and trap hundreds of thousands of Russians, but as he prepared the details, Bletchley Park read the messages. Rado relayed the plans, including the postponement of the dates of the attack through the first two weeks of April 1943, and into June. Hitler stalled, awaiting delivery of new Panther tanks, and before the attack, the Soviet army had all the details of the new tanks, down to thickness of armor, range of weapon, fuel supply, and vulnerable points.

As the Germans planned their attack at Kursk, they were able to crack some of the messages sent by Rado to Center. Not knowing the source of Rado's information, and assuming that "Werther" was a traitor in their own high command, they set about trying to close down Rado's Swiss network. One technique they employed was trying to enlist the Swiss authorities; another was to try to identify the individuals in the network in order to assassinate them. To track down the radio transmitters, the Germans used *goniometers*.

| Techint |
| --- |
| In the 1940s, mobile **goniometers,** or radio direction finders, were quite large, but they could be mounted on trucks. The Germans were not allowed to bring their goniometry equipment into Switzerland, but they could operate from the French and German sides of the border. They were able to narrow down the locations of some of the short-wave broadcast points, and tipped off the Swiss authorities. |

The Soviet army, equipped with information relayed from Ultra, defeated the Germans in the Battle of Kursk, July 5–July 13, 1943. The Germans lost another 20,000 soldiers. Between Stalingrad and Kursk, the war in the east seemed to be turning in favor of the Russians.

## Churchill Cuts Off Ultra to USSR

Although the Germans had some success in breaking up Rado's ring, Alexander Foote could still communicate to Center. However, after the battle of Kursk, Churchill ordered that the flow of Ultra information to Russia be diminished. Churchill wanted to see the Soviet army defeat the Nazis in Eastern Europe, but he did not want them to advance too quickly and overrun all of Europe. Suddenly, the data the Russians got through their networks in Switzerland dried to a trickle. It was not until well after the war, with the gradual publication of memoirs and documents, that the Russians realized that the best espionage information they got had come in a roundabout fashion from Enigma transmissions, rather than from spies in Germany.

# Enigma, Ultra, and Winning the War

The British code-breakers, like their counterparts in the United States, not only cracked the enemy's codes, but also controlled the information so that the enemy continued to use the same machines and systems. The Japanese codes that were broken and transmitted by the Americans via Magic to field commanders combined with Ultra transmissions to the United States helped MacArthur in his campaigns in the South Pacific (1942–1945).

As information about Magic and Ultra became better known 25 to 30 years after the war, a different picture of how the war was won emerged. Coral Sea, Midway, the Battle of Britain, El Alamein, Stalingrad, and Kursk—all were great victories for the Allies. In each case, the victory was at least partially possible because the codes of the enemy had been broken.

## The Least You Need to Know

- The center of the British Government Code and Cipher School was transferred to Bletchley Park outside London, where experts broke the German radio codes.

- The Enigma machine, which the Germans thought was invincible, produced ciphers that the British cracked at Bletchley Park, using prototype computers.

- The information the British obtained from breaking Enigma codes was classified as Ultra Secret, and very carefully controlled.

- Ultra Secret material was relayed to the Soviet Union by way of spies living in neutral Switzerland, without the Russians or the Germans learning the source of the information during the war.

# Part 2

# Spying in World War II

In this part, we follow some of the spies and deceptions of World War II. Using a wide variety of tricks that played on the fixed beliefs of the Germans, the British and Americans kept the enemy guessing about where and when invasions were coming.

Both America and Russia enhanced their spy apparatus during the war. The United States set up the Office of Strategic Services, which combined intelligence work and commando forces for special operations. The Soviet Union counted on its network of international sympathizers with communist ideology to recruit spies and plant undercover agents. Some, like Richard Sorge and Ursula Ruth Kuczynski, were very good at what they did, while others, like Igor Gouzenko, spilled the beans to Western counter-intelligence.

# Chapter 5

# Deception in World War II

## In This Chapter

- ◆ Deception in espionage
- ◆ Operation Double Cross
- ◆ "The Man Who Never Was"
- ◆ First U.S. Army Group
- ◆ Masters of deception

In human intelligence, a spy must deceive the enemy into believing a false identity. In World War II, there were times when the Allies needed to deceive the enemy into believing much more complex and broader false information. In this chapter, we look at several of the most successful Allied efforts at strategic deception during World War II.

## Deception as a Strategy

If intelligence is key to successful military strategy, getting faulty intelligence to the enemy can be key to their defeat. But the difficulty in doing so is that if the enemy suspects that false information has been planted, they may be able to deduce the real information from the act of trickery itself. If there are two possibilities, and the enemy suspects you're trying to force them to accept one, they may accept the other one, the true alternative, by "reading the message in reverse." Deception as a strategy is a risky game, especially where the alternative possibilities are very few.

## The Montevideo Deception

In December 1939, about three months after the war started, the British Royal Navy spotted one of Germany's few powerful surface ships, the battleship *Graf Spee*, off South America. Although out-gunned, British Commodore H. Harwood engaged the cruiser *Exeter* and the light cruisers *Ajax* and *Achilles* in a fierce fight with the German battleship on December 13. *Exeter* was severely damaged, as was *Ajax*.

After *Graf Spee* sustained light damage, the German Captain Hans Langsdorff decided to break off the action and put into the port of Montevideo in neutral Uruguay. He wanted to make some quick repairs and get medical treatment for wounded sailors.

The British were in an awkward position. If Langsdorff rapidly completed the repairs, he could finish off the remains of the British squadron and get away. If he stayed longer, it would give the British time to bring up more heavy ships. The Uruguayan government was not pleased to give sanctuary to a warship, and pressured Langsdorff to leave within a few days.

The British decided on a deception. They "leaked" a message by sending it uncoded, suggesting that several heavy British ships were already in position outside the harbor. Langsdorff got word that the ships were there, and faced two choices. If he stayed, his ship would be impounded and possibly fall into British hands. If he left the harbor, the crew could all die in the battle. Instead of choosing to stay for impoundment, he decided to save lives by steaming outside the port, setting charges to scuttle the ship, and sending the crew ashore, on December 17, 1939. In a spectacular set of explosions witnessed by thousands from the beach at Montevideo, the *Graf Spee* went down. Three days later, Langsdorff committed suicide.

The British deception worked, although not quite as they had hoped. The British might have preferred to have *Graf Spee* impounded and then to later add her to their own fleet, but at least the ship was no longer part of the German fleet.

## The XX Committee

In Britain, Operation Double Cross, or the "XX Committee," had a far more difficult and complex system of deception to operate. Headed by J. C. Masterman, the Double Cross system started slowly. A few agents working for Germany in England had been identified and *turned* into *double agents*.

**Spy Words** _____

When an agent is uncovered, it is not always the best idea to arrest and execute him. If he can be *turned,* that is, convinced through threats and ideological conversion to serve his captors, he can continue to report back with information that they control. Once working for their new masters, but reporting false information back to their original employers, they are known as **double agents**. Double agents are risky to work with, for they can pretend to be turned and either revert to their original loyalty or break down under the stress of betrayal and the double life.

The German network in Britain was not very large, and the Germans began to supplement it in 1940, by sending six agents to neutral Ireland, and then by sending another 25 by parachute or small boat into Britain. The British Security Service found most of these rather quickly, largely because they were not well trained, and their radio equipment tended to be faulty. Another problem was that each German agent was provided with only about £200, on the German assumption that they would only need to support themselves for a month or so until the German invasion and the expected defeat of Britain. Furthermore, some of the identification documents the agents brought with them included details that the British had already supplied as *disinformation* through their existing double agents, so that the Security Service could readily identify the German agents from their ID papers.

The process of "turning" a parachuted German agent had to be conducted carefully. First, the capture had to follow immediately after the agent's landing, and it had to be unobserved; otherwise the Germans would be able to figure out that the spy had been caught from news reports. The spy had to be convinced that he could save his life by working with the British. The agent's code had to be understood and messages had to be sent to convince the Germans that the agent was working satisfactorily. Although agents did not communicate by voice radio, but by encrypted Morse code, each agent had a particular "signature" or style of sending the dots and dashes. It was very risky to replace a German agent with a British substitute, so turning them and getting them to send false messages was the usual procedure.

**Spy Words** _____

Essential in double-agent work and deception is the principle of **disinformation**. If the enemy's intelligence apparatus can be convinced of one piece of false information, it can help immensely, allowing a whole chain of false ideas and data to be planted. The Soviet Union may have been the first nation to use the term.

Each of the agents was given a British code name. Summer, for example, was landed on September 6, 1940, with orders to report on air raid damage in Birmingham. As far as the Germans knew, he took up broadcasting after an illness and after contacting other German agents in Britain. In fact, Summer first attempted suicide, then tried to make his escape from England by a small boat. Although he was caught and imprisoned, it was a close call, for if he had returned to Germany and reported, it would have ruined the whole operation. From his case, the British concluded that each turned agent had to be physically and psychologically watched very carefully.

Snow was an agent who worked with the British from early in the war, as were Tricycle and Giraffe. These three were particularly useful in building the impression that Germany was successfully creating a whole network of agents, as they sent back messages reporting contact with new arrivals as they were caught and turned.

---

### Techint

The Germans developed what is now regarded as the first cruise missile, the V-1. The V-1 would fly over England, and at approximately the right distance from launch, its engine would cut off and the bomb would fall to the ground with a ton of high explosives detonating on impact. The British civilians knew them as "buzz-bombs" from the sound of their engines, dreading the ominous silence a few seconds before the explosion that could take out a whole city block. Double Cross agents relayed false reports of damage from V-1s to the north and west of London, to induce the Germans to shorten their range. They used the same trick with the V-2 rockets, and in January and February 1945, they were able to get the Germans to shorten the range by 2 miles a week, until nearly all the weapons fell outside the borough of London.

---

### Techint

In intelligence work, a **notional** agent or piece of information is one that is entirely imaginary, created as a fiction, convincing to the enemy. The Double Cross system in Britain included not only turned double agents, but also some notional sub-agents and even notional networks.

---

In most cases, the actual agent would be used to collect and relay messages. However, in some cases, the turned agent would be provided with a list of *notional* sub-agents, sending a mix of disinformation and genuine data. Enough factual material was always included to add credibility.

Gradually, the British came to realize that they effectively controlled the whole German human intelligence system in Britain. When new agents were captured, they revealed under questioning that they had been told to report to one of the most trusted agents already there, including Tate, Snow, Giraffe, and others. The British also learned from Ultra decodes that the Germans trusted the spies in Britain, all of whom were either turned or had been replaced by British agents sending false reports.

## Juan Pujol, Garbo

Perhaps the most successful part of the Double Cross system was an agent who came to the British voluntarily. A Spaniard who the Germans were convinced was working for them, Juan Pujol, volunteered to work under British direction and send false information to the Germans. The Germans, who called Pujol Arabel, were so convinced of the quality of information that he gathered from what was in fact an entirely imaginary network of sub-agents, that they awarded him the Iron Cross in December 1944. The British had already granted Pujol, whom they called Garbo, a high British award in June—the MBE or Member of the British Empire.

# Invasion Targets

Launching an invasion from the sea to a defended position ashore is always difficult, since the defenders have built-in natural advantages. While the invaders are exposed in ships and while crossing the surf zone, the defenders are able to hold defended, dug-in positions ashore, where their weapons can be protected with earthworks, concrete bunkers, and prepared trench positions. Far more material and more men can usually be moved by rail and road than by ship, so bringing reserves to a beachhead tends to favor the defenders.

These facts had been severely brought home during World War I when British, Australian, and New Zealand troops were slaughtered by Turkish troops defending high ground at Gallipoli, February 1915–January 1916. The attackers lost the element of surprise and never got off the beach. Thus when the Allies planned to attack from North Africa to southern Europe in 1943, in Operation Husky, it was essential that the German and Italian defenders be kept from preparing beach defenses. The way to achieve this was to give the impression that the attack would be directed at some point other than the true target—the island of Sicily, off the "toe" of Italy.

## World War I Precedent

The deception practiced for Sicily was modeled on a successful deception that had been accomplished during the First World War. In 1917, the British sought to push the Turks and Germans from Palestine, by driving forces under General Edmund Allenby up from Egypt through the Gaza Strip. German defense there had become so strong that Allenby decided to plant contrived documents that would suggest that the real attack was coming farther into the desert at a later date than the intended date, and that the operation through Gaza was a feint, or diversionary attack.

Colonel Richard Meinertzhagen, an officer on Allenby's staff, played a key role in the 1917 *ruse de guerre*.

**Spy Words** _____

The French expression ***ruse de guerre*** is used to apply to all sorts of deceptions or "ruses" practiced in war, including the use of false flags on merchant ships and devices to deceive or confuse the enemy, such as false preparations for attack. A *ruse de guerre* from the thirteenth century B.C.E. is found in the story of the Trojan Horse, in which Greeks constructed a large wooden horse that appeared to be a religious idol, secretly filling it with soldiers so that when hauled inside the fortified walls of Troy, they could attack from inside.

Meinertzhagen's stratagem in Palestine in 1917 consisted of a small backpack that contained a notebook, a sum of money, a personal letter to a notional officer from his wife announcing the birth of a son, a codebook, and a gossipy letter suggesting that the attack had been delayed. Meinertzhagen intentionally lost the knapsack, that had been bloodstained, together with other equipment, in the no-man's land between the fronts, giving the impression it had been dropped by a wounded officer together with his rifle and gear. Then Meinertzhagen had a radio message sent in the code contained in the "lost" codebook, confirming a false date for the attack. It all worked fairly well.

The Meinertzgehagen deception formed the basis for Operation Mincemeat or "The Man Who Never Was," planned in 1943. But by the 1940s, the deception had to be even more carefully planned than the one in 1917 in order to avoid detection.

## The Man Who Never Was

The code name "Operation Mincemeat" was a bit gruesome, as it involved planting the deceptive information, not in a bloodstained knapsack, but on a dead body. Lieutenant Commander Ewen Montagu suggested the operation and the plan was approved by Prime Minister Winston Churchill, General Dwight Eisenhower, and the Joint Chiefs of Staff in Washington.

A corpse would be planted with a briefcase containing documents suggesting the Operation Husky attack would not be against Sicily, but against the island of Sardinia, with a minor operation against Sicily as a feint. The body would be dropped by submarine off Huelva in Spain, where it was known that Germany had an agent who had good relations with the officially nonbelligerent, but pro-German Spanish authorities. The risk was that if the Germans decided the documents were faked, they would "read them in reverse," and realize that the attack was scheduled for Sicily.

A body was obtained from a London coroner, of a young man who had died from pneumonia. The water in his lungs would leave the impression he had drowned if an autopsy were performed. The XX-committee had the corpse packed in dry ice, and then gave it a new identity: Captain (acting Major) William Martin, 09560, Royal Marines. The notional Major Martin came complete with a constructed personal history: He was a staff officer at Combined Operations Headquarters, he carried personal letters, he was overdrawn at his bank, and he had a receipt for an engagement ring to a girl, from whom he carried two love letters. He even had ticket stubs from a theater performance with dates that corresponded with the whole *legend*.

**Spy Words**

A **legend** is a notional life-story made up to provide a false identity for an agent. Once the legend is created, then corroborating documents and specific details can be fitted together to make the life-story credible.

The documentary details of the legend would provide believablity for the more important documents carried by Major Martin. The most significant was a falsified personal letter to General Harold Alexander from General Archibald Nye, vice chief of the Imperial General Staff. The letter asked that, after Major Martin's expertise in landing craft had been fully used, he be allowed to come back to staff, and that he should bring some sardines, as they were rationed in Britain. The hint was planted: Sardinia.

Making sure that all the letters stayed with the body was a problem, and it was finally decided that a briefcase would be handcuffed to his wrist, similar to that used by bank couriers. It was not common practice to send dispatches in such handcuffed cases, but it was decided that handcuffing was the only way to ensure the documents would remain with the body.

The body was dropped off the coast of Spain on April 19, 1943, and recovered the next day by fishermen. When the Spanish authorities notified the British consul, the British insisted that the body be returned with the briefcase unopened. That aspect of the *ruse* was convincing, for the German agents carefully photographed the materials.

Later, the British press carried the notice of the death of Major Martin, a funeral was held in Spain, the British vice-consul erected a headstone, and the notional fiancée sent flowers.

## Operation Mincemeat Results

The British soon found out through Bletchley Park that all of the contents of the briefcase made quite a sensation, and that the Germans decided to send highly trained troops to defend Sardinia.

The deception was enhanced by some false radio traffic and the planting of false intelligence about Allied plans with the Spanish ambassador at London, who although personally pro-British, could provide a channel to the Germans. His reports to the Spanish Foreign Ministry, sent in confidence, were regularly forwarded to the German ambassador in Madrid by the Spanish foreign minister, a fact known to British intelligence. This information and other false plants suggested the attack would be against Greece and Sardinia. The Germans sent an SS brigade to Sardinia, a panzer division to Greece from Germany and two more panzer divisions from the Russian front to Greece. Rommel was assigned to command the defense of Greece.

The Allies successfully began the operation against Sicily on July 9, 1943. Forces under General George C. Patton and General Bernard Montgomery drove the defenders from Sicily by mid-August and invaded the mainland of Italy in early September. Italy surrendered in September, but the German army fought on in Italy until the end of the war.

As the major invasion of northern France was planned for 1944, the Allies kept up the appearance of threats to Greece, the Balkans, and continued the attack north through Italy. Together, the battles and the possibility of further attacks from across the Mediterranean to the so-called "soft underbelly of Europe" kept German troops tied down and away from the intended target on the northern coast of France.

Later, Ewen Montagu wrote a brief book about the episode, *The Man Who Never Was*.

## Overlord

The Double Cross system was used as part of the deceptions surrounding Overlord, the June 6, 1944, invasion of Normandy. But it was only one part of a whole set of deceptions and *ruses* employed to give the Allies some edge in the invasion.

Garbo and the other double agents and notional networks in Britain helped convince the Germans that the Allied invasion of Normandy would not take place near Cherbourg, but closer to Dunkirk. German intelligence had a whole file of Garbo ("Arabel") information that pointed to the attack to be aimed with dozens of divisions at Calais. Garbo's credibility with the Germans was increased by a last-minute transmission from him informing them of the location of the actual attack, as well as the names of the real units involved at Normandy. The British knew that it would be too late to affect German plans that had already focused on the wrong area, and that the Germans would soon learn the identity of the units. This particular deception confirmed for the Germans that Garbo/Arabel was alert, active, and getting critical intelligence.

In many small ways, the Double Cross agents provided false information, suggesting troop movements where there were none, reporting on regulations closing certain sections of the coast, and relaying rumors surrounding the false plans. Bogus radio signals (picked up by the German's "Y Service") were sent from notional units, and the Double Cross agents helped confirm that the units were there when in fact there were none.

## FUSAG

The "First United States Army Group (FUSAG)" was an entirely notional unit of many divisions, building up for an apparent attack across the straits of Dover toward Calais. Inflatable tanks and trucks, designed by theater-prop specialists, gave the impression of a huge force when viewed by spotter planes.

Leaks of information through the Double Cross network, and the rumor that General George Patton was in charge of the Army Group, all helped convince the Germans that the attack was scheduled far to the east and north of the actual Normandy beaches. Other rumors that the Normandy landings were only a feint made the Germans hesitate to commit heavy armor and troops to the defense of the region for a few days, giving the Allied invasion forces time to gain control of the beachheads.

## Deceptions on D-Day

On D-day, June 6, 1944, a whole host of deceptions were put in place. A group of launches, equipped with loudspeakers, broadcast sounds of a huge fleet off the Calais coast, miles from the true invasion beaches. The launches split into two groups: Taxable and Glimmer. Both groups of launches had radar apparatus, code-named "Moonshine," that gave the impression of a huge fleet of ships, a mass of shipping in the English channel. Taxable and Glimmer launches rattled on through the pre-dawn hours, leaving the Germans with the impression that the beginning of the attack at Normandy was only a feint while the massed attack was at Calais. The Germans bombarded the "ghost fleet," which by dawn had vanished.

The German command hesitated to send tanks to Normandy, relying on Garbo/Arabel information, holding them back to oppose the expected 25 or more divisions of the First U.S. Army Group under Patton. Hitler himself, as well as Colonel Alexis Baron Von Roenn in the field, remained convinced that FUSAG was coming to Calais, even after the Allied troops were well ashore at Normandy. Despite repeated requests from German defenders at Normandy, Hitler refused to release the armored forces from the defense against the notional attack at Calais. Rommel, who was assigned to handle the defense, grew increasingly frustrated at Hitler's refusal.

## Fortitude

In a larger operation, known as "Fortitude," public speakers and radio broadcasts to the French underground resistance continued to assert that the Normandy attack was only an initial assault. When Churchill addressed Parliament on D-Day, he spent 10 minutes describing the liberation of Rome, then mentioned the attack on the coast of France, hinting that it was the first of many such attacks scheduled. Again, the Fortitude plan kept the Germans guessing.

A possible flaw in the Fortitude speeches developed when Charles de Gaulle, broadcasting from England, asserted that the Normandy landing was the major attack and the initiation of the liberation of Europe. De Gaulle's speech to the French resistance and others in Europe was a terrible breach of the Fortitude attempt to convince the Germans another major attack was pending.

However, a carefully worded message from Garbo to Germany helped save the appearances. He had learned, he reported, that it was Churchill who had violated a pledge to conceal reference to future attacks, and it was De Gaulle who had been following a deception plan! It was Garbo's information on D-Day that the Germans trusted so much that they began the process to award him the Iron Cross.

## Sabotage

British and American agents working with the French underground coordinated their attacks with Overlord (see Chapter 6). However, to give the Germans the impression that the main attack was still pending near Calais, a few acts of sabotage around that area were coupled with a high volume of radio instructions sent to dozens of notional resistance leaders.

The actual cutting of roads, rail lines, and bridges by French resistance fighters was quite effective. In the south of France, every train leaving Marseille for Lyon was derailed at least one time in its trip, making it almost impossible for the Germans to route supplies from the south directly to the Normandy area. The combining of real acts of sabotage with deception bogged down the German effort to reinforce their troops against the growing Normandy beachhead. Some German units had to fight their way through resistance snipers and small guerilla units, not arriving to confront the Allied landing forces until D+17.

# A Great Deceiver

Although the great deceptions of World War II were those initiated to plant disinformation, the Germans had other sources that were quite reliable. Luckily for the Allies, the Germans over and over chose to rely on the false, planted information rather than on good data that came from other sources. One such good source for the Germans was a *walk-in*.

Probably the most notorious of the walk-ins who provided information to Germany was code-named Cicero. Cicero, whose real name was Elyesa Bazna, was a Turkish national of Albanian ancestry employed by the British embassy in Ankara, Turkey.

**Spy Words**

In espionage, every now and then, an individual completely unconnected with an intelligence operation will volunteer to help by conveying information, whether motivated by idealism, patriotism, or by a desire to get rich quick. In tradecraft, such a volunteer is known as a **walk-in**.

---

**Spy Bios**

Elyesa Bazna was born in what later became the Kosovo province of Yugoslavia, a descendant of the Turkish ruling classes, an ethnic Albanian. As a child, he had moved with his family south to Salonika, then held by Turkey, and when Salonika became part of Greece, moved on to Istanbul. Elyesa, by his own admission, was a "black sheep" of the well-off family, doing badly in school and getting involved in minor crimes like stealing a motorcycle or pistol.

After several petty thefts, he was arrested and sent to a prison camp in Marseilles, France, where he learned to speak and read French. When the Allies occupied Turkey at the end of World War I, he returned to Turkey and worked as a truck driver and then as a chauffeur for a British captain. His fluency in French helped qualify him for the work with the foreigners in Turkey and he was ready to spy.

---

After World War I, Bazna continued to find work in Turkey as a "*kavass*," a menial servant to a foreigner. He first worked as a servant for the Yugoslav ambassador, then for Albert Jenke, counsel of the German embassy (brother-in-law of German

Foreign Minister Joachim von Ribbentrop), then with Douglas Busk, first secretary of the British embassy. Finally, by 1943, he was employed by Hughe Knatchbull-Hugessen, the British Ambassador to Turkey.

During World War II, Turkey remained neutral, and like Switzerland, it became a hotbed of intrigue among the legations of the warring nations.

## Cicero's Methods

As a *kavass*, Elyesa Bazna was regarded as a nobody, or so he felt. Partly out of resentment at his position as valet and driver, and partly out of a desire to make something of his life by a windfall of cash, he decided to photograph documents at the British embassy and provide them to the Germans. He had taken up photography as a hobby, and he found it easy to rig up a photo stand in his small room in the embassy residence.

Despite the fact that Bazna had no training, he was a natural at the deception he had to play, perhaps because he had spent nearly two decades acting the role of humble servant while always considering himself a member of a natural elite. In any case, when he visited his former employers at the German embassy with his tale of top secret documents, he was not at first believed. Eventually, however, he contacted L. C. Moyzisch, officially the Commercial Attaché of the German embassy, but in reality an officer of the German SS and representative of the German Reich Security Department.

___

**Tradecraft** _____

In the world of espionage and counterespionage, the practice of good protection of classified information is known as operational security, or "op-sec." Ambassador Knatchbull-Hugessen committed some of the gravest errors of op-sec of the whole war. He kept top secret documents in a safe that locked with a key. Bazna made a wax impression of the key, had a duplicate made, and had no trouble getting the documents. He would smuggle the documents from the ambassador's study in his jacket, photograph them, and quietly return them when the ambassador was out with his wife attending diplomatic functions. Bazna rather delighted in outwitting the ambassador, whose disdain for him as lowly *kavass* appeared to fuel his actions.

___

Moyzisch did not think much of Bazna, and was shocked when Bazna demanded £20,000 in British banknotes for his first delivery of pictures. However, Moyzisch came to recognize the value of what Bazna supplied. He wrote later that Bazna appeared to be a man "accustomed to disguising his true feelings," the characteristic of a servant and a particularly useful quality in a spy. Moyzisch thought Bazna's French was very poor, but Bazna prided himself on the accent he had picked up in the Marseilles prison. They were probably both right.

## The Cicero Documents

The Germans code-named Bazna Cicero and soon found that he supplied them with extremely high-level material. Bazna liked to believe that the code name was chosen because the original Cicero was a Roman orator, an apparent reference to the eloquence of his documents. The ambassador had reports of correspondence seeking to get Turkey to side with the Allies. Details of war plans, information about Overlord, and British plans for the invasion of Greece all came through the ambassador's hands.

Cicero became a good source of information for the Germans, and although his identity was not known, the Allies soon realized from the information that began to show up in Enigma transmissions that there was a leak in the British embassy in Ankara. Allen Dulles, the American OSS officer in Switzerland (see Chapter 6), received a smuggled document from Germany that could only have come from a leak in the British diplomatic office in Turkey. In addition, Cornelia Kapp, an agent for the Americans, worked as Moyzisch's secretary, and she knew that someone the Germans had code-named Cicero was inside the British embassy.

Soon Ambassador Hughe Knatchbull-Hugessen received instructions to tighten up his document handling, and the flow of information to Cicero was cut off. After the Normandy invasion, the British recalled the ambassador and reassigned him to Belgium. Despite Cicero's information, when it conflicted with data from Garbo/Arabel, the Germans tended to trust the false information and distrust the real information, assuming that much of it had been planted. Moyzisch himself said that although the operation was a perfect success, it did little real damage to the British because of the German inability to believe in and take advantage of the information.

All in all, Bazna/Cicero received over £300,000 in British banknotes for the documents that he provided to the Germans. He later claimed he wanted the payment in British pounds because he believed they would win the war, even though he was working for the Germans.

At the end of the war, Bazna decided to invest his wealth, worth well over $5 million in 2003 dollars, in a new hotel. As he began to spend the money on architects, as well as in a lavish lifestyle, he received a shock. The Turkish authorities closed in on him. All of the currency he had was counterfeit, manufactured by the Germans during the war as part of an effort to cause British inflation, and used for various clandestine purposes. Bazna was broke.

The scandal surrounding the poor handling of documents, that is, bad operational security, by the British ambassador, was quietly forgotten. A memoir by Moyzisch, entitled *Operation Cicero*, was published in 1951. A fictionalized but dramatic movie starring James Mason was based on the story, *Five Fingers*, which came out in 1952. Bazna himself followed up with his own story, *I Was Cicero*, in 1962. Despite the failure of British op-sec, the failure of German intelligence to use the information, and the failure of Bazna to secure his fortune, Operation Cicero was one of the great spy stories of World War II.

## The Least You Need to Know

- The British Double Cross system of turned German agents in Britain succeeded in supplying the Germans with lots of false information during World War II.

- "The Man Who Never Was," Major Martin, was a corpse carrying a convincing set of documents establishing a false identity and providing misdirection to the Germans about the objective of Operation Husky.

- In Operation Overlord, the invasion of Normandy, the Germans were successfully deceived into believing the attacks would come elsewhere through dozens of separate deceptions, including the work of Juan Pujol, known to the British as Garbo and to the Germans as Arabel.

- In Operation Cicero, the Germans failed to take advantage of one of the war's natural great deceivers, the Albanian valet to the British ambassador to Turkey.

# Chapter 6

# The OSS

## In This Chapter

- Formation of the Office of Strategic Services
- Allen Dulles in Switzerland
- Supporting guerrillas
- Agency infighting and precedents
- The German A-Bomb

In this chapter, we look at the Office of Strategic Services (OSS), set up in World War II to provide intelligence to the U.S. armed forces and to conduct special operations behind enemy lines. A forerunner of the Central Intelligence Agency established in later years, the OSS had some notable successes, but also many frustrations and difficulties. We see how interservice rivalry and jealousies made it difficult for William Donovan to make best use of the organization. Many professionals in the Army and Navy thought of "Wild Bill" Donovan's organization as full of upstart amateurs. We look at some of the adventures of the OSS in occupied Europe, in neutral Switzerland, and as far afield as Burma and India.

# Roots of the OSS

The British Secret Intelligence Service (SIS—later known as MI-6) sought to ensure that the United States became an ally in World War II, and did not remain neutral. From September 1939 until December 1941, however, the United States was officially neutral, and as Britain faced its "darkest hour" in the bombing raids of the Battle of Britain in 1940, British agents sought to influence American opinion.

The man who led that effort was William Stephenson, a Scottish-Canadian millionaire who had been a flying ace in World War I. Stephenson was the unofficial channel for British influence in the United States following his appointment in May 1940. Known as "Intrepid," Stephenson worked with Franklin Roosevelt, J. Edgar Hoover of the FBI, and others, urging them to send a confidential expert to Britain to learn exactly what Britain was facing and to report back to the American security agencies.

## Enter Wild Bill Donovan

In July 1940, at a meeting at the White House, Secretary of State Cordell Hull, Secretary of War Henry Stimson, and Secretary of the Navy Frank Knox agreed to send William Donovan on the mission. Donovan was a successful Wall Street lawyer, and a reserve Army colonel who had won the Medal of Honor in World War I. Donovan was well-known, publicly as well as personally, to the members of Roosevelt's cabinet. William Stephenson cabled London to have the British security establishment give Donovan their full confidence and fill him in on the plight of Britain.

| Spy Bios |
| --- |
| William Donovan (1883–1959) organized "Troop 1" of the New York National Guard, and in World War I served as Colonel in charge of the 165th Infantry of the 42nd Division. He earned the Distinguished Service Cross on July 28, 1918, and the Congressional Medal of Honor three months later. In 1922, he was appointed as U.S. attorney in Buffalo, New York, and in 1924 he organized the Antitrust Division of the Justice Department in Washington. He turned down the position of governor of the Philippines to return to private law practice in 1929. He continued his interest in foreign affairs, making observation trips and reporting to the U.S. government on the Italian invasion of Ethiopia in 1935, and on conditions in eastern Europe and on the Spanish Civil War in 1938. After heading the OSS in World War II, Donovan remained an advocate of a centralized intelligence agency. |

In Britain, Donovan learned about British radar systems, and the developing Double Cross system, although at this point he was not let in on the work of Bletchley Park in cracking the Enigma codes. When Donovan returned, he met with Stephenson several times, and discussed the need for a central, coordinated U.S. Intelligence Agency. Later, Donovan's close relationship with the top British secret agent in the United States raised suspicions he was too pro-British.

His World War I nickname, "Wild Bill," seemed appropriate to some of the more conservative heads of the traditional intelligence agencies, who disliked the rumors they heard about his proposal to challenge their separate turfs. When the head of Army G-2, General Sherman Miles, heard of the idea, he said it would be "disadvantageous, even calamitous."

## Formation of COI

In late 1940 and early 1941, Donovan returned to Europe, this time visiting North Africa and the Balkans as well as Britain. He met with Churchill, and on his return, gave a public report over the radio and a confidential report to President Roosevelt. Donovan continued to press for a Central Intelligence Agency. On July 11, 1941, Roosevelt appointed Donovan to be coordinator of intelligence, reporting directly to the president, and consulting with the heads of the existing intelligence agencies: Army G-2, FBI, Navy's ONI, and State Department.

The Coordinator of Intelligence (COI) was a breakthrough. As the agencies had discovered in the late 1930s, when they tried to counter domestic activities of pro-Nazi groups and communists, it was difficult to get clear intelligence and to exchange it between the different agencies. It was hoped the new COI would bring the information together. Furthermore, the COI was established not by Congress, but by the president, acting in his role as commander in chief—showing an aspect of the growth of presidential power. Donovan jumped into the job with characteristic energy.

## COI Underway

The FBI's J. Edgar Hoover called the new agency "Roosevelt's folly," and secured the responsibility to continue FBI operations in Latin America.

Although the existing agencies remained suspicious, Donovan got right to work, recruiting people to serve as creators of propaganda, and he built an intelligence gathering and research-and-analysis team. In the first months, he drew on a class of wealthy contacts in New York and among Ivy League alumni. Among Donovan's early recruits were Archibald MacLeish, head of the Library of Congress and noted poet; James Roosevelt, the son of the president; film director John Ford; and William Vanderbilt, millionaire.

The contacts with William Stephenson paid off. Stephenson set up a school in Toronto for training COI staff, and Donovan kept in touch with British intelligence through Stephenson.

# Formation of OSS

No sooner had the COI begun to operate than the Japanese struck Pearl Harbor. The existing agencies—State, Army, Navy, FBI—all sought to split up COI personnel and responsibilities and distribute them.

Donovan sought to expand the role of the agency to meet the new war conditions, and on June 13, 1942, the COI was split. The propaganda functions and staff were transferred to the Office of War Information, and the rest of COI was incorporated in the new agency, the Office of Strategic Services (OSS), which Donovan headed. The OSS would not report directly to the president, however, but to the military Joint Chiefs of Staff. By December, the Joint Chiefs decided to use the OSS in several roles: sabotage, espionage, counterespionage, and covert action. The Joint Chiefs agreed that the OSS should work to undermine enemy morale and support behind-the-lines sabotage of enemy facilities.

**Spy Words**

It became a standing joke that **OSS** stood for Oh So Social, referring to the fact that Donovan tended to recruit as his closest advisors and operatives men and women from the wealthiest classes of Americans. These included David Bruce, a millionaire, and brother-in-law of Paul Mellon, who was also recruited to OSS, heir to the Mellon fortune of Pittsburgh.

The OSS soon grew into a major agency, operating in many of the theaters of the war. The Special Intelligence (SI) division gathered reams of intelligence, much of it from open literature such as newspapers and magazines, supplemented with information supplied from agents on the ground. The Special Operations (SO) division was in charge of sending agents, saboteurs, and guerrilla organizers behind the lines. The Morale Operations (MO) division set up a radio station, *Soldat Ensender*, to beam news and rumors in German to enemy troops.

In occupied western Europe, the OSS cooperated with the British Special Operations Executive (SOE) in supporting resistance behind the lines, particularly in France. In Yugoslavia, the British SOE and the American OSS started out by supporting different anti-German factions. In neutral Switzerland, the OSS established an information gathering and coordinating office under Allen Dulles that played a crucial role in numerous operations. However, in the Pacific Theater, General Douglas MacArthur succeeded in excluding the OSS, and Donovan had only limited success in working with the British forces attacking the Japanese through Burma.

# OSS at War

Many of the operations of the OSS remained secret during the war, and the American public only learned some of the stories in later years. Altogether, some 25,000 civilians and soldiers served in the OSS during the war, not counting the locally recruited sub-agents in various countries. Some sources put the total at 30,000.

## SOE and OSS Cooperation on the Jedburghs

The OSS helped the SOE support European resistance groups that the SOE had started. The British general in SOE who developed the concept assigned the code name *Jedburgh* for his plan to arm civilian populations to carry out guerrilla activities against enemy communication lines in 1942. The name was derived from a small town on the Scots-English border; the Scots heritage of armed resistance to the English may have influenced the name choice.

The Jedburgh program evolved into plans for a total of 70 teams, with 35 each to be supported by the British and the Americans. Later in 1942, it was decided that the teams would be headed by two officers, one from Britain or the United States, the other from the local groups of Belgian, Dutch, and French soldiers. The teams ranged in size from small groups up to 200 or more guerrillas, sometimes engaging in pitched battles that helped hold down German troops, an especially important contribution during the invasion of Normandy (see Chapter 5).

*William Donovan headed the OSS that combined intelligence gathering and special operations behind enemy lines.*

*(Courtesy of the Library of Congress)*

**Spy Words** _____

The **Jedburghs,** units of resistance troops supported by airdrops and a few military officers from SOE and OSS, were based on examples of guerrilla troops in Ireland and elsewhere. The Jedburghs operated in France, Belgium, and Holland. The French terms *maquis* and *maquisard* were derived from wild, brush-covered country on the island of Corsica. In eastern Europe, most of the local resistance forces were known as *partisans*, representing irregular troops organized on a political or party basis.

OSS officers recruited for the Jedburghs often started their training at the Congressional Country Club in Montgomery County, Maryland, where they lived in tents and attended courses in the golf clubhouse. After orientation, they were sent to the nearby Catoctin Mountains, where the OSS took over a hunting lodge, later famous as the Camp David presidential retreat. There the teams learned how to work with U.S. small arms and a mixture of foreign arms they might pick up in Europe. They also received training in compass and map work, in the French language, lots of physical training, and familiarization with the conditions they would encounter on the ground in Europe. Particularly impressive was hand-to-hand fight training with knives led by the former British chief of the Hong Kong police.

In Britain, the American OSS officers got further training with the SOE officers at Milton Hall in eastern England. Like Bletchley, it was a British estate, with a rambling mansion in the center of it. The main house at Milton Hall had the administration rooms, a lecture hall, and some recreation facilities. In the outlying fields, temporary buildings provided housing. There the teams learned radio communications, cipher use, further language training, homemade explosives for demolition work, and intensive parachute training. Other courses covered such topics as night navigation, escape and evasion, the use of couriers, ambush, and security.

**Tradecraft** _____

The British maintained the Special Air Service (SAS) as well as the SOE. The two organizations had similar missions, although the SAS sent whole units of British troops to fight behind enemy lines, rather than building up units of local French, Belgian, or Dutch forces on the ground. Sometimes the overlapping responsibilities of SOE, OSS, and SAS led to conflicting requests for resources, as there was no coordinating organization. The SAS units continued to train and receive special missions throughout the decades following World War II, although SOE and OSS were disbanded.

Once the Jedburghs, together with Special Air Service (SAS) troops landed in France, they would set up radio contact with Britain and bring in supplies, either in "packages" or "containers" dropped by parachute. The packages were large rectangular boxes and the containers were metal or plastic cylindrical cases holding supplies such as gasoline, ammunition, and explosives. Once on the ground, armed French resistance fighters would join the Jedburghs, and as new arms were brought in, more and more quiet sympathizers known as *sedentaires*, would become active and armed.

---

### Techint

The Jedburghs had their own weapons, including a special handheld anti-tank weapon known as a Piat (projector, infantry, anti-tank) with a range of 100 yards, but weighing only 32 pounds. A favorite weapon of the Jedburghs was the Bren gun, a British modification of a Czech machine gun that fired .303-inch ammunition, holding 30 rounds in a magazine. The Jedburgh local recruits and partisans elsewhere were often supplied with the Sten gun, a small semiautomatic weapon fondly known as a "pipe and a bedspring," that was cheap to make, easy to dismantle, and quite rugged.

---

The Jedburghs eventually had more than the originally planned 70 teams. Most of them were in occupied France, with six more in Holland and Belgium, and another 20 or so operating in southern France. Each team had an innocuous code name, such as Alfred, Arnold, Andrew, or Jacob, each with a designated area of operations.

Although the SOE and OSS were theoretically co-equal in sending in these teams, the SOE was the senior partner, partly because of experience and partly because of control of the operation out of Britain.

After the Allied invasion of Normandy, the Jedburghs harassed the German rear lines, often engaging German armored and infantry forces in hot firefights. With information sources on the ground and radio communications to Britain, the teams could relay valuable information about German troop movements, supply centers, and transport details.

### Spy Bios

David Bruce headed up the Special Intelligence Division of OSS, then was appointed by Donovan as commanding officer of the whole OSS operation in the European theater. He operated his office out of a facility at 70 Grosvenor Square in London, later expanded to the adjacent buildings. Bruce was a Princeton graduate, a lawyer, and gentleman farmer, well received by the British. Later, he served as U.S. ambassador to France, and then to West Germany.

## OSS in Holland and Norway

On a much smaller level, OSS teams parachuted into Holland and Norway to provide tactical intelligence and to work with resistance units in those countries. To operate in Holland, General Donovan personally recruited Lieutenant Jan Laverge, an American-born son of Dutch refugees in England. The OSS team eventually set up to help in the liberation of Holland consisted of six officers and about eight enlisted men. The mission was code-named Melanie, and was to focus on transmitting information from the Dutch underground. In Operation Market Garden, later made famous in the book and movie, *A Bridge Too Far*, OSS agents worked behind the lines to provide intelligence to the advancing Allied troops.

In Norway, Major William Colby (who would later serve as Director of Central Intelligence) led a behind-the-lines sabotage operation called Operation Rype. His story of the operation remained unpublished until the winter of 1999, three years after his death. Colby later noted that it was the first and only combined ski-parachute operation ever mounted by the U.S. Army. Twenty American OSS soldiers and four Norwegian underground members set out to blast a bridge at Grana.

### Spy Bios

William Colby (1920–1996) was son of an Army officer and college professor. He attended Princeton University, graduating in 1940, and then he enrolled in Columbia Law School for one year. He joined the Army as an officer and took parachute training at Fort Bragg before joining the OSS as a recruiting officer. After training in guerrilla warfare in Britain, Colby had missions behind the lines in France and Norway. After World War II, he finished his law degree and joined William Donovan's law firm. In 1950, he joined the Central Intelligence Agency, and served in several positions with the agency. President Richard Nixon appointed Colby Director of Central Intelligence in 1973 and he served in that post until 1976.

Colby's group had originally planned to steal a train, but the group settled for blowing up a bridge. With recruits and more explosives, they destroyed more railway lines, took on some German patrols, and shot their way out of Norway to safety. They were still on the ground in May 1945 when Germany surrendered, never accomplishing very much in the way of damage to the German war effort.

## SOE OSS Troubles in Yugoslavia

The lack of coordination between allied special operations groups created some dangerous mix-ups. In Yugoslavia, the British SOE provided support to the partisan units fighting under Marshall Tito, whose forces were dedicated to establishing a communist regime in postwar Yugoslavia and Albania. The Americans supported the anti-German forces of the Serbian Monarchist Colonel Draza Mihailovic known as Chetniks. Oddly enough, the Soviet Union was supporting Mihailovic as well.

Soon the Chetniks and the Partisans were fighting each other. The Partisans bought or stole weapons from the Chetniks and used them to fight Chetnik forces. Meanwhile, the heir to the throne, King Peter, lived in London, where the British pressured him to dismiss his minister of war, Mihailovic. Eventually, the Americans pulled out, and both the British and the Russians cooperated in supporting Tito.

## Piercing the Reich

Sending teams to work in occupied sections of Europe was difficult, but sending OSS agents into Germany itself presented more serious problems. Nevertheless, before the end of the war, some 100 teams had parachuted into Germany, with a total of more than 200 agents. William J. Casey (1913–1986) in London headed the German operation. Casey later served as Director of Central Intelligence under President Ronald Reagan.

| Techint |
| --- |
| A problem confronting OSS agents in Germany was that their radio reports could give away their location, as the Germans used truck-mounted goniometers or radio-direction finders. Steve Simpson, a former RCA electronics engineer, presented a solution. He developed a radio that broadcast, not in every direction, but straight up. The messages could be picked up by a U.S. Air Force plane circling overhead and then recorded or relayed to headquarters. An additional advantage was that the agent could broadcast in plain English, not requiring elaborate encoding and deciphering. Simpson called the radio the Jane-Eleanor system, for two of his girlfriends. Apparently, he had trouble choosing between them! |

David Bruce of the Special Intelligence (SI) office of OSS, in charge of all penetrations, appointed Casey to organize the penetration of Nazi Germany in June 1944.

Sixteen of the teams to go into Germany were made up of Poles who had every reason to hate the German regime. However, when the Allied leaders met at Yalta in February 1945, they agreed with Russian demands to cede part of Poland to the Soviet Union. The morale of the Polish teams evaporated almost at once.

Other teams had other problems. Some groups would land, and in a few days, begin to send back shortwave radio messages. Others would simply disappear, perhaps killed in the parachute fall or shot on landing.

Recruiting the teams was difficult. Prisoners of war, some of whom might have been anti-Nazi, could have presented a pool of recruits, but the Geneva Convention prohibited such recruitment. American boys fluent in German and healthy enough to parachute would be suspect if they tried to pass themselves off as German civilians,

### Tradecraft

To ready the agents, Casey equipped them with legend identities, forged documents, money, and suitcases filled with clothes, toothbrush, wallets, shoes, and combs, all bought from refugees or requisitioned from prisoners of war. Casey estimated that their cover stories were thin: ten percent fact, ninety percent invention based on guesswork.

because all young men were in the German military. The best source was refugees in Britain from some of the occupied countries, since Germany had drawn civilian workers into their factories from France, Poland, and other conquered territories. Another choice was German communist refugees, and Casey opposed their use. However, Donovan insisted that he would accept them, and Casey reluctantly went along.

Casey, trained in law, found a way around the ban on recruiting prisoners of war. If in discussions, they chose to *volunteer* to fight against Hitler, no one could say they were recruited. He got a few in that fashion.

Another source was German nationals who had fled Germany because of their labor union activity. The recruitment of this group was headed up by SI's Labor Division led by a New York labor lawyer, Arthur Goldberg (later appointed to the Supreme Court by President Kennedy). Goldberg urged recruiting among a group of left-wing German unionists organized in a National Committee for a Free Germany. Although dominated from Moscow, the Free Germany movement provided some solid recruits for Casey's operation, not all of whom were communists.

### Spy Bios

Paul Lindner was 34 years old when he parachuted into Germany on the Hammer mission. He had been born in Berlin, and grew up in a social democratic home, becoming active in the German labor movement as a teenager. He helped organize the German Metal Workers' Union, and in 1930, he spoke out against the Nazi plan to draft German youth. In 1932, Nazi storm troopers attacked and beat him up, and when Hitler was appointed chancellor, the Nazis arrested Lindner and beat and tortured him for 12 days. He organized a hiking club as a cover for a resistance group and continued distributing anti-Nazi literature. He smuggled Jews into Czechoslovakia and fled himself in 1939 to Britain. He was deported to Canada in 1940, then was finally released. He and his English wife moved back to London in 1942 and he eagerly jumped at the chance to join the OSS penetration effort against the Reich.

Some of the teams were quite successful. One named Hammer sent out messages relayed by a circling aircraft, pinpointing a power plant that supplied electricity to a tank factory in the suburbs of Berlin. The two men on the Hammer mission, Paul Lindner and Anton Ruh, were both recruited from the Free Germany movement. Another mission, named Chauffeur, set up in Regensburg, Germany. There, two French girls who had been forced into prostitution for the Germans cooperated. The OSS agents hid in a closet, listened to discussions by German officers after their visits with girls, and radioed information from an open field outside of town, detailing the movement of German troops.

A team named Luxe gave targeting details for a bombing raid on rail yards at Weilheim. Unfortunately, the American bombs missed the target there and hit a residential neighborhood and a hospital.

**Tradecraft**

Casey gave explicit instructions to agents parachuted into Germany on what to do if captured. If the agent could not escape, he or she could bite down on the "L Pill," consisting of a cyanide pill in a rubber casing, that resulted in immediate death. At the last minute, the agent could reconsider, and swallow the pill, passing it harmlessly because of the coating. If they decided to tough it out, they were to hold out for 48 hours before answering questions. By that time, any accomplices had time to get away or cover their tracks.

Casey in London recruited a German refugee by the name of Hilde Meisl. She was flown to France, went through Switzerland to the Austrian border and under code name Crocus set up an intelligence network among Austrian socialists. The German SS spotted her trying to sneak back into Switzerland and wounded her, but she killed herself with her poison pill before they could question her.

Some other teams were captured or killed on landing, one even landing on an SS unit watching an outdoor movie. At first Casey planned all drops on moonlit nights, but soon found that the agents hit their drop pinpoints just as well if they flew on dark nights, which was safer for the aircraft.

Altogether, just over 200 OSS agents were sent into Germany, and 36 were killed or captured. The 18 percent casualty rate was high, but considering the risks, surprisingly good.

# Italy

For the OSS, Italy was a special case. Part of the Axis, Italy was an enemy country. But so many Italians regarded their fascist leader, Benito Mussolini, as a tyrant that it was possible to construct partisan bands like those operating in Yugoslavia and like the Jedburgh groups of *maquis* in France. Later estimates calculated that the Italian partisans tied down seven German divisions, and actually obtained the surrender of two German divisions, helping in the liberation of Genoa, Turin, and Milan.

One group of 1,200 partisans, known as the 36th Garibaldi Brigade, was armed by airdrops from the OSS. The Germans' own intelligence officer estimated that between June and August 1944, the partisans killed 5,000 German troops and wounded another 25,000. The 28th Garibaldi Brigade was commanded by a brilliant partisan officer code-named Bulow. Later, the OSS discovered that Bulow was a thin, young peasant man from Romagna, yet a brilliant strategist who helped the British 8th Army Chief of Staff plan a surprise attack that liberated Ravenna.

The OSS partisans and communist partisans worked together in the Committee for National Liberation (CNL). The CNL particularly spotted SS and fascist officers known for their atrocities, ordering them executed. The CNL also agreed to the immediate execution of Mussolini when he was captured trying to escape from Italy via the Brenner Pass.

# Our Man in Bern—Allen Dulles

Just as crucial as the armed partisan and Jedburgh units to the war effort was the flow of intelligence out of Switzerland, from the OSS office there headed by Allen Dulles. Known as "Agent 110," Dulles arrived in Bern in November 1942. He carried a special codebook, and a letter of credit for $1 million, with instructions to set up an office of the OSS. Although his mission was secret, the local press realized something was up, and he was reported as the personal representative of President Roosevelt. Dulles claimed that the publicity was not a bad idea, since it helped informants get in touch with him. He was the last American to enter Switzerland legally for a year and a half.

---

### Spy Bios

Allen Dulles (1893–1969) had worked with his brother, John Foster Dulles, at the prestigious New York law firm of Sullivan and Cromwell. His international career began in World War I, when he represented the United States at the funeral of the emperor of Austria-Hungary in Vienna in 1916. He was recruited into the OSS by David Bruce, and after service in Switzerland during World War II, he returned to private law practice. In 1953, President Eisenhower appointed Dulles Director of Central Intelligence, and he served in that post until 1961.

No more Americans could get into Switzerland, as Axis-controlled territories surrounded it. To build up a staff, Dulles tapped into the country's American community, including executives from Standard Oil, National City Bank, and others. He radioed out his information, and after October 1943, began smuggling out microfilm to be relayed by the French underground to Corsica, where it was flown to Algiers, taking about 10 or 12 days.

Dulles collected information from a wide variety of sources, including anti-Nazi German exiles, German clergymen and laborers, and a variety of walk-ins. Among the most important sources was walk-in Fritz Kolbe, who worked in the German foreign office and who Dulles called George Wood. In fact, in his memoirs published years later, Dulles continued to call Kolbe by his code name, Wood.

Dulles supplied key information, not all of it believed at the time. He provided details on the V-1 and V-2 rockets and their factories, information about the German atomic bomb project, and liaison for planning the surrender of German forces in Italy a week before the final surrender of Germany.

## Moe Berg and Werner Heisenberg

One of the more colorful OSS agents to pass through Switzerland on Dulles' watch was a former baseball player by the name of Moe Berg. Donovan sent Berg to Switzerland to investigate the German atomic bomb project, and to make contact with Werner Heisenberg, the German physicist who headed up the Nazi effort in nuclear research.

Berg attended a lecture by Heisenberg in Zurich in November 1944, later claiming he sat in the front row with a pistol in his pocket, ready to assassinate the physicist. Berg came to conclude that the German project was lagging behind, and that the German physicists already thought that Germany was losing the war, so he left the pistol in his pocket. No doubt Berg's memoirs exaggerated his role quite a bit.

However, Berg's reports of Heisenberg's comments were right on the mark. The German A-bomb project was underfinanced and by the end of 1944, had not achieved even the controlled chain reaction that the Americans had accomplished two years earlier. And Germany fought on only for another six months.

## Nazi Gold

During World War II, the Nazi government stole the gold reserves worth hundreds of millions of dollars from Belgium and other countries. In a German plan known as

Safehaven, the Germans passed the gold through banks in Switzerland in order to have reserves that could be called upon after the war, if Germany were defeated, to revive an international Nazi movement. American intelligence knew of the plans through Enigma decrypts and other sources. Working with sources in Swiss banks, Dulles began to relay back through OSS details of the transactions that passed through banks to Sweden, Portugal, Turkey, and Argentina.

Much of the money remained in Switzerland, however. In the post-war world the Swiss made a token payment of $58 million back to the victim nations, and OSS information kept the Americans posted on the details as the settlements were negotiated.

# OSS in Burma

By contrast to the role played in Europe by the OSS, its role in the Pacific Theater of the war was much smaller. According to OSS memoirists, the reason was that General Douglas MacArthur simply refused to work with OSS, relying only on Army G-2 and Ultra information, while the Navy had its own sources of information through code-breaking and ONI. The Navy, like the Army, refused to work with the OSS.

It was true that the type of penetration operations into Germany would have been almost impossible to achieve in Japan as any American agent would be quickly spotted as a foreigner. But an effort similar to the Jedburgh operation was successful in one backwater of the Pacific Theater: Burma.

## Detachment 101

In Burma, the OSS "Detachment 101," like the Jedburghs and the OSS operations with Italian partisans, worked closely with the irregular forces fighting the Japanese. Originally only 21 OSS officers, under command of Major Carl Eifler, worked with local tribesmen known as Kachins to build up an irregular force eventually numbering about 1,000 insurgents. Working in northern Burma along the Chinese border, Detachment 101 provided information to the U.S. 10th Air Force to bomb Japanese targets.

Through 1943 and 1944, the Allies tried to push through a road from Ledo in the Assam province of India to Myitkyina in Burma. From there a road over the mountains into China could be used to truck in supplies to the nationalist Chinese fighting the Japanese in southern China. Detachment 101 and its Kachin fighters assisted a special force of American troops, "Merrill's Marauders," in defeating the Japanese at Myitkyina in the spring of 1944. Detachment 101 and its native allies suffered only 89 dead while killing at least 5,400 Japanese troops, the highest ratio of any unit in the war.

## Other OSS Ops in SE Asia

From bases in New Delhi, India, and on the island of Ceylon, other OSS agents supervised a network of informants and saboteurs in Burma, Malaya, and Indonesia, working with refugees from the countries. Probably the most highly placed agent of the OSS in the region was Mom Rajawongse Seni Pramoj, whose code name was Ruth. Former ambassador to the United States, he became prime minister of Thailand immediately after the war.

# OSS Legacy

Military officers look to history for lessons learned, and the experience of the OSS provided many such lessons, from large questions of strategy, to details of tactics and operational security or op-sec. What worked and what did not work were reviewed for years, and later intelligence officers in the United States reviewed the details of operations in the countryside of France, in London, in Bern, and in the airdrops behind enemy lines.

The legacy of the OSS took other forms, too, in the orientation of a whole generation of leaders who continued to influence American intelligence policy over the next decades. On a more sinister level, it was later learned that Soviet agents had successfully penetrated the OSS. Intelligence officers in the United States would recall such breaches of security and try to guard against their recurrence.

## Some Lessons Learned

OSS officers were frank to admit that they learned a lot about special operations from the British. Memoirs and reports gave repeated accounts of the type of training that applied, of the penchant for masses of data and background information that Donovan inspired, and the exact tactics of airdrops of men and equipment. The legacy of sending armed men and women to operate as irregular military forces in the heart of land held by the enemy would become a hallmark of many of the "secret wars" conducted by the United States over the next 50 years.

The failure to act on good intelligence when it came through always troubled agents like Dulles, Colby, and Bruce, who were closer to the sources than the officers back in Washington. And more outrageous, most OSS veterans agreed, was the refusal of some regular officers, especially MacArthur, to even make use of OSS efforts.

Providing a central clearinghouse for intelligence remained a goal. If all the sources, whether provided from signals intelligence and code-breaking, or from agents and walk-ins, could be coordinated and interpreted wisely, American security would be enhanced. Such an agency, perhaps, could prevent future Pearl Harbors.

## HST Nixes OSS

After months of bureaucratic infighting between September 1945 and January 1946, President Harry Truman dissolved the OSS. He was not going to have any "American Gestapo," he said. Like many others, he feared the development of a strong intelligence agency in peacetime, and may have seen Donovan as a political rival. Intelligence planning over the next two years remained a hot topic in Congress, in the press, and in the Pentagon. It was said that the only battle the OSS really lost was the one in Washington, D.C.

## People

The veterans of the OSS were a powerful contingent, including many bright and accomplished people. Some who worked in Donovan's early information agency, like Archibald MacLeish and Arthur Schlesinger Jr., went on to teach at Harvard. An agent who had worked in France was Julia Child, later famous for her TV cooking show, *The French Chef.* Another young lady, Aline Griffith, who served in the OSS, later married a Spanish count and published her memoirs as the Countess of Romanones, *The Spy Wore Red.* It was such a hit that she wrote two sequels.

Out of veterans of the OSS would come the next generation of leaders of the intelligence and diplomatic communities, including David Bruce, William Casey, William Colby, and Allen Dulles. They would remember the lessons and try to apply them to the cold war that emerged after World War II.

## The Least You Need to Know

- ◆ The Office of Strategic Services at first drew on ideas provided by the British in their Special Operations Executive.

- ◆ OSS agents succeeded in helping resistance fighters against the Nazi occupiers in France, Holland, Belgium, Norway, and Italy.

- ◆ Although excluded from the Pacific Theater of the war, the OSS, with Detachment 101, was active in Burma.

- ◆ The OSS provided a generation of leaders who would influence American intelligence operations over the next 40 years.

# Chapter 7

# Soviet Heroes, Soviet Defectors

## In This Chapter

- Soviet Union's human intelligence
- Illegals and legals
- Richard Sorge and Sonia: Master spies
- Gouzenko and his revelations
- Rudolf Abel—artist at work

In this chapter, we take a look at the tradecraft of the spies who worked for the GRU and the NKVD (or KGB). We follow the stories of a few who were extremely valuable to the Soviet effort, such as Ursula (Ruth) Kuczynski who worked in Britain and in Switzerland, Richard Sorge who served in China and Japan, and Rudolf Abel who went underground in the United States.

Although these loyal agents served the cause of the USSR well, all spy agencies suffered from defectors and traitors. The agencies of the Soviet Union were no exception. A few important agents became disillusioned in the international communist cause and switched sides. At the end of World War II, the defection of Russian agent Igor Gouzenko in Canada sent shock waves through the intelligence world. Because of Gouzenko, Canadians, Americans, and Russians alike had to rethink their *op-sec* or operational security. His revelations helped touch off some of the first intelligence scandals of the cold war.

# Soviet Tradecraft

Like other countries in the 1930s and 1940s, the Soviet Union had agencies that sometimes overlapped and even competed. The Soviet GRU (*Glavnoe Razvedyvatelnoe Upravlenie*) or army intelligence maintained a separate overseas apparatus from the NKVD (which evolved into the KGB—see Chapter 2). The GRU worked directly for the chief of staff of the army of the Soviet Union, in a role similar to the U.S. G-2, who reported to the Assistant Chief of Staff-Intelligence (ACSI). However, the GRU maintained a more elaborate organization overseas than did the American G-2. Both Soviet agencies were excellent at *humint* while the British and Americans tended to rely more on *sigint*.

> **Spy Words**
>
> The Soviet Union's intelligence agencies tended to rely on **humint** (human intelligence), that is, networks of recruiters, controllers, and informants who relayed on-the-spot information to Moscow. By contrast, the British Bletchley Park and the Army Signals Security Agency in the United States relied on **sigint** (signals intelligence). The two categories of work were abbreviated as humint and sigint.

The Soviet GRU and the KGB sometimes fought turf battles. However, the two agencies apparently cooperated at times better than their counterparts in the United States. Once in a while an agent or contact handled by the GRU would be shifted to the NKVD or vice-versa. The NKVD/KGB used the code word Neighbors to describe the GRU, and it seemed that the two agencies did help each other out in a neighborly way.

## Illegals and Legals

Both the NKVD and the GRU sometimes attached an agent to a trade mission, to an embassy, or to a consulate. With diplomatic status, the agent was legally posted to a foreign country. Of course, if the host country found that the diplomat was a spy, they could declare the agent *persona non grata*, withdraw the person's diplomatic status, and require him or her to go home. During the cold war, from time to time, there were waves of such expulsions, when the United States or Britain expelled dozens of diplomats suspected of spying for the Soviet Union, and Moscow would respond by making the Western nation remove an equal number of diplomats from the Russian capital.

However, during World War II, when the Soviet Union, Great Britain, the United States, and Canada were allies, Soviet agents attached to official legal diplomatic missions in the United States, Britain, and Canada went largely undetected, or were quietly tolerated.

The Soviet Union also maintained secret agents, some of whom were citizens of the USSR, and others who had been recruited, usually through the communist international or Comintern, to recruit local informants to supply intelligence. Either entering the target country with forged papers to indicate they were citizens of the country, or traveling under an assumed name on business, this class of agents was known as *illegals*. Unprotected by diplomatic immunity, the illegals could be arrested, and in time of war, executed for espionage. It took guts to be an illegal.

## Dead Drops and Cutouts

Whether illegal or legal, agents of the Soviet Union were experienced in compartmentation, or insulating one group of agents from knowledge of other groups. Often an agent was unknown by his actual name to his sub-agents or suppliers of information. To reduce risk when documents were handed over, they would be placed in a *dead drop*, often a location in a public place that could be inconspicuously approached, such as a park bench.

A signal indicating that the dead drop contained either cash or documents would be posted where it could be innocently seen, often consisting of a chalk mark on a lamppost, a mailbox, or a fence, or signaled by a thumbtack in a particular spot. Thus if an agent or sub-agent were suspected and followed by counterintelligence forces, at least he would never have to meet face to face with his contact more than once to set up the arrangements.

### Tradecraft

The **cutout** was an intermediary who would pick up information or payments, and then deliver the material up or down the chain of command. In a **block cutout**, the contact person knew the name of all the agents working in a particular operation or cell. In a **chain cutout**, the contact knew only one agent, linking only the person below and the person above him in the chain of information flow. Thus if a cutout were apprehended, he would only know that he picked up material from one person with a code name like Rest, and delivered it to another, with a code name like John.

As a further protection, sometimes material would be delivered to the agent through a third party, so that the agent and those providing information never met at all. The Soviets were excellent at using different types of *cutouts*.

The complex safety mechanisms were not always followed, but together they added up to good operational security when used. Perhaps the tradition of working in revolutionary conspiracies against the tsar in Russia had enriched the espionage culture of the country. After training in Moscow, agents became inventive in creating networks that were difficult to penetrate.

**Tradecraft**

Frequently *Moscow Center*, either the GRU or NKVD headquarters, would arrange for a contact to meet a new agent in the field. Since the two had never met, it was important to establish a *recognition signal*. Some of the signals were so intricate that they became the subjects of ridicule when later exposed. A contact might be expected to show up at a particular street corner, carrying a green book and a tennis ball on every Friday at two in the afternoon for a month. The person meeting him would be wearing one pair of gloves and carrying another. After a few rehearsed lines, the two would be sure that they had made contact. Sometimes agents or informants forgot their recognition-signal lines, creating many nervous moments.

# Richard Sorge—The Great Illegal

Some writers have claimed that Richard Sorge was probably the greatest spy of all time. The claim is hard to substantiate, since Sorge was eventually caught, and others who achieved a great deal were never caught or exposed. However, he certainly was smooth, and he did provide excellent, high-level intelligence. If not the greatest he was indeed one of a very few super spies.

For more than four years, Richard Sorge managed a network of agents in Japan, providing information to the Soviet Union of the highest quality. The root of Sorge's loyalty to the Soviet cause was his fervent belief in the communist cause.

## Sorge's Background

Born in 1895 in the Caucasus region of Russia, Sorge was the son of a German oil-drilling engineer. His grandfather gave him a copy of Karl Marx's *Das Kapital*, which he read as a child. When World War I broke out, he was 19, and enlisted in the

German army. Convalescing from wounds, he read extensively in communist theory, and in 1920, became an early member of the German Communist Party. He went on to earn a Ph.D. in political science from the University of Hamburg.

He was recruited in the 1920s to serve as an intelligence agent, and eagerly went to Moscow to receive training. In 1927, he briefly went to Hollywood, California, to help try to set up party cells in the film industry. He showed his ability with languages, gaining fluency in English, French, Russian, and later in Japanese and Chinese.

The GRU recruited Sorge and sent him to Shanghai, China, with the cover story that he was a German newspaperman. While there, Sorge also went under the alias of William Johnson, American journalist. Jan Berzin, the head of the GRU, developed a plan to have Sorge move to Japan, where he would be able to gain insight into German plans. Berzin saw a Tokyo assignment for Sorge as a backdoor means of learning what the Nazi regime in Germany was planning. Berzin selected Sorge and gave him a free hand to develop his own network in Japan. Berzin was later executed in a Soviet purge.

## Sorge Builds His Network

Sorge took two agents with him to Japan from his work in China: Max Klausen, a devoted German communist and good radio operator, and Branko de Vokelic, a former officer in the Yugoslav army, knowledgeable about military information. In addition, Sorge identified two Japanese citizens he could trust: Ozaki Hozumi, a Japanese political journalist, and Miyagi Yotoku, a young man with extensive contacts among liberal Japanese politicians who opposed the government's militarism. It was an excellent network. Ozaki Hozumi became an unofficial advisor to the Japanese cabinet in the period 1937–1939, and then an official of the South Manchurian Railway.

Sorge solidified his own position by returning to Germany and developing a new legend. He joined the Nazi Party, and even made friends with officials in the retinue of Nazi propaganda minister Joseph Goebbels. With this connection, he got appointed as the Japanese correspondent for several leading German newspapers. With everything set up, he arrived in Japan in 1938, with good credentials as a Nazi, a friend of Japan, and a political correspondent. Fluent in Japanese, he made himself useful to Colonel Eugene Ott, the German military attaché at the German embassy in Tokyo. Since Ott could not speak any Japanese, he began to rely on Sorge to help provide him with material that he could file in official reports. Soon, the Soviet Union had an agent in the enviable position of providing Germany with intelligence about Germany's ally, Japan!

Sorge kept building up his network of sub-agents, until he had between 11 and 20 people getting information to him, many of them in important positions in the Japanese government and military. Sorge carefully collected and analyzed the data he received, collating bits of information and putting together a picture from random facts. Sorge soon learned of German plans to invade the Soviet Union and relayed them by radio. However, in Moscow, the Soviet leadership did not believe Sorge's information any more than they believed the relayed Enigma information coming through Switzerland, or other intelligence from within Germany, all pointing to the impending German attack. Unlike Britain and the United States, the Soviet Union had no real intelligence analytic capability.

## Sorge's Op-sec

Sorge realized how dangerous his position was. Japan, after all, was not a democracy. Japanese secret military police or *Kempeitai* remained constantly on the lookout for suspicious activity, as did the civilian *Tokko*, or Special Higher Police. Sorge moved his radio transmitter from one house to another, trying to foil radio-detection work. He even installed it aboard a small sailboat, and Klausen would transmit from the boat from various locations, using the practice of high-speed burst transmission to foil detection.

Sorge used code names for his agents. Thus Klausen did not know who Ozaki was, since Sorge always referred to him as Otto. Max Klausen was known as Fritz to the others. Similar code-names kept all the Sorge sub-agents isolated from knowledge of each other.

The *Kempeitai* knew there was a network of some kind, simply because they picked up bursts of shortwave encoded messages, sent from a hidden clandestine radio. In 1939, the *Kempeitai* arrested Ritsu Ito, who had been leader of the Japanese Communist Party. Under torture, he revealed the names of everyone he knew in the Japanese party who might have been involved in underground work. In this way, the Japanese secret police got the names of two of Sorge's Japanese contacts, Hozumi and Yotoku. The *Kempeitai* began following them to find out their contacts. By 1941, the Japanese were suspicious of all *gai-jin* or foreigners, and noted that Sorge was constantly meeting with high officials. Even though his cover as a German journalist would make such meetings seem natural, they drew attention.

## Sorge's Information

By 1941, Eugene Ott, the military attaché in 1938, had become Germany's ambassador to Japan. Sorge kept in touch with him, meeting often. In this fashion he learned a crucial piece of information. As German forces attacked across Russia, they hoped the Japanese would attack Russia from the East. The Axis treaty did not oblige Japan to attack, but Germany urged them to do so. The Japanese debated whether to assist the Germans. From their bases in Manchuria, China, and Korea, they could have seized vast areas of the Soviet Far East. However, in 1941, the Japanese decided to move to the South—gaining petroleum and other natural resources in Indonesia and Malaya.

Sorge discovered that fact and relayed it to Moscow. This time he was believed. The Soviet Union moved crack troops from the Far Eastern defenses, shipping them by railroad across Siberia back to help defend Moscow from the attacking Germans. The fresh, well-equipped troops combined with the severe Russian winter helped to repel the Germans from the Russian capital.

Sorge even picked up word that the Japanese planned to attack the U.S. Navy, probably in Hawaii, before the end of 1941. Before he could transmit that particular fatal piece of news, however, the *Tokko* closed in.

## Arrest and Prison

The Japanese military and civilian secret police had a tug of war over who should arrest Sorge. The foreign section of the civilian *Tokko* and the military *Kempetai* both suspected Sorge, and were growing nervous about his continued contact with the German ambassador. In August 1941, the local police called in Sorge's mistress, Hanaco-san and told her to break off her relationship with him. Sorge responded by inviting the police chief to dinner.

On October 18, 1941, the *Tokko* rounded up Sorge, Klausen, and Vukelic. Searching Sorge's house, they found not only cameras, but also a partially encoded report, as well as other reports and charts of information. Under questioning, Sorge first claimed to be spying for the Germans. However, confronted with evidence, Sorge began to confess to the Japanese authorities that he was a spy for the Soviet Union. Later investigation into the Japanese records of the case focused on the question of whether Sorge was tortured to get his confession, and most analysts have concluded that he was not.

> **Tradecraft**
>
> The Japanese civilian secret police *Tokko* and the military *Kempetai* military secret police did not cooperate very well. The rivalry between military and civilian security services was an international pattern in the 1940s: G-2, OSS, and ONI did not get on well with the FBI; GRU and NKVD/KGB, although "neighbors," were suspicious of each other; and the German military SS and civilian Gestapo were never comfortable colleagues.

Apparently Sorge concealed the fact that he worked for GRU, fearing that if it became known that he worked for Soviet military intelligence, he might be turned over from the *Tokku* to the *Kempetai* and immediately shot. Eventually Sorge wrote a 200-page autobiographical statement that was published after the war. Although a confession, the document successfully evaded giving details about the espionage apparatus.

After nearly three years of confinement and interrogation, Sorge was executed in April 1944. Altogether, the Japanese arrested 35 men and women in connection with the Sorge case, including 18 who were later found innocent.

Later, an American G-2 officer who had worked with General MacArthur, General Charles A. Willoughby, published *Report of the Sorge Case* that itself became a center of controversy, as it tied American communists to early work of Sorge in China. Other later works, based on released documents, have provided even more details of the *Greatest Illegal* of them all. The Soviet Union later honored Sorge by making him a Hero of the Soviet Union and issuing a postage stamp with his picture on it.

# Ursula (Ruth) Kuczynski

Although the Sorge story has been told and retold, many Soviet agents lived out their lives in relative obscurity, doing their job and quietly retiring. In a few cases, we know of their existence only from memoirs and confessions published many years later. One such case is that of Ursula Ruth Kuczynski.

## Sonia's Background

Ruth Kuczynski, code name Sonia, hardly looked like a spy. In 1941, when British police set out to investigate her in Oxford on reports she had a secret shortwave transmitter, they encountered a nice lady by the name of Mrs. Ruth Beurton, living in an ordinary house, with two ordinary children. But appearances were deceiving.

Ursula Ruth Kuczynski was born in 1908, the daughter of Rene Kuczynski, a prominent German communist and economist. She and her brother, Jeurgen Kuczynski, would become two of the most agile agents for the GRU through the 1930s, acting as talent scouts and recruiters of communists in Britain to serve the Soviet cause as agents.

In 1926, at age 18, she went to New York to operate a bookstore, and there married Rudolph Hamburger. In 1930, Hamburger and Ruth went to Shanghai, China, where he had a job as an architect. There in 1933, Richard Sorge recruited her into the

GRU. She went to Moscow for training, and in 1935, she divorced Hamburger. Apparently on orders from Moscow, she married a GRU agent named Alfred Schultz, who two years later was executed in a Soviet purge.

## Sonia and the Red Orchestra

Sonia, as she was known to the GRU, soon proved very helpful in Europe. She was sent to Switzerland to set up a network based on communists and pro-communist individuals from Britain who had fought for the loyalists during the Spanish Civil War. There she recruited, among others, Alexander Foote (see Chapter 4). Whether Foote was a double agent really serving the British, or whether he served the Soviet cause and defected to the British later, depends on which source you read.

After recruiting Foote and others in Switzerland, Sonia moved to Britain, where she married Leon Beurton (also known as Len Brewer), a veteran of the Spanish Civil War. But Sonia kept at work as a talent scout for the network of World War II agents, who reported by shortwave to Moscow, known as the Red Orchestra. She was in a good position. Her father taught economics at Oxford, and her brother, Jeurgen, got a position as an economic analyst with the British Air Ministry, and later, served with the American OSS (see Chapter 6). In both positions, Jeurgen was able to provide information to the GRU and to develop new contacts.

Meanwhile Ruth (Sonia) met with German communists and other left-wing youth who had fled from Nazi Germany to Britain. Among them she encountered and made contact with a crucial young physics Ph.D. candidate, Klaus Fuchs (see Chapter 8). Learning of his interesting work on the British "Tube Alloys" project, equivalent to the Manhattan Project, she obtained a radio for sending reports back to Moscow.

| Techint |
| --- |
| Sonia had two small children, one fathered by Shultz and one by Beurton. She took her older son to London—just another middle-aged mother traveling with her child. He carried a large teddy bear. Following GRU methods, she met her contact in a park, where he handed over a package that she put in the hollowed-out tummy of the teddy bear. The package contained parts for a shortwave radio. Stringing up an aerial as a clothesline, she broadcast details of Klaus Fuchs' work on the Tube Alloys project. |

## A Close Call and Getaway

In 1947, Alexander Foote explained Sonia's role in recruiting him in the 1930s to MI-5. When Fuchs confessed in 1949 (Chapter 8) he never mentioned Sonia, claiming he had not been recruited into Soviet espionage work until later. When the MI-5 agents questioned her in 1947, she invited them in for tea. They could not believe that this friendly, disarming, middle-aged housewife could be a secret agent. She realized they might come back, however, so she and her husband and children left for East Germany.

**Spy Words**

After a **recruiter** or *talent scout* identified a potential informant, he or she was passed on to a *control* or **controller**. The control made sure the informant kept in contact and relayed the information back to Center, whether GRU or NKVD.

She had not only *recruited* Fuchs and other agents in Britain, but had served as the *controller* of several, including Melita Norwood. Norwood worked in the British Tube Alloys project, and provided a steady stream of nuclear espionage to the GRU and the NKVD. Norwood was handed off from one agency to the other, but supplied data to GRU through Sonia.

Sonia and her husband retired to a comfortable home near the Baltic Sea. After she published her memoirs in 1977, under the title *Sonia's Rapport*, the world learned a little more about the valuable Soviet agent. Her book became a bestseller and she was interviewed on East German television, finally getting public credit for her quiet but steady work for Soviet intelligence. Ruth Kuczynski was the only woman to ever have been made an honorary colonel of the Red Army. She was awarded two Orders of the Red Banner.

# Igor Gouzenko—The Great Defector

The extent of Soviet penetration by secret agents into Britain, the United States, and Canada during and after World War II became obvious only gradually. One revelation led to another, and the onion-like layers seemed to go on and on. Although U.S. G-2, FBI, and the OSS knew that the Soviet Union spied on the United States during the war, they had little proof and only unsubstantiated rumors to work on. MI-5, the British internal security apparatus, seemed either reluctant to act on tips, like those about Sonia, or perhaps was itself so penetrated by Soviet agents as to be ineffective (see Chapter 9). It was the Royal Canadian Mounted Police who helped crack the first major post-World War II espionage case, and that resulted, not from diligent counterespionage work, but from the greatest defector of them all, Igor Gouzenko.

## Gouzenko's Cover

Although Igor Gouzenko was a lieutenant in the GRU, he was a legal in the role of a cipher clerk in the Soviet embassy in Ottawa, Canada. In later years, references to him often identified him as cipher clerk, overlooking his actual espionage role as a GRU officer.

Gouzenko had been stationed in Canada during the war, and had grown to like its freedoms and economic prosperity. Although living conditions in Canada in 1944 and 1945 were pretty austere, they were a great improvement over those in the Soviet Union. Gouzenko got word in September 1945, that agents would be returning home. He knew Soviet policy—many of those who had been stationed overseas were frequently regarded as contaminated, suffering low paid positions, demotions, or even imprisonment or worse in the paranoid conditions of Stalin's Russia.

If he simply walked out of the embassy and sought political asylum, the Canadians would probably turn him over to the Soviet authorities, and he would face certain punishment. He decided to remove some documents, with which, he hoped, he could purchase recognition.

On the day of his defection, he stuffed in his shirt a packet of more than 100 decrypted messages from Room 12 at the legation that he knew provided details of recent espionage against both Canada and the United States. He had to suck in his stomach, his wife later said, to keep from looking pregnant.

The documents were decoded to plain text, but agents and contacts, as usual, were represented only by their code names. However, the packet contained details of espionage in Washington (see Chapter 10) and against the Manhattan Project (see Chapter 8). He did not bring out any code keys or manuals.

**Tradecraft**

The NKVD chief, Lavrenti Beria, was outraged at the Gouzenko defection, and thought it pointed out the incompetence of the GRU. Beria noted, "The most elementary principles of security were ignored, complacency and self-satisfaction went unchecked." The neighbors were not always friendly!

## Won't Anyone Listen?

September 5, 1945, the day of Gouzenko's defection, was a nightmare for him. He could not get anyone to listen to his claims. He visited the *Ottawa Journal* newspaper, and they found his story incredible, refusing to look at the papers, missing the spy story scoop of the decade, if not of the century. The Ministry of Justice turned him away. Returning home after several hours of trudging the streets of Ottawa looking for someone to whom he could defect, he was terrified that the embassy would send security agents for him.

Fortunately, his neighbor, a noncommissioned airforce officer, believed his story and hid him on a back porch while the Soviet agents raided Gouzenko's apartment. The NCO put Gouzenko in touch with the Royal Canadian Mounted Police, who at first considered turning him over to the embassy. But on hearing out his story, they finally analyzed his information and informed the Canadian Prime Minister William Lyon Mackenzie King, who relayed the news to President Harry Truman and British Prime Minister Clement Attlee.

## The Aftermath of Gouzenko

Gouzenko's documents caused a stir. One of the first Soviet informants detected was a British scientist who had worked on the atom bomb project in Montreal, Alan Nunn May. He had passed on details of the project and, in August 1945, had provided through the Ottawa embassy of the Soviet Union minute samples of Uranium 235 and Uranium 233. At the end of the war, Nunn May was teaching at King's College in London University back in Britain. Although Mackenzie King's government was slow to act, by February 1946, they arrested 13 individuals turned up from the Gouzenko documents, and notified Scotland Yard about Alan Nunn May. When Nunn May was questioned, he confessed to passing on the information and material to the Soviet Union.

At his trial, Nunn May's defense attorney, Gerald Gardiner, made the point that May had not transmitted information to the enemy, since Russia and Britain were allies in 1945. But the crime, the prosecution pointed out, was transmission of information to unauthorized persons. Alan Nunn May was sentenced to 10 years in prison, despite many pleas from other scientists that he be given a lighter sentence.

But finding some of the others identified only by code names in the Gouzenko documents took much longer. One was Elli, a mysterious figure high in the British government, who had served the Soviet cause. Other code-names also remained elusive, although the documents pointed to a few specifically named individuals in the United States. Despite the fact that the Canadians shared the information with the FBI, no U.S. arrests could be made until evidence that would stand up in court could be assembled.

Gouzenko's revelations, published in a Canadian White Paper in 1946, meshed with testimony of another defector from the Soviet cause, Elizabeth Bentley (see Chapter 10). The hunt for spies in the United States was on, sometimes reaching a pitch of excitement as the press followed one disclosure after another through the late 1940s.

The Canadians provided Gouzenko with a changed identity, and he and his wife settled down in something like the American witness protection program. In 1975, a member of the Canadian Parliament, Thomas Cossit, sought an increase in Gouzenko's government pension, and the Soviet authorities assumed that Gouzenko must have been living in Cossit's parliamentary district. They never tracked down the great defector, although the KGB kept him on its death list, marked for elimination if ever found.

# Colonel Rudolf Abel

In the three years following Gouzenko's defection, the carefully constructed network of Soviet agents in the United States, built on Communist Party members, began to come apart. Part of the reason was the investigations sparked by Gouzenko and Bentley as discussed in Chapter 10, and the unraveling of one ring after another. But in the Soviet Union, repeated purges also weakened both the GRU and NKVD organizations.

With both agencies finding their networks drying up at the very time when the Soviet Union wanted to learn more of American military and technical strengths with the beginning of the cold war, the KGB decided to plant at least one illegal agent in the United States. Their choice to be illegal *rezident*, based in New York, was the man who became known as Colonel Rudolf Abel.

## A Man of Many Names

Although the name Rudolf Abel has gone down in history as one of the great undercover agents, the name itself was a fabrication. Years later, the story of Abel was partially pieced together. Abel was originally William Fischer.

William Gerrykovich Fischer was born in England in 1903, the son of a Russian family of German ancestry who had immigrated to England in 1900. Henry Fischer, the father, became involved in the British labor movement and was an early member of the British Communist Party. Until age 14, William grew up in Britain, learning English at school and from playmates and speaking Russian at home. With the Russian Revolution of 1917, the Fischers returned home. As loyal communists, they were welcomed. William, already speaking English like a Brit, was recruited into the Soviet intelligence service in the 1920s.

 **Tradecraft**

As soon as Kayotis (Fischer) arrived in Detroit, a new name appeared. Emil Robert Goldfus was born August 2, 1902, in Manhattan. Somehow, the KGB had acquired the birth certificate. The fact that the real Goldfus had died in 1903 did not matter. Birth certificates and death certificates in New York were not correlated.

By 1948, at age 45, but looking a few years older because he was prematurely balding, Fischer received an assignment to work in the United States. He entered the United States from Canada, landing on November 14, 1948, in Quebec from the passenger ship *Scythia*, from Germany.

As he got off the ship, his papers identified him as Andrew Kayotis, 53 years old, headed for Detroit. The original Kayotis was a naturalized citizen who had lived in Detroit, born in Lithuania. He had returned to Lithuania in 1947, where he passed away in a hospital. The KGB acquired Kayotis's papers, and they provided a convenient identity for Fischer.

For the next few years, Emil Goldfus (Fischer) set up a cover in New York City. The name that finally stuck in the American press, Rudolf Abel, did not surface until some years later.

## Artist at Work

"Emil Goldfus" was a semi-retired photographer, interested in painting. He established a bank account in New York, and began to make regular deposits in 1950. He lived very quietly, learning the bus and subway routes, scouting public places such as theaters and parks that might provide dead drop spots, and setting up an apartment and a studio.

During the period 1950–1953, little is known of Goldfus's activities, although he did make contact with Lona and Morris Cohen, later identified as Soviet agents who worked in the United States, then left after the revelations of the Rosenberg case to work in Britain. (See Chapters 8 and 9.)

In 1953, Goldfus set up an apartment in Brooklyn, and rented studio space in a seven-story building, Ovington Studios, in Brooklyn Heights. The building was full of artists and writers who paid very low rent for large, well-lit studios. Goldfus began to meet the other occupants, mostly younger men trying to get a start in the art world. Burt Silverman, a young army veteran who painted portraits, thought Goldfus had a slight accent, perhaps Scot.

For the fellow artists in the Ovington Studios, Goldfus was a man of contradictions. He knew photography all right, but he seemed to have a broader range of intellectual interests. He knew U.S. labor history and could talk about the radical labor movement, including the Industrial Workers of the World, with some authority. His taste in art was quite traditional or conservative, but so was that of some of the others. He was vague about his background, but always a good companion. When the conversation drifted into politics, he sounded like someone who might have been an early radical, but who had stopped being political in the mid 1930s. He was always more of a listener than a talker.

## Reino Hayhanen

Fischer had as an assistant, Reino Hayhanen, a lieutenant colonel in the KGB, whose job was to operate a radio set and help build a network. But Hayhanen proved not to be up to the job. He never grew proficient in English, he began to drink heavily, and he had loud fights with his wife that disturbed their neighbors. At one point when Fischer was traveling to the West in the United States, Hayhanen misused KGB funds. On his return, Fischer gave Hayhanen a dressing-down, and then, apparently on orders, told Hayhanen he was to return to Moscow for a short vacation.

Hayhanen smelled trouble. Agents did not go back to Lubyanka for vacations. His 1957 flight home took him through Paris, where he decided to defect. As a walk-in at the American embassy, he gave a few details of information, including the name of a U.S. sergeant who was spying for the Russians at the American embassy in Moscow, Roy Rhodes. But more interesting were the details regarding Fischer. Hayhanen had no idea what Fischer's real name was, knowing him only as Mark.

Under questioning in the United States, Hayhanen bragged about how he had misused KGB funds, and how he and Mark had not gotten along. He also provided information on drops that he and Mark had used. Although he did not remember exactly where the Ovington Studios were, the FBI drove him around Brooklyn until he spotted the building.

## Arrest and Trial

With Hayhanen's description of Mark, the FBI staked out the building, finally spotting him and following him to a hotel where he had taken up residence. Perhaps Fischer was careless, since he should have known that Hayhanen never got to Moscow. In any case, when the FBI searched his hotel room and studio, they found incriminating evidence—a few devices with concealed compartments. However, they found no secret documents and no real evidence that Mark had stolen or purchased any classified information.

The FBI questioned the fellow artists, and various contacts that Mark had made, learning that he was known to most as Emil Goldfus, and to a few others as Martin Collins. Although he could not be arraigned on espionage, the charge was initially illegal entry as an alien, and then conspiracy to commit espionage. The final indictment included three charges: conspiring to transmit to the USSR information relating to U.S. national defense; gathering such information; and remaining in the United States without registering as a foreign agent.

In prison, the arrested master spy wrote to the warden, asking that he be deported, and stated that his real name was Rudolph Ivanovich Abel. His request for deportation was denied, and he went to trial. But the press picked up his new name, and he was known henceforth as Colonel Abel.

No evidence of any documents showed that Abel (or Goldfus, or Martin, or Mark) had obtained any military secrets. Nevertheless, the physical evidence of espionage equipment, the testimony of Hayhanen, and various odd circumstances, such as a safety deposit box rented in a friend's name that contained $15,000 in cash, were enough to convince the jury. Colonel Abel was convicted and sentenced to 45 years in prison and a total set of fines of $3,000 on November 15, 1957.

After serving five years as a model prisoner in the Atlanta Federal Penitentiary, Colonel Abel was traded to the Soviet Union for the pilot of the American U-2 spy plane, Francis Gary Powers. That is a story we get to in Chapter 13.

## Some Unanswered Questions

Although the arrest and conviction of Colonel Abel was big news—the FBI had broken up a spy ring—the case left a whole series of questions. Was Abel the spy's real name? Although at first confirmed in the Soviet press with the publication of a letter detailing what a great family man R. I. Abel was, reporters were later allowed to discover the headstone detailing the life of William Fischer. He had been buried in Moscow after his death from lung cancer in 1971.

Was the name Abel a signal to the KGB to inform them how he had been betrayed and what little information the FBI might have? Did he allow himself to be caught, and if so, was that on orders? Why was he so apparently competent at tradecraft, and his assistant Hayhanen so obviously incompetent? Was that simply an accident of KGB personnel work? And perhaps most important, how much information had he gathered and transmitted? Although the KGB later let the world think that Colonel Abel had been extremely effective, could those hints themselves have been propaganda or disinformation?

So the story of Fischer/Kayotis/Goldfus/Martin/Mark/and Colonel Rudolf Ivanovich Abel, the man of many names, while reading like a spy novel, yielded little information about the accomplishments of Soviet espionage. After his return, the KGB kept alive his reputation, even spreading hints, no doubt to worry Western agencies, that he was again hard at work overseas. More likely, he was comfortably engaged in teaching humint technique to future agents. With the revelations of some Soviet archives in the 1990s, it became clear that his job had been to set up a new illegal espionage network and that he had little luck, partly because the American Communist Party was in decline and could not provide recruits when he operated.

## The Least You Need to Know

♦ Overseas espionage by the Soviet Union was conducted through two agencies, the GRU or Army Intelligence, and the NKVD/KGB State Security.

♦ The espionage techniques of the Soviet Union in planting agents, building networks, and collecting information were carefully practiced to prevent detection.

♦ Although a truly successful spy was by definition not known to the public, some of those uncovered appeared to be quite competent, including Richard Sorge in Japan, Ruth Kuczynski in Britain, and William Fischer (Colonel Rudolf Abel) in the United States.

♦ When a GRU colonel, Igor Gouzenko, defected, it had a great impact in unraveling the espionage efforts of the Soviet Union.

# Part 3

# Spying During the Early Cold War

Through the first years of the Cold War, Americans were shocked to discover that the Soviet Union had planted spies inside the Manhattan Project to learn how the atomic bomb was designed. Meanwhile, the British learned that there were Russian spies high in their own government. The Cambridge Five were members of the upper crust of British society, trained at Cambridge University, and secretly working for the Soviet Union for decades.

After disbanding the Office of Strategic Services, President Truman decided that the nation needed to coordinate its intelligence work and created the CIA. In its first years the CIA pulled off some daring exploits, like tunneling under the dividing line in Berlin to tap Russian phone lines.

# 8

# The Atomic Spies

## In This Chapter

- ◆ The Manhattan Project
- ◆ From Venona to Harry Gold
- ◆ Klaus Fuchs
- ◆ The Rosenbergs
- ◆ Kurchatov, Beria, and Fat Man

Although Germany, Japan, and the American public knew nothing about the Manhattan Project until after the first bomb was dropped on Hiroshima, Japan, on August 6, 1945, the Soviet spy apparatus had been hard at work, through several separate networks, learning about the new weapon. When the Soviets detonated their first nuclear weapon four years later, they surprised the American intelligence establishment. In 1949–1950, the FBI began to close in on some of the spies who had provided the Soviet Union with key information that helped them build their bomb. The FBI never caught all the spies, but we look in this chapter at how the bureau, with the help of code-crackers, broke some of the atomic spy cases.

# The Manhattan Engineer District

In 1939, nuclear physicists Leo Szilard and Albert Einstein wrote to President Franklin Roosevelt, urging him to finance studies of how new discoveries in knowledge of the atom could be turned into weapons. The fact that Germany had recently taken over Czech uranium mines suggested that it would be doing the same work, and Roosevelt heeded the warning. Starting slowly, scientists at universities began to work on contract on various aspects of the subject. By 1942, it was clear that a nuclear weapon was a real possibility, but it would be too large and expensive for such contract-lab work. The project to build the bomb was turned over to the Army Corps of Engineers, and a special district of the Corps was established, code-named the Manhattan Engineer District (MED), to build the weapon.

The code name was a good one, because as huge amounts of money were diverted from other war priorities, Army staff members simply believed it was being shuttled to New York. Only after the war, when reports were published, did the name Manhattan Project come into use. By then, $2 billion had gone into the work, a goodly amount in 1940s dollars. The total national debt run up by all of the government's deficit spending during the Great Depression before the beginning of the war had been only about $4 billion.

## Op-Sec on the Manhattan Project

Keeping the project secret was difficult. Over 50,000 people, counting construction workers, were engaged in parts of the job, building complete secret cities at Hanford, Washington; Oak Ridge, Tennessee; and Los Alamos, New Mexico. Thousands of scientists, engineers, and technicians, recruited from universities, the military, and industry worked on the job. Although the weapon was designed at Los Alamos, the core of the weapon needed fissionable materials. One type of weapon could use plutonium manufactured in nuclear reactors built secretly at Hanford, and another type could be made from the fissionable rare isotope, Uranium 235, that was separated in a massive plant built at Oak Ridge.

Although most of the workers had no precise idea why they were building the huge facilities, they did know that the structures were part of the war effort, and that they did not have a need to know any more. Scientists who were informed were cleared, or as the British would say, "vetted," with background investigations. If acceptable and hired for the project, they were sworn to secrecy.

Notes and documents were locked in safes at night, and each of the facilities was surrounded by chain-link fences, with guards at the gate who checked all IDs. Some of the academic scientists were irritated by the restrictions. Even the idea of putting away their notes at night seemed like interference for many who were used to working amidst a comfortable clutter. They balked at the idea of compartmentation between specialists, because science makes better progress when there is a free exchange of ideas. A compromise at Los Alamos was to allow the leading scientists from different divisions to meet weekly at seminars, where new ideas and solutions to problems often came out of the give and take.

The Army officers who ran security were suspicious of some of the academics, especially many who were refugees from central Europe, and those who had associated with left-wing causes. Two of the security men, Boris Pash and Peer de Silva, were convinced that the civilian head of the project, J. Robert Oppenheimer, well known for his left-wing views, was spying for the Soviet Union. Despite finding some damaging associations and evasive answers to questions, they never uncovered any convincing evidence for their suspicions (see Chapter 12). Security officers were nervous about the British and Canadian scientists who helped on the project.

## Atomic Secrets

The purpose of the Manhattan Engineer District was a secret. The War Department did not want the Germans to learn that the United States was working on a nuclear weapon, fearing that the advanced German nuclear physics community might beat the Americans to the bomb if Hitler learned how big an effort the United States was mounting. After the war, Americans learned that Germany did have a nuclear project, headed by Werner Heisenberg (see Chapter 6), but the German bomb program never had the resources to make much progress.

Not only the central Manhattan Engineer District's purpose, but also all the specific new technologies were closely guarded. The methods of separating plutonium from the reactor slugs at Hanford, the Oak Ridge methods of getting U-235 from the more plentiful U-238, the exact amounts required to achieve critical mass for a detonation, and of course, all of the designs of the *gadgets*—the bombs themselves—were classified as Top Secret. All documents, blueprints, plans, reports, notes, and administrative correspondence were classified. Even the materials were given code-names and code words, and the weapon itself was sometimes called "S-1" for Special Weapon Number 1.

## Espionage Revealed

When GRU officer Igor Gouzenko defected from the Soviet embassy in Ottawa, Canada, in September 1945, his revelations shocked the American intelligence community (see Chapter 7). He named several spies who had worked in Canada, the most important of whom was Alan Nunn May. But more disturbing were some decoded messages that Gouzenko brought out, referring to other nuclear spies in the United States, only by their cover names. Over the next four years, the FBI and the Army's Signals Security Agency (SSA) worked on trying to figure out exactly who the other spies had been. They made progress, but only slowly.

**Tradecraft**

The body of coded diplomatic messages from the Soviet Union's consular offices in the United States to Moscow, some 2,900 between 1940 and 1948, was stamped "Venona" by the SSA (although at first the batch of material was known by other code-names, such as Bride and Drug). The American public only learned about the Venona messages and the brilliant job of cracking them much later, in the 1980s and 1990s. (See Chapter 19.)

## Venona Messages

One source of information was a body of encoded messages, sent from a busy Soviet consulate in New York City and from other diplomatic posts to Moscow. Although the enciphered messages were recorded and kept by the Signals Security Agency, the messages were extremely difficult to crack. Even when partially deciphered, they still contained code-names for individuals rather than their real names.

At Arlington Hall, in Virginia, a code-cracking unit struggled with the Venona messages. Meredith Gardner at SSA (later known as Army Security Agency or ASA), provided information to Army G-2. At first, the FBI was not notified.

**Tradecraft**

Even when a Venona message was decrypted, it would contain only tantalizing hints as to the identity of spies. In 1947, Meredith Gardner transmitted Special Report No. 1, to G-2, noting that the records indicated a mysterious, unidentified informant for the Soviets.

"LIB?? (Lieb?) or possibly LIBERAL was ANTENNA until Sept. 1944. Occurs 6 times, 22 October–20 December 1944. Message of 27 November speaks of his wife ETHEL, 29 years old, married (?) five years. ..." Gardner, quoted in Robert Louis Benson, *Venona: Soviet Espionage and the American Response, 1939-1957.*

The ASA did not have resources to do the necessary detective work to uncover the identity of LIBERAL.

The trail to ANTENNA or LIBERAL was a twisted one.

Gradually, the separate American intelligence agencies began to cooperate, and by 1948, Meredith Gardner of ASA met regularly with Robert Lamphere, from the FBI. Together, the two agencies began to zero in on a few of the Soviet Union's agents, trying to sort out from various clues, who had been conducting espionage at Los Alamos and elsewhere in the Manhattan Engineer District. Gardner and Lamphere's work in breaking the case remained classified for decades.

# Unraveling the Tangle

One particular code name was tantalizing, for it represented a highly placed scientist who had worked at Los Alamos. The name Rest and the name Charles referred to the first of the atomic spies tracked down by the joint ASA/FBI investigation, Klaus Fuchs.

## Finding Fuchs

One of the decoded Venona messages was a verbatim report on the progress of the Manhattan Project written by Klaus Fuchs. Fuchs, who had fled Germany as a communist youth, studied in Britain, became a British subject, and then was sent to the United States to work on the bomb at Los Alamos. After the war, he had returned to Britain and was at work at the British nuclear establishment at Harwell.

| Spy Bios |
| --- |
| Klaus Fuchs was born in Germany and as a youth was active as a communist. He studied physics at Leipzig University. When the Nazis came to power in 1933, Fuchs, like many communists, knew he would be rounded up for a concentration camp if he stayed. He left and settled in Britain, continuing his study for a doctorate in physics under Rudolf Peierls there. Sometime between 1938 and 1940, he was recruited by Sonia (see Chapter 8) to provide information to the Soviet Union. Later, he would work on the Manhattan Project, and provide top-level scientific data to the Soviet Union. Arrested in Britain in 1950, he served nine years of a 14-year sentence, before being released for good behavior. He returned to the communist German Democratic Republic settling near Leipzig, where he settled into a comfortable life. |

At first, Lamphere and Gardner were unclear as to whether the Fuchs report on the "Fluctuations and the Efficiency of a Diffusion Plant" had been stolen and sent by agent Rest to Russia. However, when another decoded message indicated that Rest was a British spy whose sister was attending an American university in 1944, it narrowed the field. Investigation showed that Fuchs had a sister named Kristel who had been studying at Swarthmore College. It looked like a match. It seemed likely that Fuchs had somehow sent his own report to the Soviet Union.

## Fuchs Interrogated

The FBI notified MI-5, the British internal security agency, and the task of confronting Fuchs was given to James Skardon, a skilled officer who had successfully questioned other spies in the past. While Alan Nunn May had refused to name others with whom he had worked, Skardon hoped to get more information from Fuchs. In December 1949, Skardon visited Harwell and began to interrogate Fuchs.

*Despite his studious and mild-mannered demeanor, Klaus Fuchs was probably the most important of the atomic spies for the Soviet Union.*

*(Courtesy of the National Security Agency)*

After listening to Fuchs' tale of his youth and education, Skardon took a bit of a chance with a bluff. He asked Fuchs whether he would care to comment on the precise information that he had been in touch with a Soviet agent during the war. To Skardon's pleasant surprise, the ploy worked. Fuchs began a lengthy confession, admitting that he had supplied Russian agents with information from the British Tube Alloys project even before he left for the United States, and that he had spelled out the principles of design of the plutonium bomb for an agent when he was in the United States. He confessed in January 1950, and was arrested February 2.

He promptly came to trial and was convicted on March 1 to a 14-year sentence for passing military secrets to a foreign ally. It was not a capital crime, much to his relief.

## Looking for Raymond

Although Fuchs gave a fairly complete confession of his own crimes, like Nunn May, he did not want to implicate others. However, Skardon was able to extract some interesting information. Fuchs explained that he had provided the details to a courier, a man who he knew only by the code name Raymond.

Before transferring from work with a team at Columbia University to Los Alamos, Fuchs had met four or five times with Raymond, providing him information. But when Fuchs moved to Los Alamos in 1944, the contact was broken. Trying to re-establish contact, Raymond looked up Fuchs' sister, Kristel, then living in Cambridge, Massachusetts, and later, when Fuchs came back to Cambridge for a visit, she helped put the two in touch again. Raymond took a trip to Santa Fe, New Mexico, near Los Alamos, where he met Fuchs in June 1945, receiving details about the weapon. They met near a bridge over the Santa Fe River. For years, the bridge bore a small plaque that said something like "On this spot, in June 1945, Klaus Fuchs transmitted to the Soviet Union the secret of the Atomic Bomb."

On that June 1945 visit, Fuchs explained the plans to test the Fat Man weapon. The test was held a month later, at Alamogordo, in southern New Mexico.

Although Fuchs confessed all this, he did not know Raymond's real name. But he offered Skardon a description of Raymond and a few details. Kristel and her husband, under questioning by the FBI, gave more description of the man they knew under a different code name, Gus. They thought he was Jewish and a chemical engineer. Even with the descriptions and details, several million men would look about right.

*Fat Man. The nuclear weapon tested at Los Alamos and dropped on Nagasaki looked like this one being loaded onto an aircraft. The Soviet Union used information supplied by atomic spies to faithfully duplicate the weapon, down to the last bolt.*

*(Courtesy of the National Archives and Records Administration)*

However, a clue from the Bentley revelations (see Chapter 9) suggested that several Soviet spies had worked through an engineering firm of Abraham Brothman in Queens, New York. One man at that firm who the FBI had already questioned in connection with Brothman, Harry Gold, met the description provided by Fuchs, Kristel, and Kristel's husband for Raymond, alias Gus.

---

### Spy Bios

Harry Gold was born in Switzerland and immigrated to the United States with his parents when he was two years old. The family settled in Philadelphia, and his father worked for the Victor Talking Machine Company in Camden, New Jersey. Harry grew interested in the Socialist Party as a youth, and studied briefly at the University of Pennsylvania. Working as a chemical engineer at a sugar factory, he earned enough to study nights at Drexel Institute of Technology. Through communist friends, he was recruited by AMTORG, the Soviet trade mission, to conduct industrial espionage in the 1930s. It was only in 1943 that he was recruited to serve as a courier to pick up nuclear information from a scientist from Britain. That man, he would later learn, was Klaus Fuchs.

---

The FBI asked Harry Gold if they could come to his house and look through his belongings. With advance notice, he nervously tore up and disposed of what he thought was all the incriminating evidence of various courier trips. Among the items he overlooked was a street map of Santa Fe, New Mexico, a place he had denied ever visiting. When confronted with it, he broke down. He admitted he was the man the FBI was looking for. It was May 1950.

When shown Harry Gold's picture, Klaus Fuchs at first claimed he could not be sure it was the right man. Eventually however, the two confessions added up. Both Gold and Fuchs had stories that matched, and both were guilty of espionage. Whether Fuchs stalled to protect Gold or whether he simply couldn't remember at first remained an open question.

## From Gold to Greenglass

The FBI subjected Harry Gold to intense questioning about his travels, his aliases, his contacts, their code-names and locations, the hotels he had stayed in, and everything else he knew about Soviet espionage. Although he, like the others, did not want to rat on his associates, he did mention that on one of his trips to Santa Fe, he had stayed at a hotel in Albuquerque. Traveling by train, it was easier to get off at the Lamy station near Santa Fe without going to Albuquerque, and this raised another question for the FBI. What was he doing in Albuquerque, some 50 miles away from his Santa Fe appointment with Fuchs?

### Tradecraft

When Harry Gold served as a courier to two different informants, Klaus Fuchs and David Greenglass, on the same trip to New Mexico in June 1945, that represented a breakdown in the traditional careful NKVD/KGB tradecraft of compartmentation. The reason was, according to Yakovlev, the NKVD/KGB controller in New York, that the regular courier for Greenglass, Lona Cohen, was ill and her job was temporarily transferred to Gold. In espionage terms, it was "bad op-sec."

Lona and her husband Morris quietly left the United States when the atom spy case began to unravel. Yakovlev urged them to go, he later remembered. The couple settled in Britain, changed their names to Helen and Peter Kroger and continued to spy for the Soviet Union.

Gold had boxed himself in. He confessed to meeting a soldier in Albuquerque, whose name he could not remember. He had gone to the soldier's home, but he did not remember the precise address in Albuquerque. Under questioning, he provided a description of the house. Slowly, he remembered other details. The soldier's wife was named Ruth. The soldier had provided him with some sketches connected with the atom bomb, and Gold had given him $500. The soldier was a draftsman or machinist, working at Los Alamos. He had a Brooklyn or Bronx accent, and was probably Jewish. Almost accidentally, the FBI, when reviewing files of previous individuals questioned, came across someone who matched the description, with a wife named Ruth. It was David Greenglass.

### Spy Bios

David Greenglass was the brother of Ethel, who married Julius Rosenberg. Greenglass dropped out of Brooklyn Polytechnic Institute and married Ruth in 1942. He was active in a communist youth movement in New York, and he was drafted to the Army in April 1943. He worked as a machinist at Oak Ridge, and transferred to Los Alamos to work on the nuclear project, and later informed Julius Rosenberg that he had information about the atomic bomb project to submit through channels to Moscow.

The FBI took a movie of the house in Albuquerque that Greenglass had lived in, and despite the fact that it had been remodeled, Gold identified it as the house he had visited. When the FBI got a picture of Greenglass as he had looked in 1945, Gold identified Greenglass as the soldier he had met on his June 1945 visit.

## From David to Julius

When the FBI questioned David Greenglass, they had very little evidence to go on implicating him in espionage, none that would have stood up very well in court. Gold's identification was fairly tenuous. However, Greenglass immediately broke down, confessed, and named his wife, Ruth, and his brother-in-law, Julius Rosenberg, as involved in espionage.

Although both Gold and Greenglass were fairly complete in their confessions, Julius Rosenberg and his wife, Ethel, refused to admit to any involvement in espionage. What resulted was one of the most controversial investigations and trials in American history.

### Tradecraft

In his confession, David Greenglass claimed that he and his brother-in-law, Julius Rosenberg, worked out a recognition signal. In the kitchen of the Rosenbergs' apartment, they cut a Jell-O box lid in half. Later, Harry Gold claimed he was provided with the half and when he showed it to Greenglass, and said he brought greetings, Greenglass invited him in, matching the box lid with the other half from his own wallet. Gold never quite remembered whether he was to have said, "I bring greetings from" Ben, or from Phillip. On prompting from the FBI, he finally decided that the recognition comment was "I bring greetings from Julius."

Arrested on July 17, 1950, Rosenberg refused to budge. A few days later, his wife was arrested. Despite the effort of the FBI and the Justice Department to build a case, they had little physical evidence. The Jell-O box recognition signal was long gone, but a new one was later cut up as a demonstration for the court. The testimony of Harry Gold and David and Ruth Greenglass could be regarded as a little tainted, as Gold received a lighter sentence for his confession, as did David. For David's testimony, the government agreed not to prosecute his wife.

## The Rosenberg Ring

The members of the Rosenberg Ring were:

♦ Harry Gold. Courier for NKVD. Arrested May 22, 1950. Confessed to passing information from Fuchs to John—code name for Soviet agent Anatoli Yakovlev in New York. Gold identified David Greenglass. Sentenced to 30 years in prison.

- David Greenglass. Brother of Ethel Rosenberg. Arrested June 15, 1950, confessed to conspiracy to commit espionage. Sentenced to 15 years in prison.

- Al Sarant. Defected to Czechoslovakia and Soviet Union, changed name to Philip Staros and contributed to founding the Soviet Union's microcomputer enterprise.

- Mort Sobell. Had worked in Navy Ordnance. Fled to Mexico, kidnapped there and forcibly returned to United States; arrested mid-August 1950; convicted of conspiracy to commit espionage; sentenced to 30 years in prison.

- William Perl. Had worked on classified aircraft projects. Arrested March 15, 1951; convicted of perjury to grand jury; sentenced to two concurrent five-year sentences.

- Joel Barr. Defected to Czechoslovakia and Soviet Union, changed name to Joseph Berg and with Sarant contributed to founding the Soviet Union's microcomputer enterprise.

When tried for conspiracy to commit espionage in time of war, both Julius and Ethel Rosenberg refused to make any confession. The FBI's case was difficult—the testimony of David Greenglass, obtained on the grounds he would receive leniency, could be suspect. Morton Sobell refused to give evidence. Harry Gold testified that he remembered that when he met Greenglass, he said, "I come from Julius." Although his memory had earlier been fuzzy, the statement was pretty convincing for the jury.

### Tradecraft

In June 1950, Robert Lamphere of the FBI wrote a classified memo to Meredith Gardner of the ASA, later released:

... it has been determined that one JULIUS ROSENBERG is probably identical with the individual described as ANTENNA and LIBERAL ... It is also believed now that DAVID GREENGLASS is identical with the individual described as KALIBR, and that RUTH PRINTZ GREENGLASS is identical with the individual known under the code name OSA. From the information available to date it is believed that ANATOLI ANTONOVICH YAKOVLEV is identical with the individual described under the code name ALEKSEY ... Reprinted in Robert Louis Benson, *Venona: Soviet Espionage and the American Response, 1939–1957.*

Anatoli Yakovlev was an agent of the MGB (NKVD) stationed at the Soviet consulate in New York City.

Some who came to the Rosenbergs' defense charged that they had been framed. The FBI did not wish to reveal the fact that some of their evidence was based on Venona materials, as the mere existence of the decrypting effort was still classified. The FBI/ASA work in identifying Fuchs and Gold and establishing the connection to the Rosenbergs through Venona documents was not revealed fully until decades later.

When both Julius and Ethel Rosenberg were put to death in June 1953, the world was shocked. It was the first time a husband and wife had both been executed by the U.S. government, and the fact that the executions created two orphans was even more horrifying. Later balanced analyses of the evidence against them supported the conclusion of the jury that they were guilty, but left open the question of whether they deserved the death penalty, and whether their trial had been fair.

*In prison, Julius and Ethel Rosenberg had few opportunities to meet, and then they were separated by wire mesh.*

*(Courtesy of the National Archives and Records Administration)*

The death sentence was questioned on several grounds. The espionage ring that Julius operated was primarily concerned with electronics information from the New York and Norfolk, Virginia areas, and Gold and Greenglass were almost accidental additions to his ring. Others, who were much more central to atomic espionage, like Alan Nunn May and Klaus Fuchs, received much lighter sentences. The death sentence seemed an effort to make the Rosenbergs scapegoats of the cold war. It was handed down during the Korean War, and in light of the fact that the atomic espionage appeared to have accelerated the Soviet nuclear program, it showed that they had been singled out as symbols of cold war tensions.

# Assessments

The atomic espionage revelations of the 1950s left many questions that were debated for decades. The guilt of the Rosenbergs was difficult to believe for many who thought they were persecuted for their political affiliation with the Communist Party and/or for being Jewish.

Conspiracy theories abounded, supported by the FBI's tactics of bugging their defense attorney's conversations, the illegal kidnapping of Morton Sobell from Mexico, the agency's use of threats and deception during questioning, the prosecution's use of dramatic evidence (such as a substitute Jell-O box) that could be challenged on legal grounds, and the fuzzy memory of Harry Gold. The fact that the link through Venona could not be discussed also made the case look a little fishy in spots.

The two sons of the Rosenbergs, who were later adopted by friends of the family, took the adoptive name Meerapol. After 1974, Michael and Robert Meerapol began to publicly argue that their parents had been convicted on trumped-up evidence. Their book, *We Are Your Sons*, published in 1975, was a moving statement of their continued faith in their parents, but did not provide any solid evidence for their position. In 1983, a well-researched study, based on documents and interviews by Ronald Radosh, *The Rosenberg File*, reviewed all the available evidence. Radosh had set out to confirm the Rosenbergs' innocence, but had to honestly conclude that the evidence showed their guilt.

## Did the Russians Need the Atom Secrets?

Even for those who accepted the evidence that the Rosenbergs were guilty, however, the question remained: Did the Soviet Union really need the espionage information to develop the atomic bomb? After all, Russian science was highly advanced, and in some areas, the technology of the USSR matched or exceeded American achievements. When the Soviet Union detonated a weapon that they claimed was a hydrogen bomb in 1953, before the United States developed one, many Americans began to doubt that the atomic secrets had really been so crucial to the Soviet Union. In 1957, the Soviet Union placed an artificial satellite in orbit, fully two years before the United States. Didn't that prove, some asked, that the Russians never really needed the spy material provided by Klaus Fuchs?

## Kurchatov, the Beard

Legend had it that Igor Kurchatov, the civilian head of the Soviet Union's program to build a nuclear weapon, grew a beard and claimed he would not shave it until the project yielded a successful weapon. Known as *The Beard*, Kurchatov had to wait until August 1949, for the clippers.

*Igor Kurchatov, the Soviet scientist in charge of the nuclear weapon project, vowed not to cut his beard until the weapon was detonated. Here he is shown about two years into the project with the beard.*

*(Courtesy of the Library of Congress)*

Kurchatov wrote that he was extremely impressed with the intelligence information that came from Fuchs and from other agents in the Manhattan Engineer District. As a physicist, he understood the great strides that were being made, and he admitted that the information supplied some valuable shortcuts and answers to technical barriers that might shave years off the schedule. Later, Premier Nikita Khrushchev wrote that the Rosenbergs had provided significant help in accelerating the atom bomb project, as did Vyacheslav Molotov, who had served as foreign minister of the Soviet Union, 1939–1949 and 1953–1956.

## Joe One and Fat Man

Although Premier Joseph Stalin entrusted the technical work on the bomb to nuclear scientists, he put the head of the KGB in overall charge of the program. Lavrenti Beria, it was said, made it clear that there were to be no mistakes. When the Russian scientists sought to make a weapon of their own design, rather than imitating the

U.S. plans, Beria insisted that the first weapon be *an exact duplicate* of the plutonium-core Fat Man design, the one tested at Alamogordo on July 16, 1945, and the design used for the weapon dropped on Nagasaki on August 8, 1945. Beria was reputed to have told Kurchatov that if the bomb did not work, he would have Kurchatov killed, and then Stalin would have Beria himself killed. They were both a bit relieved when the test went successfully in 1949.

The Western press began to call the August 1949 detonation of the Soviet Union's first nuclear device, "Joe One." Later investigation of the record has shown that the plans developed by Fuchs, the explosive lens work of David Greenglass, and the other technical material smuggled out by at least two other highly placed Los Alamos scientists, were all incorporated in the August 1949 Joe One test. Joe One was a Soviet-built Fat Man, identical down to the size of the bolts.

## MLad, and Pers

The Venona messages contained references to other spies at Los Alamos. One was MLad, a Russian word meaning "lad" or "youth." Eventually, the young scientist Theodore Hall was identified as MLad. He moved to Britain, was never arrested, and lived quietly into the 1990s. Another code-name was more puzzling. Experts have debated whether Pers or Perseus really existed, or whether the Soviet Union had planted the term as a piece of disinformation. In any case, it appeared that in addition to Ted Hall, there were at least one or two other spies at Los Alamos who were never apprehended. That was the claim of Anatoli Yakovlev, the Soviet agent running the spy rings, in later interviews.

## How Did Fuchs Get Cleared?

At the heart of the successful atomic espionage by the informants and spies for the Soviet Union was of course a failure of the elaborate operational security methods set up under the Manhattan Engineer District. Once the FBI began to look into the background of Klaus Fuchs, they quickly found captured German records that indicated he had fled Germany because he was a communist. Although those records were not available when Fuchs went to work on the Tube Alloys project in Britain, and when he was recruited by Sonia there, the British had plenty of evidence, if they had looked for it, about the political leanings of Klaus Fuchs.

At the beginning of World War II, all German aliens were rounded up, and Fuchs was sent to an internment camp in Canada, and then to another on the Isle of Man in the Irish Sea. At the camp in Canada, Fuchs had been active in the pro-communist and anti-Nazi group of internees. While that may have made him seem a good security risk when it came to possible loyalty to Germany, British MI-5 had a 1934 report from the German consul in Bristol, England, that Fuchs was a communist. MI-5 had another confirming report from a German refugee about Fuchs' Communist Party politics.

When Rudolf Peierls, who later headed the British scientific group to join the Manhattan Engineer District, recruited Fuchs in 1941, he asked the British Air Ministry if Fuchs could be hired. The Air Ministry checked with MI-5, and then stated that it would be all right, as long as Fuchs was restricted to information on a need-to-know basis. Peierls said that scientists could not work that way, and the ministry dropped the condition.

When the British team came to the United States, the American security officials accepted the assurances of the British that their people had been vetted properly. Fuchs had slipped through.

Later, as evidence that the Soviet Union had planted moles within MI-5 began to surface (as discussed in Chapter 9), observers wondered whether letting Fuchs through had been an intentional step, rather than an oversight. But so far, there is no evidence that was the case.

For every great intelligence success on one side, there is a great intelligence failure on the other. Probably the success of Klaus Fuchs in spying for the Soviet Union should be regarded, as so many other successful espionage efforts, as simply a major failure of op-sec by the outfit that got penetrated. And similarly, the mistakes that led to the capture of Fuchs can be traced to one or two poor op-sec practices on the part of Harry Gold and his boss, Anatoli Yakovlev.

## The Least You Need to Know

♦ Soviet espionage into the Manhattan Engineer District provided crucial information that helped the Russians build their first atom bomb.

♦ The most important of the spies captured was Klaus Fuchs, a German-born British scientist who had worked at Los Alamos.

♦ Piecing together evidence, the FBI and the Army Security Agency tracked down Harry Gold, who had served as a courier for Klaus Fuchs.

♦ Harry Gold's confession led the FBI to David Greenglass, who confessed he worked through his brother-in-law Julius Rosenberg.

♦ The trial of Julius and Ethel Rosenberg and their execution in 1953 created a storm of controversy.

# Chapter 9

# The Cambridge Five and Other British Cases

## In This Chapter

- ◆ Cambridge in the 1930s: The Apostles
- ◆ KGB talent scouts and recruiters
- ◆ Sleepers and moles
- ◆ Burgess, Maclean, and the Third Man
- ◆ Who was the Fifth Man?

In the 1930s and 1940s, the KGB and the GRU recruited British citizens to spy for the Soviet Union. Several of the informants achieved high ranking positions in the British government, continuing to send important intelligence back to Moscow for years. In this chapter, we take a look at the features of British society that made it difficult to uncover the agents: the nature of the British Left in the 1930s, the British respect for privacy, trust based on personal relationships that grew out of family and school connections, and the persistence of a defined class structure.

The identity of the individuals in the network was a running detective mystery for more than three decades. Even after two agents defected to the Soviet Union, the search for the third, fourth, and fifth members of the Cambridge Five represented one of the longest-running espionage scandals of the twentieth century.

# British Intellectuals and the Communist Party

During the 1930s, communist ideas appealed to many intellectuals in the United Kingdom, France, the United States, and Canada. Disillusioned with capitalism because of its apparent failure to produce a just and stable economic system during the Great Depression, they found communism and the Soviet Union's system an attractive alternative. The argument that communism was built on a scientific set of principles and that society and economics was planned, rather than a matter of haphazard development, appealed to intellectuals whose training and background made them appreciate logical order and structure. Two noted British socialists, Beatrice and Sidney Webb, visited the Soviet Union and published a book in praise of the Soviet Union's attempt to build a new society.

In Britain and the United States, however, communist parties had trouble recruiting large numbers of permanent members, even during the Great Depression (1929–1939). One reason was that both parties, the CPUSA and the CPGB, were directly financed and controlled out of Moscow, through the *Comintern.*

**Spy Words** _____

The **Comintern,** the international league of communist parties, was established in Moscow in 1920. The Comintern financed communist parties all over the world, and decided who should serve as local chairman and party secretaries, as well as setting policy. The Comintern charter made it clear that to be a member party, foreign parties had to support the aims of the Soviet Union. Especially dedicated members of these overseas parties would sometimes be identified and selected to assist either the KGB or the GRU in their espionage activities.

In Britain there were several reasons why the party had limited growth. One was that British intellectuals who tended to be critical of their own society were an independent-minded lot. The kind of person who was attracted to communism as a method of criticizing authority would often find it intolerable to take orders they disagreed with from CPGB leadership. When they realized the orders came from Moscow, the party seemed even less attractive. For this reason, the two leaders of the British Party, Harry Pollitt and Rajani Palme Dutt, tended not to admit prominent intellectuals to leadership circles in the party.

Another consequence of the party's policies was a rapid turnover in membership. A young intellectual might join and be a member for a few months or years, and then drop out. The same situation prevailed to some extent in the United States. Even when the CPGB supported a popular cause, like the loyalist side in the Spanish Civil War, many British intellectuals had doubts about the central control of the party and its adherence to a line dictated in Moscow. Most notable among those complaining of Moscow control was George Orwell, whose later books *Animal Farm* and *1984* were critical of this aspect of the Soviet Union's type of Marxism.

Another reason for the limited appeal of the CPGB was that it was possible to be active on the left in Britain in the 1930s through other groups. A splinter group of the Labour Party sought to organize left-wing opinion, and the Left Book Club, although generally sympathetic to the CPGB, was independent and attracted hundreds of thousands of members.

For a few crucial individuals, however, the CPGB and even recruitment into the Soviet Union's overseas espionage establishment held great appeal.

## Cambridge in the 1930s

The two great universities of Britain, Oxford and Cambridge, drew students from the upper and upper-middle classes. Both ancient universities include many separate colleges. Both were founded in the twelfth century, and during the 1930s, Cambridge University consisted of 22 colleges. The *scions* or heirs of many of the leading families of Britain attended both universities, with many who sought careers in government service clustered in a few of the Cambridge University colleges, including Trinity and Kings Colleges, both of which had strong foreign language faculties. Several who became active as members of communist groups at Cambridge had known each other from their days in "public" schools, what Americans would call private schools. Some of the students attracted to Communist Party ideas and to socialism were members of a college club that had been founded in the early nineteenth century, the Apostles.

## The Apostles

The formal name of the Apostles was the Cambridge Converzatione Society, and it had been founded in 1820 by 12 fundamentalist Christians, who jokingly called themselves the Apostles. By the 1920s, most of the members of the Apostles Club were from Kings College, and in order to become an *embryo* or new member, one had to be approved by the existing leadership. Only one or two new members of the brightest students were admitted each year, and over the first century of its existence, the club had hosted many of the most famous and brilliant British subjects, including poet Alfred Lord Tennyson, physicist James Clerk Maxwell, historian Thomas Macaulay, philosopher Bertrand Russell, and economist John Maynard Keynes. Despite the club's almost obsessive secrecy that could be traced back to its origins as a hotbed of religious reform in the nineteenth century, some of its history leaked out.

By the 1920s, the club regularly met on Saturdays, had a snack of whales (sardines on toast), and discussed liberal topics ranging from socialism, homosexuality, and anarchism to post-impressionist art. Although homosexuality had been fairly common at Cambridge since the 1890s, by the 1920s, it began to come out of the closet, with numerous overt homosexual affairs. A few of the Apostles in the period were well known as announced gays, and a few other members of the club were gay, but not out.

As the Soviet Union sought recruits in Britain in the 1920s, one of their first targets was Cambridge University, and within it, the cluster of young intellectuals who would be likely to represent the next generation of leadership found at Kings College, Trinity, and in the Apostles Club.

### Tradecraft

Although less than 1 percent of Cambridge undergraduates in the 1920s and 1930s were interested in Marxism, an unusually high percentage were concentrated in the Apostles. British espionage historian John Costello analyzed all the 26 members of the Apostles who were admitted to the club between 1919 and 1939, and identified 20 of the 26 as either socialists, marxisant, or open or clandestine communists. He defined as marxisant those who had explicitly adopted a Marxist worldview. The peak of recruiting to the party came between 1927 and 1937.

## Recruiters and Talent Scouts

Tracing exactly who recruited whom into the Apostles Club, into the Communist Party, and into espionage for the Soviet Union has been made difficult by the secrecy surrounding all of the activities. However, several individuals appear to have played key roles in the late 1920s, as indicated in the following table:

## Apostle Club Members

| Member # | Year | Admitted Name |
|----------|------|---------------|
| 266 | 1923 | G. D. Thompson |
| 268 | 1925 | A. R. D. Watkins |
| 271 | 1927 | A. G. D. Watson |

| Member # | Year | Admitted Name |
|----------|------|---------------|
| 273 | 1928 | Anthony Blunt |
| 281 | 1932 | Guy Burgess |
| 287 | 1936 | Michael Straight |
| 291 | 1937 | L. H. Long |

Although only a few of the Apostles became recruits for the Soviet Union, three of those listed above later confessed to espionage for Moscow: Anthony Blunt, Guy Burgess, and L. H. Long. Watson, who later worked on sonar research in Britain, was eventually suspected by MI-5 of supplying information to the KGB, but he never confessed and was quietly switched to nonsensitive work in the late 1960s. Blunt later told interviewers that he had been recruited by Watson, and investigators have tracked down many other connections and crosscurrents among the members of the Marxisant Left at Cambridge in the late 1920s and 1930s. Michael Straight, an American who later applied for a security clearance, told investigators that Blunt had recruited him to the Communist Party in the 1930s, and it was Straight's information that led to questioning of Blunt.

Despite confessions, memoirs, MI-5 investigations, scholarly studies, and journalistic exposés, we may never learn the exact connections among the Cambridge Five both from inside and outside the Apostles Club. But this elite organization was certainly a recruiting ground for several that ended up working for the Soviet Union.

KGB records credited one Soviet agent for taking the lead in recruiting the Cambridge Five: Arnold Deutsch. Deutsch was an Austrian who worked for the KGB in London in 1934, and he reputedly recruited another 15 British subjects besides the recent Cambridge graduates. Deutsch may have been the mastermind behind recruitment at Cambridge. He suggested that the recruits from among communist-leaning students be encouraged to adopt a publicly more conservative image as they matured.

# The Cambridge Five

The world did not learn about the espionage activities of the young men until more than 20 years later. For two or more decades, the recruits worked their way up in their careers. Some were troubled by alcoholism, by conflicts in their love lives with both men and women, and by the stress of leading a double life. Eventually the stories of these *moles* ended up among the most publicized espionage tales in the English language.

**Spy Words**

Until the novels of John Le Carre, which fictionalized the experience of men like the Cambridge Five, agents who had been recruited early in their careers and who quietly worked their way up to positions of authority from which they could obtain important information were known as sleepers or simply as traitors or spies. Le Carre introduced the term **"mole"** in his 1974 novel *Tinker, Tailor, Soldier, Spy* to describe their underground existence, and for years it was assumed he had invented the term. However, Walter Pforzheimer, a retired CIA officer, discovered that the term had been used in a 1622 biography of King Henry VII to describe spies working to undermine opponents. So it appears the term itself had an underground existence for several centuries.

## Getting Access

At the suggestion of the KGB, Blunt worked to get into British intelligence. At the beginning of World War II, he joined Field Security of army intelligence, but was dismissed when investigators turned up his communist affiliations at Cambridge. He then turned to a close friend, who may have been a lover as well, Guy Lidell, who held a position at MI-5, and Lidell got Blunt a job in that agency. Guy Burgess joined MI-6, the overseas branch of British intelligence about the same time. Burgess brought in Harold A. R. (Kim) Philby to MI-6. Donald Maclean joined the Foreign Office.

For a period during World War II, Blunt worked as a double agent. Using a group of young men and women who were on the payroll of MI-5, Blunt had them seduce couriers attached to neutral embassies in London. The diplomatic bags would be opened and photocopied, with copies going to MI-5, and with duplicate copies going to the KGB. Blunt also reported to the KGB on the activities of several governments-in-exile that had been set up in London, particularly the Czech and Polish governments.

Blunt's access improved during the war. In 1944, he was appointed as the MI-5 liaison officer with the Supreme Headquarters of the Allied Expeditionary Force, and apparently had access to ULTRA materials (see Chapter 4).

## Blunt Protected

After the war, Blunt, whose field of study had been art history, was appointed keeper of the royal pictures—in effect, curator of the art collection of the royal house.

According to some accounts, this appointment was a reward for his work in recovering documents from Germany that showed German plans to install the duke of Windsor as monarch if Germany had conquered Britain. The duke had served as King Edward VIII briefly in 1936 before abdicating the throne to marry an American divorcée, Wallace Simpson. The duke had expressed pro-German political views, so the conspiracy theory was plausible, even if evidence for it was never published.

In any case, Blunt was well connected with the royal family, and his position appeared to protect him from exposure for many years. In the meantime, Burgess and Maclean, and then Philby, were exposed and defected to the Soviet Union. Their membership in the establishment also protected them for quite a while.

## Kim Philby

Harold (Kim) Philby came from an illustrious family, and despite a rather strange political career in the 1930s, his family and institutional connections helped assure him a place in MI-6 during World War II.

Kim's father was Harry St. John Philby, a graduate of Trinity College at Cambridge, who had served in the British administration in India, and then as a special emissary to King Ibn Saud in Arabia. A bit of a character, the elder Philby had been dismissed from the British service for disobedience of orders. He became a Muslim and settled in Jidda, Arabia, where he became an adviser to King Saud, often in direct opposition to British policy. So it was not the loyalty of the family, but its prominence that mattered.

Kim, like his father, attended Trinity College, and even belonged to the same club as his father, the Athenaeum. He started to study history, but switched to economics, where he met Guy Burgess.

## Philby in Vienna

Philby left Cambridge in 1933, and traveled to Vienna, Austria, by motorbike, where he immediately got involved in a local communist group. He met Litzi Friedman, an active worker in the Viennese communist underground. When the Austrian government clamped down with troops on the communists, Philby married Litzi, got her a British passport, and together they fled back to Britain in 1934. He would later divorce her and marry three more times.

Whether Philby had been recruited or only identified as a possible recruit at Cambridge, by the time he and Litzi came back to Britain, he was working for the Soviet Union. In his memoirs, he claimed he had been recruited as early as 1933, but it may not have been until his return to Britain in 1934.

# Philby as Pro-Fascist

On his return to Britain, Philby began to construct an alternate image of himself as an anticommunist, pro-fascist conservative, following the pattern that Arnold Deutsch recommended. He went to Spain early in 1937 to report from the anticommunist side, headed by Francisco Franco. Although at first not hired by the London *Times*, his freelance articles began to appear in that newspaper. He later got official credentials as a correspondent for *The Times*. His reports were so favorable to the fascist cause that Franco personally granted him a medal in March 1938. Philby later claimed that during this period, he provided information in code to the Soviet Union regarding Franco's forces. Another motive for working with *The Times* may have been the fact that British Intelligence often recruited from among *Times* staffers. He may have been trying to set up the sort of career that would get him into intelligence. He succeeded.

| Spy Bios |
| --- |
| Key dates in the life of Harold Adrian Russell (Kim) Philby: |
| 1912: Born in Amballa, India, son of Harry St. John Philby |
| 1929: Enters Trinity College, Cambridge. Joins University Socialist Society |
| 1933-1934: Goes to Vienna, marries Litzi Friedman, returns to London; recruited by the Soviet Union |
| 1937: Goes to Spain to report on Franco's side of Civil War |
| 1938: Receives medal from Franco |
| 1940: Joins MI-6 under Guy Burgess |
| 1941: Works in MI-6, Section V: Iberian Section |
| 1944: Appointed head of anticommunist section of MI-6 |
| 1946: Stationed with MI-6 in Turkey |
| 1949: Stationed in Washington |
| 1951: Learns of suspicions surrounding Maclean |
| 1955: Government denies Philby is Third Man, but he is dismissed |
| 1963: Philby defects to Moscow |
| 1965: Awarded Red Banner |
| 1988: Dies and is buried with military honors in Moscow |

# Philby in MI-6

At the beginning of World War II, Philby was accepted into the British MI-6 or the Secret Intelligence Service (SIS) with overseas responsibilities. Although the rival agency with MI-5 (or Security Service) that focused on domestic security, those who worked in the two agencies often socialized. The history of both agencies was surrounded with folklore. For example, the director of MI-6 was always known as "C," supposedly because the first director, Mansfield Cumming, had signed his name with his last initial. Or perhaps, others claimed, "C" stood for "Control" or "Chief."

In 1939, Stewart Menzies took over as C at MI-6, and served until 1953. Under Menzies, Philby was entrusted with several key responsibilities. Later, after the revelations that Philby had spied for the Russians, Menzies refused to talk about it, although he did tell one reporter, "What a blackguard Philby was!" Working his contacts, Philby was put in charge of Section V, concerned with Spain and Portugal. He ran his section efficiently and was admired by his staff and his superiors. When officials from the American OSS sought to establish liaison with both MI-5 and MI-6, the two agencies at first resisted. However, Philby made himself useful by agreeing to serve in a liaison capacity.

### Tradecraft

When spies retire, they sometimes write their memoirs detailing their careers, or even full-length autobiographies giving the story of their lives. If the retired spy is living under the jurisdiction of the nation for which he or she spied, the work is often selective with the truth. For this reason, such books can be full of disinformation, false leads, stories that disparage the agencies on the side they worked against, and plain falsehoods, mixed with some truths that can be verified from the public record. Espionage experts who have worked with Kim Philby's *My Secret War* (1968) have found it full of subtle and not-so-subtle distortions of the truth.

In 1944, Philby was transferred to head Section IX, which was concerned with countering Soviet espionage in Britain. It was quite a triumph for the KGB to have their own man heading the agency intended to prevent their espionage! Following the war, Philby was stationed in several postings in Europe and two years in Turkey, but his most significant help to the Soviet Union may have been in 1949–1950.

In 1949, Philby secured a position to act as liaison with the CIA, and moved to Washington. There, he was able to provide to the Soviet Union information about CIA and British-trained agents that MI-6 sent to Albania. As soon as they landed on the beaches, they would be arrested and after interrogation, executed. He also learned of the efforts to decipher the Venona materials (see Chapter 8) and the tracking of the atomic spies. One of the revelations developed from cracking the Venona messages was that someone highly placed in British Intelligence had been feeding information to the Soviet Union. From the details, it appeared to be someone in the British Foreign Office.

# Tracking the Moles

The American Army Security Agency identified the British leak from the Venona materials as code-named Gomer, or in English, Homer. Despite the fact that MI-5 appeared slow or uncooperative in evaluating who would have had access to the leaked materials, by May 1951, the list of possible Homer suspects had been narrowed to one: Donald Maclean of the Foreign Office. As the investigation proceeded, Philby kept posted and relayed the information to Moscow.

*Donald Maclean. Of all the Cambridge Five, Donald Maclean was probably the least stable and the most likely to blow the whole operation. Code name: Homer.*

*(Courtesy of the National Security Agency)*

Philby and the KGB knew that Maclean was notoriously unstable. When William Skardon had questioned Klaus Fuchs early in 1950, he had succeeded in getting lots of information (see Chapter 8). If Skardon had gone to work on Maclean, the results could be disaster, with exposure of numerous agents, and perhaps the unraveling of the whole KGB network in Britain.

## Maclean and Burgess Defect

On May 25, 1951, a Friday, Donald Maclean and Guy Burgess quietly left Britain. They knew that Maclean was scheduled to be arrested, and trusting the fact that bureaucrats did not operate between closing hours on Friday and opening on Monday, they got clean away. Blunt later suggested that Burgess had to defect along with Maclean because Maclean could not be trusted to make it all the way to Moscow without breaking down. He may have had to be convinced that it was best to defect, and it took the arguments of an old friend. Maclean spoke no Russian and had no desire to leave Britain.

Within an hour of the decision to arrest Maclean, Burgess was out buying luggage and canceling weekend appointments. Clearly, he had been tipped that the arrest was imminent. It seemed unlikely to later investigators that the warning had come from Philby, who was in Washington at the time, but rather from some other source within MI-5. However, Philby was known to be friends with the two.

## The Hunt for the Third Man

Burgess had left some incriminating papers behind, which Anthony Blunt calmly rescued. They included love letters from Burgess to Blunt, and letters in the handwriting of the fifth member of the Cambridge Five. The fact that Burgess and Maclean defected as soon as the arrest was authorized created shockwaves. The Americans, already incensed at the slow procedures of MI-5, smelled a rat. The press had a field day. With two spies defected, they borrowed the title of a popular film of the era that had starred Orson Welles, and began a hue and cry for "The Third Man."

Suspicion soon focused on both Blunt and Philby. Blunt was questioned 10 to 14 times between 1954 and 1963, before finally offering a secret confession, not made public until 1979, when MI-5 agents leaked the story to author Andrew Boyle. He published *The Fourth Man*, spelling out the cover-up.

Both the CIA and MI-5 suspected Philby, and he was forced to resign his position in 1955. Despite the fact that there was no evidence against Philby that could be presented in court, the CIA insisted that he be dismissed, or the relationship between the British and American intelligence communities would be severed. When Philby was confronted with the suspicions, he claimed he was a victim of false accusations, but did resign with a small cash settlement.

For the next several years, he lived in Beirut, Lebanon, as a correspondent for the *Economist* and the *Observer*, where he continued to provide the KGB with information. In 1956, Dick White became head of MI-6, and he was convinced that Philby was a Soviet spy. Philby disappeared from Beirut on January 23, 1963 and moved to Moscow. Two years later, he was awarded the Soviet Union's Red Banner Order. He claimed to journalists that he was appointed to colonel in the KGB, although KGB records did not confirm the story. Philby claimed that even after he had formally left MI-6 under pressure, MI-6 kept him on in Lebanon. That claim may have been further disinformation designed to make the agency look worse than it already did.

# The Fourth Man and the Fifth Man

Although Anthony Blunt provided a fairly complete confession of his activities in 1963, the conditions that he obtained for his confession were that it not be made public, and that he continue in his position with the royal household. Thus, when the British public learned about his confession 16 years later, with the publication of *The Fourth Man*, his activities were already history. Yet revelations and scandals continued to unfold well into the 1980s, with echoes of the work of the Cambridge Five.

## The Spycatcher Affair

Searching for the Fifth Man became another extended struggle in Britain. Suspicion focused on several highly placed individuals, including Sir Roger Hollis, head of MI-5. One investigator, Peter Wright, became convinced that Hollis was a KGB agent (see Chapter 18).

Although the charges against Hollis proved spurious, the efforts to suppress publication of details of the investigations ensured that events of the 1940s and 1950s had ugly continuing echoes down to the 1980s.

| Spy Bios |
| --- |
| John Cairncross finished at Cambridge in 1933, and worked in treasury until the war. Then he joined the groups at Bletchley Park working on decoding the Enigma materials from German radio transmissions. Working in Hut 6 at Bletchley, Cairncross never had access to the early computers developed at Bletchley, but he did work with the translated and decoded messages. He passed Ultra Secret materials to the Russians for four years between 1940 and 1944. When Cairncross confessed in 1963, he explained that he had been recruited by James Klugmann, and that his Soviet control officer was Anatoli Gorski, the same controller for Blunt, Burgess, Maclean, and Philby. Klugmann, an open member of the British Communist Party, was an active talent-spotter and recruiter for the KGB. |

## Another Cambridge Man

The Fifth Man, ELLI, was finally identified, through Soviet bloc revelations and other evidence, as John Cairncross. Cairncross had been one of the men found by Deutsch at Cambridge; his espionage career had been at a much lower level than those of Burgess, Maclean, Philby, and Blunt.

Even though Cairncross had confessed to espionage in the 1960s, his identification as the fifth of the Cambridge Five had to wait until the publication of some of the records of the KGB in the 1990s.

# Other USSR Moles and Spies in Britain

The number of agents working in Britain for the Soviet Union during and after World War II will probably never be known with certainty. KGB claims that as many as 29 were active at once may or may not be true. But a number of individuals beyond the Cambridge Five have been identified.

## The Krogers

Lona and Morris Cohen had played roles in the espionage efforts of the Soviet Union against the Manhattan Engineer District in the United States. Morris Cohen (code-named Volunteer) had a small network that included his wife, Lona (code-named Leslie). Lona had worked as a courier, getting information from Ted Hall at Los Alamos, and perhaps from David Greenglass as well. With the exposure of the Rosenbergs in 1951, the Cohens fled to Mexico, where they lived with two members of the Spanish Communist Party in exile there.

| Techint |
| --- |
| Microdots and high-speed transmission, although two different media, are both methods of compressing messages to evade detection. |
| The microdot system was invented in Germany in World War II. A page of a document would be photographed with a lens similar to that of a reverse microscope, onto film that was nearly free of grain. The resulting *micropunkt* or dot was so small that it could be pasted over a period in a book or newspaper. The document it contained could be read by an ordinary microscope. |
| High-speed radio transmitters allowed an agent to send encoded messages in extremely rapid bursts. By changing frequency and compressing parts of a message into a few seconds, it became nearly impossible to track down a clandestine radio transmitter. |

They surfaced again a few years later. After obtaining false New Zealand passports with the name of Peter and Helen Kroger, they set up shop in London as antiquarian booksellers. When the Polish agent Mikhail Goleniewski defected (see Chapter 14), his revelations led to the search of the Kroger's house. There, MI-5 found a powerful high-speed radio transmitter and a shortwave receiver hidden under the kitchen floorboards, a set of one-time cipher pads, a microdot reader, and seven sets of false passports.

At their trial in 1961, the Cohens were sentenced to 20 years. They had been working with Soviet agent Konon Molody, who operated under the name Gordon Lonsdale. As Lonsdale, Molody had recruited a filing clerk named Harry Houghton who had access to top secret British information about submarine warfare and nuclear submarines.

Goleniewski's information had led to Houghton, Houghton to Lonsdale, and Lonsdale to the Krogers. Lonsdale (Molody) was later traded for a British agent captured in Russia (see Chapter 14).

## George Blake

The story of George Blake seems like a version of the book and film, *The Manchurian Candidate*. Blake had been captured by the North Koreans during the Korean War (1950–1953), when he had been serving as an MI-6 agent with the cover as vice-consul at the British consulate in Seoul, South Korea. After three years of captivity in North Korea and Manchuria, he was released as part of the prisoner-exchange program. For nearly two decades after his release, he worked as a mole for the KGB.

| Spy Bios |
| --- |
| George Blake had been a communist before his capture in Korea. He was born George Behar in 1922 in Holland. Raised in Cairo, Egypt, as a teenager, he was recruited into the party and into the KGB by Henri Curiel, a relative of Behar's and a KGB officer in Egypt. Behar returned to Holland to complete secondary school, and was there when Germany invaded in 1940. He joined the Dutch resistance, changed his name to Max de Vries, and then fled to Britain where he again changed his name to George Blake. Blake worked in Naval Intelligence during the war, and in 1948, working as an undercover agent for the KGB, he was assigned to Seoul. |

After his return from Korea, Blake was assigned to Berlin by MI-6. There he learned of the CIA operation to construct a tunnel through which they would tap East German-Russian phone lines (see Chapter 11). The Soviets, learning of the tunnel from Blake, could have used the tapped lines to transmit some disinformation mixed in with real information. Apparently the KGB didn't want to tell the GRU about the wire tap, so military information began leaking to the Americans.

Following the 1961 defection from the Soviet Union of Mikhail Goleniewski (see Chapter 14), the CIA learned that George Blake had been working for the KGB while in Berlin. Recalled from Lebanon to London, Blake was confronted with the charge. He broke down and confessed.

After revealing how his espionage had led to the capture and execution of many Soviet double agents, he was tried and sentenced to 42 years in prison. However, in 1967, Blake escaped with the aid of a fellow prisoner, Sean Bourke, a member of the Irish Republican Army. Blake settled down to a comfortable life in Russia, and later boasted of his successful work as a KGB agent.

# Damage Assessments

The damage done by British moles and agents like the Cohens, Blake, and the Cambridge Five was difficult to assess. Some of it was direct, as in the exposure of agents that the Americans and British tried to infiltrate into the Soviet Union and Albania, who were caught and executed.

Other effects were less direct, such as the sowing of seeds of distrust between the British and American agencies, and within the agencies as suspicion fell on innocent people. Victims of false charges included prime minister Harold Wilson, Sir Richard Hollis, and many loyal intelligence officers.

## How Did It Happen?

Like the exposure of Klaus Fuchs, the exposure of the Cambridge Five raised serious questions about the British method of vetting candidates for security clearances. The British had relied on a system of agents vouching for others on the basis of acquaintance. Character references, based on family connections and affiliations with schools, clubs, and professions, were preferred to investigations of political affiliation. The attraction of Marxist ideas that some had openly shown in the 1930s was dismissed as a combination of youthful enthusiasm, intellectual fad, and a symptom of the times, just as the KGB had anticipated when recruiting the young men.

The fact that several key agents, including Blunt, Burgess, and Maclean, were known to be homosexual or bisexual, was similarly dismissed. After all, many perfectly loyal British and American citizens were homosexual. On the other hand, the fact that, in the 1930s, homosexuality was a crime and was often concealed, opened some individuals to blackmail, reputedly one of the techniques employed by Blunt in recruiting younger men. Furthermore, homosexuality in that era often led to a double life for those who had not come out of the closet. Such dissimulation could mean that some might be better prepared for the double life of espionage.

## Propaganda Value

Although the key agents were exposed, the KGB continued to extract useful mileage from them even afterward. By playing up the successes of the KGB in outwitting MI-5 and the CIA, Moscow could make good propaganda out of the cases, often ensuring that copious amounts of disinformation misled readers. The release of autobiographies by men like Philby and Blake became part of the propaganda of the cold war. For this reason, students of the subject have a difficult time sorting out the facts.

## The Least You Need to Know

◆ The Cambridge Five were Donald Maclean, Guy Burgess, Kim Philby, Anthony Blunt, and John Cairncross.

◆ The penetration of British intelligence agencies by the KGB caused serious suspicion within the agencies and between the United States and Britain.

◆ The slow exposure of secret agents over the years of the cold war served as one of the propaganda tools of the Soviet Union.

◆ Some lesser agents and moles like Morris and Lona Cohen and George Blake were only uncovered when information came from defections of Soviet bloc agents.

# American Moles

## In This Chapter

- ◆ Aboveground and underground communists
- ◆ Agents of influence and spies
- ◆ HUAC and spy hunting
- ◆ Chambers and Hiss
- ◆ Elizabeth Bentley

After the United States and the Soviet Union opened diplomatic relations in 1933, Soviet agents began to recruit informants and couriers to work in America secretly. Both the civilian and military espionage agencies of the Soviet Union sought to build networks that could be used to gather information and to place people in positions of authority or influence. "Agent of influence" became a term the Russians used to describe highly placed political figures who would be friendly to the Soviet Union. As noted in Chapter 3, the Soviet agency that became the KGB went through several name changes over the years, and to keep things easy to follow here, we will call the agency the "KGB" in this chapter, even when it went by other initials in earlier periods. The military agency was the GRU.

# The Soviet Networks in the United States

As a target for intelligence operations, the United States seemed attractive for several reasons. In the mid-1930s, intelligence officials in the Soviet Union believed that the United States would play an important part in world affairs, and they also believed that the United States would be a good listening post for intelligence regarding potential enemies such as Germany and Japan. Furthermore, American advances in technology in numerous fields were interesting to the Soviets as they sought to modernize, and although much information could simply be gathered through sources like magazines and technical reports, access to technical trade secrets and to classified military technology would require more than just visits to the public library. Among the technical areas that interested Soviet intelligence the most were aircraft design, aluminum production, weapons capabilities, and after about 1941, the nuclear bomb.

## Recruiting and Recruits

Soviet agents found that a good recruiting ground for informants was among the growing numbers of young people disillusioned with American society and capitalism after the Great Depression, and who had turned to the Socialist and Communist Parties. As in other countries, the American Communist Party had both an open and a secret, or underground, membership.

Early in the 1920s, as the Communist Party of the United States of America (CPUSA) organized out of the various language sections of the Socialist Party and other groups of radical Marxists, some of the members had operated secretly and others openly. The dual structure of open and admitted party membership for some, and secret, clandestine membership for others was well suited to the mission of Soviet intelligence operations.

The KGB and the GRU recruited from among party members, seeking out those who seemed ideologically correct, trustworthy, and intelligent, and those whose early careers suggested that they might have a role to play in government circles. As in Britain, the Soviet agencies hoped that the young recruits of the 1930s would be part of the leadership generation a decade later. From evidence that came out over the rest of the century, it is now known that they had some limited success in planting a few moles and in winning over a few agents of influence. In some cases, the American recruits to the cause of the Soviet Union became as notorious as their British counterparts, but the Soviet recruiters themselves, as in Britain, generally succeeded in keeping low profiles.

Soviet agents were adept at using aliases, and those who operated in the 1920s and 1930s in the United States were no exception. I. V. Voldarsky, code-named Brit, went by the name of Armand Lavis Feldman, whose main task appeared to be economic and technical information. Valentine Markin, code-named Davis, operated out of New York and from about 1934 began to recruit Americans to work with the Soviet intelligence agencies. Markin got a few agents to provide information from the U.S. State Department. He worked with another Soviet illegal, Itzhak Akhmerov, known as Bill and code-named Yung.

Akhmerov married the niece of the American Communist Party leader Earl Browder, Helen Lowry, who served as a contact between open party members and the under-ground network. In 1939, Helen Lowry Akhmerov moved with her husband to the Soviet Union and continued as an agent with the KGB. Earl Browder, the head of the CPUSA through the 1930s and World War II, himself became a Soviet agent, and was convicted in 1940 of illegal use of false passports.

When Markin was accidentally killed in an auto accident in 1934, his replacement as a new station chief was Boris Bazarov or Nord. Nord had the specific assignment of building the Soviet network in the State Department, and to organize information sources in the military.

## Good and Bad Tradecraft

Despite the professional espionage training received by agents like Markin, Akhmerov, and Bazarov, they could not always apply good tradecraft in the United States. Their American recruits, even when bright and articulate, had character traits that often made it difficult. Some, like young Whittaker Chambers, liked to brag about their secret activities to friends or overdramatize their underground life.

Others were in it for very romantic or psychological reasons, and cared little about compartmentation, combining their clandestine information gathering with openly meeting with radical friends in discussion groups. Still others worked for Soviet intel-ligence for purely financial reasons. Leo, one of Markin's sources, pretended to be getting information from two other sources, one with a $500 per month fee, and another receiving $400 per month. When Markin figured it out, he cancelled the payments.

Despite the sometimes amateurish or unauthorized behavior of the American agents, the networks continued to grow, and a few of the recruits worked their way into posi-tions of some importance with connections that got them access to valuable informa-tion. Among the more unique American recruits to the Soviet intelligence cause were the daughter of an American ambassador, a U.S. Congressman who headed a committee investigating un-American activities in the 1930s, and a young millionaire who had first been recruited at Cambridge University in Britain.

## The Ambassador's Daughter

Martha Dodd, the daughter of U.S. ambassador to Germany, William Dodd, fell in love with Boris Vinogradov, a Soviet diplomat, while her father was stationed in Berlin in 1934. He recruited her to begin providing material from her father's files. When Vinogradov was transferred to other posts, she became an active Soviet agent, providing material based on files and overheard discussions. Even after her father's retirement in 1937, Martha continued to work directly for the KGB, and her controllers there regarded her as an important agent because of her social connections. Although Martha had several lovers during the 1930s, she continued to try to arrange a marriage with Vinogradov, but neither he nor his superiors approved the idea.

In 1937, Martha Dodd married an American millionaire, Alfred Stern. Later, her husband, her younger brother William, and several of her social contacts became recruits for the KGB. At times, her handlers in Moscow found it difficult to decide what to make of her. Her various love affairs, her sometimes-open promotion of communist causes, and her tendency to talk too much put them off. Nevertheless, they continued to use her as a talent scout up to about 1949. Later, the Sterns left the United States, first for Mexico, living in Castro's Cuba for a while, and finally settling in Czechoslovakia.

## Code-Name: Crook

Another of the unusual cases was Congressman Samuel Dickstein. Dickstein headed the House Committee on Un-American activities in 1937, which then focused on the activities of fascist groups in the United States. Dickstein met with the Soviet ambassador, and offered to sell information uncovered by the committee regarding pro-fascist Russian groups in the United States. The KGB assigned Dickstein the code name Crook. Dickstein asked for $2,500 a month to supply information and after the Soviets offered $500 a month, he counter-offered at $1,250 a month.

As time went on, Dickstein's handlers agreed that he was certainly living up to his code name. When Congress selected Martin Dies to head the committee, Dickstein's value to the Soviets fell off. After a series of arguments over the value of his continued services, the Soviets broke off contact with him in January 1940. Altogether, Dickstein (Crook) had received $12,000, estimated by historian Allen Weinstein, who published the story later in 1997, to be the equivalent of more than $133,000 in dollar value of that year.

## Michael Straight

Michael Straight was the son of a wealthy American family, and he had studied in Britain in the early 1930s. After finishing his university education at Cambridge, where he had been identified as a promising plant in the United States by Anthony Blunt (see Chapter 9), he returned home to seek a position in the government. He first hoped to get a job on the personal staff of President Franklin Roosevelt or in the Treasury Department. His family knew Henry Wallace (then secretary of agriculture), the president's personal aide Harry Hopkins, and Henry Morgenthau, secretary of the Treasury Department.

Straight landed a position on the National Resources Board and then took a job with the State Department. At first the Soviet handlers were convinced he would be a useful agent, following a career like the Cambridge Five, moving into a position of influence and certainly a position with access to sensitive materials.

However, Straight did not get much chance to view important documents at the State Department, and he continued to believe that the information he provided was channeled to the Comintern, not directly to Soviet espionage agencies. Often, both the KGB and the GRU would allow willing American agents to think that they were providing information to the Communist Party or to the Comintern, rather than to Soviet espionage agencies.

Straight really confused his Soviet handlers. He was quite wealthy, and the income from his investments netted him over $50,000 per year. Unlike some of the other American contacts who wanted to be paid, Straight kept offering to *give* money to the Soviet Union for the cause. They were further frustrated by the fact that he refused to give up his contacts with other Communist Party members and sympathizers. Again, bad tradecraft.

Like other Americans who were pro-communist in the 1930s because they believed it was the best way to express their anti-fascism, Straight became suddenly disillusioned in 1939 with the announcement of the pact between the Soviets and Nazis. After wavering, he broke off contacts with his Soviet handlers. He later told both Anthony Blunt and Guy Burgess, friends from Cambridge, that he had completely abandoned his faith that communism was an extension of progressive ideas.

# The Red Spy Queen

The activities of strange characters like Martha Dodd, Samuel Dickstein, and Michael Straight were not fully understood until years after their espionage careers, with the opening of Soviet archives and the research of diligent historians like Allen Weinstein, whose 1997 bestseller, *The Haunted Wood*, pieced together the accounts. But in the 1940s, several self-confessed spies told stories that made headlines and brought the activities of the Soviet agencies to the attention of the general American public. One of them, Elizabeth Bentley, became known in the print media of the day as the Red Spy Queen.

## Bentley and Her Revelations

Jacob Golos, a Russian-born communist who had lived in the United States from 1910 to 1926, recruited Elizabeth Bentley into espionage. He went back to Russia briefly in the late 1920s, and returned to the United States by 1930 to work for Soviet intelligence in the KGB. Golos's first job was arranging to get false passports for Soviet illegals and U.S. Communist Party members who needed to travel overseas under assumed names. His cover was a tourist agency, World Tourist, that specialized in arranging trips to the Soviet Union. The agency was so successful that it began providing revenue to the American Communist Party. By 1937, Golos began to recruit merchant seamen and others who could work as couriers.

Golos recruited Elizabeth Bentley, whose ancestors included some of the first settlers in the United States, and a signer of the Declaration of Independence. She had graduated from Vassar College and had studied at Columbia University, she and had held jobs as a librarian and teacher.

At first Bentley worked as a courier for GRU informants, and then in 1938, she was transferred to work officially with the Golos network and the KGB.

Golos and Bentley became lovers, and remained so until his death in 1943. Golos was arrested and convicted of operating an espionage operation in 1939, but after his release, he continued to recruit agents in Washington and New York. Two of them were fairly highly placed: Nathan Silvermaster, code-named Pal (later, Robert) and Harry Dexter White, code-named Richard. Silvermaster coordinated a network at the Treasury Department, and Harry Dexter White also worked at Treasury.

The fact that Golos had been arrested and was watched by the FBI after his release made the Soviet agents nervous that the American authorities would spot his networks. Golos's operation was even more at risk because one of the early Soviet agents, Volodarsky, was a double agent and reported to the FBI.

Together, Golos and Bentley worked with American communists during the first part of World War II, identifying individuals who could be helpful in espionage. Golos suffered from a heart condition, and as his health worsened, the KGB sought to transfer his networks of agents to Akhmerov. When Golos died from a heart attack in

1943, Bentley inherited his contacts, and like Golos, she sought to manage them herself without turning them over for direct control by Soviet agents.

## Bentley's Defection

Other aspects of Bentley's operation bothered the Soviets. She not only tried to prevent meetings between the Soviet agents and the members of her networks, she was careless about tradecraft, letting different members know of the activities of each other, giving out her home phone number, and otherwise violating the rules about compartmentation.

Furthermore, she began dating a man, Peter Heller, whom the KGB suspected worked for the FBI. By October 1945, she had decided to cooperate with the FBI. Soon, Kim Philby (see Chapter 9) informed the KGB office in London that Bentley had begun to cooperate with the FBI as they started to investigate leads to the agents mentioned in the materials taken from the Soviet embassy in Ottawa, Canada by Igor Gouzenko (see Chapter 7).

Philby continued to relay information to Moscow about the progress of the FBI investigation into the Bentley revelations. Quickly, Moscow moved to protect Maclean, who was stationed in Washington, and began ordering the Soviet agents to come home. In memoranda and discussions, the KGB considered ways to liquidate Bentley, but constantly postponed coming to grips with exactly how it should be done and by whom. As Bentley moved from quiet discussions with the FBI to testimony before Congressional committees, and then to the front pages as the Red Spy Queen, the damage she did to the Soviet networks in the United States mounted.

What was revealed was that several networks of American sympathizers with the communist cause who worked in Washington and in ways that seemed amateurish and characterized by poor tradecraft, had infiltrated numerous agencies. With members scattered through different parts of the government, and at least one congressional staff member, the networks established by Golos and Bentley provided information on war production statistics, aircraft technical specifications, plans for postwar Germany, trade policy, and related issues.

The defection of Bentley in late 1945 caused panic in Moscow. Perhaps we should put "defection" in quote marks, because Bentley was an American citizen, and she simply dropped her role as traitor and decided to confess to U.S. authorities. When she began to provide the FBI with information, the KGB closed down all communications with numerous informants and issued instructions for their subsources to cut off contact. Whole new recognition signals, code names, courier channels, and contacts had to be established. The organization was suddenly in disarray.

*Elizabeth Bentley. Known as the Red Spy Queen, Elizabeth Bentley named a long list of spies in the U.S. government who had worked for the Soviet Union. Her revelations put a serious crimp in Soviet spying for several years.*

*(Courtesy of the National Security Agency)*

# Whittaker Chambers and Alger Hiss

Perhaps the best remembered and most notorious of all the espionage cases of the era was that of Whittaker Chambers and Alger Hiss. There are several reasons why the case was kept alive over the decades. One was that Alger Hiss, although confronted with clear evidence that he had lied to Congressional investigators about his past, continued to deny that he had ever worked with Soviet intelligence. Another was that the politician most responsible for bringing the Hiss case before the public and to court was Richard Nixon, one of the most controversial figures in American politics of the twentieth century.

## Chambers and Hiss: A Study in Contrasts

In some ways, Whittaker Chambers and Alger Hiss were very different, and in some ways, rather similar. Both came from what we would now call disfunctional families, with suicides of family members and an absent or hostile father. The differences however, were noteworthy and almost always noted in news accounts of the period.

Hiss was a successful graduate of Johns Hopkins University and Harvard Law School, a man whose career seemed typical of many of the bright young graduates who worked in the New Deal and World War II agencies of the Franklin Roosevelt administrations. After serving as a clerk on the Supreme Court, he held a position as a staff member on the Nye Committee, investigating munitions sales and the politics of America's involvement in World War I. He worked in the agricultural adjustment administration, and during the war, served with the U.S. State Department. There, he attended the international conference at Yalta, and helped arrange the first conference of the United Nations in San Francisco in 1945. After the war, he was selected as president of the Carnegie Institution, a very prestigious non-profit think-tank in Washington.

By contrast, Whittaker Chambers had dropped out of Columbia University, and had become an admitted and open communist by 1930. He worked as a writer and then editor for the Communist Party's paper, the *Daily Worker*. Recruited to serve as an underground recruiter for intelligence agents and as a courier for the growing networks in Washington, Chambers adopted a double (or sometimes, triple) life. However, with the purges of the Communist Party in the Soviet Union, he became troubled with the strain, and dropped out of espionage work in 1938.

He provided reports to the U.S. government of his activities. By the end of the war, he was a writer for *Time* magazine, starting as a book review editor and then promoted to a senior editorial position. In his work at *Time*, he not only took on a strongly anticommunist position, he was highly critical of the Roosevelt New Deal and New Deal liberalism.

*Alger Hiss. Alger Hiss and Priscilla Hiss denied any involvement in espionage, and their confident air of good breeding convinced many they were wrongly accused.*

*(Courtesy of the National Security Agency)*

Not only had the two careers of Hiss and Chambers seemed very different, the two men differed in appearance. Hiss was handsome, well dressed, with excellent manners.

Chambers was always described as unkempt or rumpled, diffident, and unimpressive. On first impression, most people would trust Hiss more than Chambers.

## Hiss Recruited

Alger Hiss had worked with the GRU in the 1930s, and although others knew his pro-Soviet positions and politics, he appeared to be a diligent and loyal worker for the United States. He had first been recruited by Whittaker Chambers in about 1934 to become an agent of influence, but he also began to provide classified documents through Chambers and later, through others, to the Soviet army intelligence. Sometimes he would bring documents home, and his wife Priscilla would retype them so that the originals could be returned to the files.

The KGB was embarrassed when Michael Straight, who they had asked to serve as a talent spotter, opened discussions with Alger Hiss in 1938. When the KGB realized that their man was trying to recruit someone with whom the GRU was already working, they had to ask Straight to back off. They had to do it without explaining why, in order to protect compartmentation.

## Breaking the Case

When Chambers left his espionage career, he was afraid that the Soviet agents would track him down, and he secretly kept a batch of documents that he hoped he could use to ensure his safety. If threatened, he could claim that on his untimely death the incriminating documents would be released. Perhaps he had seen too many movies. On the other hand, the murder of one or two Soviet agents who had defected, and the intense purges back in Russia that led to the deaths of others, may have given him a basis for caution.

He stored the documents, and late in 1939, went to Under Secretary of State Adolf Berle, whom Roosevelt had appointed to try to coordinate counterintelligence work, and gave details of the espionage network with which he had worked. Berle apparently did very little about the information, which included a denunciation of Alger Hiss. This conversation took place in early September 1939, immediately after the German invasion of Poland that began World War II, and Berle may have overlooked the Chambers matter in the press of war-related duties.

Berle never reported the conversation to the FBI, and did not follow up on Chambers's request that he be offered immunity from prosecution for testifying. Berle later made quiet inquiries about the loyalty of Alger and Priscilla Hiss at the State Department, and was assured by Dean Acheson and Felix Frankfurter that Hiss was perfectly reliable and that the charges by Chambers that Hiss was a spy were groundless.

When the *House Committee on Un-American Activities* was interviewing Chambers, in August 1948, he described his earlier espionage work, and identified Alger Hiss. News media seized on the story. After all, Hiss had been a high-level New Deal official, and now held a prestigious position with the Carnegie Institution. When Hiss read the news items describing Chambers's testimony, he denied ever having met Chambers.

### Spy Words

The **House Committee on Un-American Activities** became incorrectly abbreviated as "HUAC"; the correct acronym would have been "HCUA" or "HCOUA." Since it was difficult to pronounce either of those two versions, "HUAC" (pronounced hew-ack) caught on in the press and on radio and television. The committee was always controversial and in the 1960s, it became such a target for criticism that Congress closed it down. A basic problem was that the definition of what constituted un-American activities was a political one, and for Congress to investigate the political behavior of citizens could infringe their First Amendment rights to free speech and political association.

### Techint

When Chambers produced documents that he claimed had been recopied from classified material by Priscilla Hiss on a typewriter, the FBI tracked down the typewriter. By tracing its sale from one party to another over a period of more than 10 years, the FBI turned up the original Woodstock typewriter owned by the Hiss's. Slight differences in type-font could allow experts to match a typewriter with typed manuscript, and in this fashion, a piece of technical evidence was introduced that helped convict Hiss of perjury. Supporters of Hiss claimed the evidence was faked; his critics saw the typewriter-document match as proof he had been a spy.

Over the next weeks, Congressman Richard Nixon, then a junior member of the committee, had himself appointed as chairman of a subcommittee to investigate the problem of the discrepancy between the story of Chambers and that of Hiss. As testimony of the two developed, it soon became obvious that Chambers knew many details about the life of Alger Hiss in the 1930s, that he had rented an apartment from Hiss, and that Hiss had given Chambers an automobile. He even knew details of Hiss's hobbies and interests that only a close friend would know.

Hiss continued to protest that he had never met Chambers, and when finally confronted with more facts, he began to admit that indeed, he had known him, but under another name. But Hiss denied he had ever conducted any espionage or ever worked in a cell providing information to the Soviet Union. As Hiss began to correct his story, it became clear he was not being entirely truthful with the committee.

**Spy Words**

When Whittaker Chambers was asked to provide some proof of his charges against Hiss, he produced the documents that he had saved years before. Some of the documents came from an office in which Hiss had worked. Chambers had microfilmed the documents and he hid them temporarily in a pumpkin on his farm in Maryland. When he led investigators out to retrieve the microfilm and the story got out, the press dubbed the evidence *The Pumpkin Papers.*

Hiss sued Chambers for slander, and lost the suit. Since the civil lawsuit in effect ruled that Chambers had told the truth about their relationship, the Congressional committee pressed perjury charges against Hiss, and he was found guilty and imprisoned on that charge.

Despite his conviction, Hiss continued to insist that he had been framed. Public opinion soon divided, almost along predictable political lines. Democrats, liberals, and those opposing an irrational red-hunt in Washington tended to side with Hiss. Republicans, conservatives, and outspoken critics of the New Deal found the Hiss case an ideal issue, as it could be used to argue that Roosevelt, and then his successor, Harry Truman, were both soft on communism.

**Tradecraft**

In the light of the fact that the Rosenbergs were executed for conspiracy to commit espionage, and that other spies received prison sentences for their crimes, the public often asked why Hiss was not tried for espionage but only for perjury. The answer was that the evidence against him pointed to acts of violation of security procedures in time of peace, more than 10 years before. It was far easier to bring charges of perjury for having lied to Congress, charges that had already been demonstrated in his slander civil law suit against Chambers, than it was to prove espionage.

# The Politics of Counterespionage

The publicity surrounding the Alger Hiss case made the obscure junior congressman from California, Richard Nixon, suddenly very famous. He was good at timing information releases and he played up the dramatic episodes of the Hiss case for all they were worth. He was elected to the U.S. Senate in 1950, and in 1952, Dwight Eisenhower selected him to run as his vice-presidential candidate. Nixon's career was launched on the Hiss case.

For democrats and others who then and later disliked Richard Nixon, the story put out that Alger Hiss had been framed seemed to fit. But careful sifting of the evidence by Allen Weinstein, Sam Tannenhaus, and other objective historians showed that indeed, Chambers had told the truth, and that Alger Hiss had been an active agent for the Soviet Union. In fact, when the Venona documents were finally published in the 1990s, Hiss was identified as code-named Ales by the GRU (see Chapter 19).

## Professional Red Hunters

Elizabeth Bentley and Whittaker Chambers, among others who had once been active in the Communist Party and in espionage, reformed and confessed their past crimes. For many Americans, it was difficult to believe the stories of such people, for several reasons. In the first place, Americans tended to be uninformed and naïve about espionage, considering the stories to be works of fiction. The sensationalized fiction-mixed-with fact that surrounded people like Mata Hari, Sidney Reilly, and Herbert O. Yardley, as discussed in Chapters 2 and 3, made all espionage stories seem either like pulp fiction or like a wild conspiracy theory. Now and then the arrest of a real-life spy, like Judith Coplon, seemed like a spy fiction script.

---

### Spy Bios

Judith Coplon was a committed communist who decided she wanted to help out the cause. Working at the FBI, she volunteered to provide information. At first, like some other spies, she was told that the information would be channeled to the American Communist Party. However, when she learned that the data was going to the Soviet Union, she claimed she was proud to be working directly for Soviet intelligence. She became one of the KGB's best sources, since like the agents who penetrated Britain's MI-5, she could keep track of counterespionage work for Moscow. As a result of code-cracking, Coplon was arrested March 4, 1949, on a New York street, carrying top-secret documents in her purse when she met with her contact Valentin Gubitchev. In the Venona documents, her code name was Sima.

---

Another fact was the personalities of people like Chambers and Bentley. Could you really trust the statements of people who by their own admission had once led a double life and had lied to their friends and sometimes to their employers about their politics and their secret work? Once a liar, people believed, always a liar.

And then there were the politicians and the professional red hunters. Some of the congressmen asking questions in committee used the charges of espionage or disloyalty to discredit political positions they did not like. People who had been active in labor organizing, in supporting the loyalists in Spain, in agitating against Nazis and fascism, or who had supported various New Deal reforms could be conveniently smeared through association with those a little further to the left who had been so pro-Soviet as to commit espionage. Many Americans simply were disgusted with the politics of accusation and guilt-by-association.

## Making Political Hay

When conservative congressmen like Richard Nixon, Karl Mundt, Martin Dies, and later, Joe McCarthy gained headlines by beating the drum about communists and espionage, it became even harder to sort out the real cases from all the political hot air. Unfortunately, the careers of many perfectly loyal Americans were damaged in the process. Some of the real and phony scares of later years are explored in Chapter 12.

## The Least You Need to Know

- In the 1930s and 1940s, both the GRU and the KGB built networks of spies in the United States, frequently recruiting from among members of the Communist Party.

- When several of the spies became disillusioned with working for the Soviet Union, they confessed their past activities, exposing the networks.

- The most famous of the self-confessed spies were Elizabeth Bentley and Whittaker Chambers.

- Richard Nixon earned national fame as a red-hunter with his controversial exposé of Alger Hiss based on testimony and evidence supplied by Whittaker Chambers.

# CIA Formation and Early Successes

## In This Chapter

- ◆ Setting up the CIA
- ◆ Inter-agency issues
- ◆ Direct Ops in Italy, Albania, Ukraine
- ◆ Tapping landlines
- ◆ The CIA in Korea and Guatemala

From its first years, the late 1940s through the mid-1950s, the Central Intelligence Agency had the heavy responsibility of coordinating intelligence gathered from other agencies. But as the newest agency, it lacked the seniority and prestige of army G-2, Office of Naval Intelligence, the FBI, and the State Department. One issue was unclear from the first: How much should the agency itself get involved in direct operations? Direct Ops, as they were known, could involve clandestine payments to foreign political groups, bribery, sabotage, support for armed resistance groups, kidnapping, even assassination, along the lines of the operations run by the

OSS during World War II. Stories of a few successes of the new agency circulated, and the CIA started to gain stature in American intelligence circles in this period.

# Setting Up the CIA

President Harry Truman refused to keep the OSS in operation after World War II because, he said, he did not want any Gestapo type of organization in the United States. He never liked Bill Donovan and cutting the budget seemed a good idea. However, as the cold war intensified, and as the operation of Soviet agents in Canada and the United States became better known through the defections and testimony of Igor Gouzenko, Elizabeth Bentley, and Alger Hiss, Truman became convinced that the United States needed to better coordinate its intelligence sources.

Examination of the failure of intelligence represented by the surprise attack on Pearl Harbor suggested that bits and pieces of information had not been properly or promptly shared (see Chapter 3). In an age of nuclear weapons and long-range bombers (and the looming prospect of long-range missiles), the next surprise attack could be far more devastating than the one on December 7, 1941. Coordinating information to prevent such a surprise would be a major responsibility of the new agency.

## Two-Step Creation

Even before the agency itself was created, Truman set up the post of Director of Central Intelligence (DCI) by executive order in 1946 to head the Central Intelligence Group. The CIA itself was created by the National Security Act passed by Congress on July 26, 1947, and it began operation in September 1947. The enabling legislation gave the new agency extraordinary freedom from oversight, explicitly allowing the CIA to expend federal money with-out accounting for it in the usual fashion. The agency, operating by direction of the president, simply advised Congress how much had been spent.

From January 23, 1946 to June 10, 1946, Admiral Sidney Souers served as Director of Central Intelligence by executive authority, and he headed the Central Intelligence Group. Hoyt Vandenberg, a General in the Army Air Force, replaced him. Admiral Roscoe Hillenkoetter was appointed DCI #3 in May 1947, and when the National Security Act established the Central Intelligence Agency, effective September 18, 1947, Hillenkoetter continued to serve as Director. The new CIA replaced the Central Intelligence Group.

The overlapping history of these years creates a bit of confusion sometimes, because there was a Director of Central Intelligence during the period of the Central

Intelligence Group. The CIA was created three and a half months into Hillenkoetter's term as DCI #3.

In April 1950, the National Security Council (also created in 1947) issued directive number 68 or NSC-68, which summed up the moral, ideological, and political obligation of the United States to uphold free institutions worldwide, and to oppose the attempted expansion of the Soviet system. However, the tougher position of the United States in foreign and defense policy toward the Soviet Union is usually dated to a speech in 1947, when President Truman asked Congress for $400 million to support aid to Greece and Turkey to oppose communist-aided rebels in those countries.

*When Harry Truman and Joseph Stalin met at Potsdam in 1945, the espionage that would characterize the cold war was already at work. Truman did not know that Stalin knew more about the Manhattan Project than he had known while serving as Franklin Roosevelt's vice president.*

*(Courtesy of the Library of Congress)*

## Surprises

Despite the fact that the DCI and his new agency, the CIA, were supposed to coordinate information and predict the flow of events, over 1948–1949, a series of international developments came as surprises, critics claimed. In February 1948, communists conducted a coup in Czechoslovakia, converting that country into a satellite of the Soviet Union. On June 28, 1948, the Soviet Union expelled Yugoslavia from the Cominform, heralding a split in the Soviet bloc. In 1948, the small new nation of Israel won a war even though vastly outnumbered by the surrounding Arab states. On June 24, 1948, the Soviet Union closed access to Berlin, establishing a blockade that lasted over 10 months. On September 21, 1949, the Chinese Communist Party proclaimed the People's Republic of China in Beijing. Where was the DCI in all this? journalists asked.

In answer, the director of the CIA, Admiral Roscoe H. Hillenkoetter, noted that the reports were incorrect, and that the CIA had indeed predicted the split between Tito in Yugoslavia and Stalin in Russia, that it had repeatedly predicted that the nationalist forces in China were disintegrating. He admitted that the agency had been surprised at the quick Israeli victory over the Arab states, but had underestimated the aid the new Israeli state would receive from overseas. With regard to Czechoslovakia, Hillenkoetter admitted that the CIA had not been very accurate in prediction.

---

### Techint

As the United States tested nuclear weapons by detonating them above ground in 1946–1949, the Atomic Energy Commission and the Air Force cooperated to track the fallout of radioactive particles. While most of the hazardous fallout was on or near the Nevada test site north of Las Vegas, radioactive materials rose high into the upper atmosphere and blew entirely around the planet. Gradually the heavy isotopes and the unfissioned plutonium from the weapons would fall to earth. The Air Force developed a system in which filters aboard aircraft would pick up minute dust particles. Early in September 1949, filters picked up plutonium particles, and the AEC/Air Force experts determined that a nuclear explosion had gone off about a week earlier. They knew it was not one of theirs. To keep the detection method secret, President Truman delayed announcing the Russian nuclear test until the end of September.

---

Perhaps most disturbing of all the surprises was the discovery in September 1949, that the Soviet Union had detonated a nuclear device sometime in late August. Just weeks before the detonation, the CIA had predicted that the low supply of uranium in the Soviet Union would prevent the manufacture of a nuclear device until about 1953. In answer to questions in Congress, Hillenkoetter stated that the detonation of the nuclear device required that the Central Intelligence Agency reassess its estimates. No kidding!

When the North Koreans attacked South Korea in June 1950, the ability of the CIA to make predictions came under even more serious public and political scrutiny. President Truman replaced Hillenkoetter with General Walter Bedell Smith on October 7, 1950, with a mandate to reform the agency.

## Coordination Problems

Souers, Vandenberg, and Hillenkoetter faced some difficult problems, characteristic of many intelligence agencies, not only in the United States, but also in Britain,

Germany, the Soviet Union, and Japan. Although an agency can control its own op-sec, it usually has little influence or control over that of a sister agency. Sharing information can have the consequence of revealing a source, simply because good op-sec on the other side may have limited the distribution of information to a very closed number of individuals. The nature of the information itself can reveal exactly where the leak occurred.

### Tradecraft

Intelligence operations consist of several phases, each of which is crucial to the process. Information must be gathered, analyzed, communicated, and incorporated in policy or strategy. Furthermore, to protect information from being acquired by the enemy or potential enemies, good op-sec must be in place, limiting access to information to those with a legitimate and authorized need to have the information. Built into these requirements or goals is the basic intelligence dilemma. For information to be analyzed, communicated, and used in policy, it must be shared. However, sharing it too widely runs against good op-sec, simply because those outside the gathering agency might be careless and reveal information.

Op-sec is not a simple jealous guarding of turf; it is essential to the continued gathering of information. If a source, whether in the form of a human informant, or a method of breaking into the secure communications of the opponent, is compromised, the source will dry up. If the enemy can detect a traitor in their own camp, the traitor will be apprehended or provided with false information, or doubled or turned. If a communication pathway is leaking, and the enemy discovers the leak, corrective measures will be taken. Either the transmission system will be changed, or it will be used to send disinformation.

For such reasons in the period 1946–1947, as the DCIs tried to coordinate information, and then as the CIA began to get established under Hillenkoetter, the agency ran into severe problems, as other agencies guarded their own sources. Some of the resistance to the DCIs seemed to spring from turf concerns, or from separate agencies having separate missions.

The FBI, which had jurisdiction over civilian intelligence in Latin America, had agents working as the legal attachés in embassies. When the CIA was given jurisdiction and was to replace the FBI, the CIA station chiefs showed up to find that the FBI had cleared out their offices, taking all their files with them. J. Edgar Hoover was notoriously uncooperative with the new agency.

In addition, the military agencies, Army G-2 and the Office of Naval Intelligence, remained suspicious of the CIA, assuming the new agency would be as difficult to control or use as the OSS had been under General Donovan. Furthermore, each military service and its intelligence agency had an incentive to see the Soviet buildup as worse in its own area. For example, the Air Force would estimate that the Soviet Union had more bombers than would the Army or Navy.

The State Department, which had an extensive intelligence network, found the mission of the new agency disturbing. Some at the State Department wanted to run their own covert operations and disliked the idea of an independent agency outside of State Department control.

---

### Spy Bios

General Walter Bedell Smith was known to his friends as "Beedle" or "Beetle" Smith. Short and wiry, and tough as nails, the name seemed appropriate. Born in 1895, in Indianapolis, he served as Chief of Staff of the Allied forces in North Africa and the Mediterranean in World War II, and then as Chief of Staff to General Eisenhower. In the period 1946–1949, he served as U.S. ambassador to the Soviet Union. President Truman appointed Smith the fourth Director of Central Intelligence, and he served from October 7, 1950 until February 9, 1953. Smith reorganized the agency, establishing firmer chain of command, with three directorates: intelligence (CDI), plans (DP), and administration (DA).

---

The DCIs argued that all the other agencies naturally had to shape the intelligence they gathered to serve the interests of their departments. The DCI and the CIA, on the other hand, were charged only with coordinating intelligence for the White House, and did not have to satisfy the goals of a larger department. Eventually, the CIA began to gain some clout from the fact that the DCI had direct access to the president, through the National Security Council. By contrast, the military agencies, and the intelligence officers of the State Department all had to report to the president through their department heads.

## Some Direct Ops

During the first few years of the agency's work, only scraps of information leaked out about its clandestine activities, as one might expect. The stories of direct operations that emerged during the first years of the agency's life were a mix of failures and some successes. The critics of the agency hashed over the stories many times, so that even some of the agency's more notable success stories became the subject of two types of criticism. Conservatives tended to find failures in operational security, while liberals tended to find failures in the agency exceeding its authority or operating unethically. In the long view of history, both kinds of criticism were sometimes justified.

# Albania

Efforts to offset the penetration of communists into Greece by infiltrating Albanian resistance fighters along the coast of Albania were constantly stymied by the rapid apprehension of the CIA-supported agents. In a joint British-American effort, called Operation Valuable, agents were sent in by parachute and small boat. One group of so-called *pixies* managed to survive for two months in Albania but could not raise any resistance.

One CIA agent was Hamit Matjani, known as the Tiger. He made 15 trips into Albania, but was ambushed on his sixteenth trip in 1953, when he had been enticed by disinformation that suggested a growing resistance movement. After the Americans realized they had dropped Matjani to his death, the CIA got out of the Albanian operation altogether. Later, it was learned that the Soviet mole in the British service, Kim Philby, had been responsible for leaking the plans to the KGB who in turn provided the Albanian communist regime under Imre Hoxha the names, dates, and locations of the penetration efforts. (See Chapter 9.)

**Spy Words**

When the CIA and MI-6 supported Albanian refugees in their efforts to infiltrate into communist Albania in hopes of building a resistance movement there, the Anglo-American agencies called the little groups **pixies**. Whether the code name was a disparaging reference to the ineffectiveness of the agents, or an allusion to the fact that they were supposed to remain invisible, was debateable.

# Ukraine

In the Ukraine, a republic within the Soviet Union, pockets of resistance to the communist regime survived. The Ukrayinska Viyskova Orhaniztsiya (known by its English acronym for Organization of Ukrainian Nationalists—OUN) had been founded in the early 1920s in Paris by refugee Ukrainians, and it had survived World War II, supported and armed by the Germans. When the Germans withdrew, some 50,000 armed OUN troops were spread across Poland, Ukraine, and parts of Czechoslovakia. As late as 1947, the OUN claimed to have 100,000 or more resistance fighters ready to oppose the Soviet Union. Efforts to support those troops against attacks from Polish, Russian, and Czech forces were a case of too little, too late. Although the British thought the OUN would be a good basis for resistance, the Americans believed the OUN was riddled with ex-fascists and Nazi sympathizers and was therefore unreliable.

## Looking for a Good Underground

The OUN continued to fight through August 1949, but in September 1949, decided to disband the military groups and go underground. Two days later, the CIA decided to support the military operation of a rival group, mostly ethnic Russians, in a National Labor Alliance (known by its Russian acronym, NTS). Meanwhile, the British MI-6 continued to support the OUN. Both MI-6 and the CIA sent in small groups by parachute, and trained others. Disagreement between the CIA and MI-5 over the OUN versus the NTS was regularly reported by Philby to the KGB, who used his detailed information to track down the agents sent to help both resistance groups.

Even after Philby was cut off from the information, Soviet intelligence had other sources. A constant flow of refugees and displaced persons from Eastern Europe provided the CIA with new information about conditions behind the Iron Curtain. However, the KGB was well aware of this and could use the flow of refugees to their own advantage. Captain Nikita Khorunshy defected in Berlin, claiming he had fallen in love with a German girl. He moved to Frankfurt, and his up-to-date information about life in the Soviet Union became useful to émigré groups. A CIA-sponsored school to train infiltration agents for the NTS at Hamburg hired Khorunshy, who reported back to the KGB on plans for infiltration.

Khorunshy also identified several NTS leaders resident in Germany, and the KGB then targeted them for assassination. While they did not always succeed, the KGB arranged murders of Ukrainian leaders Lev Rebet in 1957, and Stepan Bandera in 1959, and at least two speakers who regularly broadcast over Radio Free Europe. Radio Free Europe was an American-sponsored station that beamed news and information to listeners inside the Soviet bloc.

All of the efforts to send freedom fighters into Albania, the Ukraine, and the Soviet Union itself were frustrating for the American agents who tried to set up the systems in the late 1940s and early 1950s. In later years, many agreed that the operations had done little more than send a number of idealistic patriots to their deaths.

## Italy

The National Security Council, in NSC directive 4a, ordered DCI Hillenkoetter to undertake some direct action to prevent a Communist Party victory in the upcoming Italian elections. He set up a Special Procedures Group (SPG) in December 1947, to direct the effort run by Frank Wisner. James Jesus Angleton worked in the operation, and he would emerge as a major influence in the CIA in later years (see Chapter 14).

Aside from a number of open activities, the SPG sponsored some clandestine operations to affect the elections. Among the open actions were a letter-writing campaign by Italian-Americans, threats by Truman to withhold financial aid if the new government included communists, and a heavy program of food and grain assistance to alleviate hunger during the election months. The SPG channeled secret funds to several Italian parties in the political center. SPG planted news stories and articles detailing the brutal actions of Soviet troops in occupied Germany, as well as some forged documents purporting to have originated with the Italian Communist Party. The communists did not do very well in the elections, and whether or not the SPG efforts made any difference, at least the CIA did not need to view the SPG campaign as a failure.

# Korea

On June 25, 1950, North Korean forces invaded South Korea, and the United States came to the aid of South Korea. The Soviet delegate to the UN Security Council had been boycotting the meetings of the council since January 1950, because the United Nations had refused to seat the communist Chinese as members to replace the defeated nationalists who had withdrawn to Taiwan on December 8, 1949. It was bad luck for the Russians, because when the United States introduced a resolution condemning the pro-Soviet North Koreans for the invasion and calling on UN members to come to the military aid of South Korea, the Soviet Union was not present to veto the measure. They learned their lesson and gave up the boycott.

With the UN Security Council vote, the American effort to support South Korea was cast in the guise of a UN police action, a term American troops resented. What the veterans, the American public, and the news media called the Korean War lasted until a truce was signed July 27, 1953. The CIA's operations during the war were quite covert and did not receive much publicity until years later, with the gradual release of information and some memoirs.

## Tofte to Atsugi

The CIA's Office of Policy Coordination (OPC) ran much of the CIA operation in Korea. A former OSS officer, Danish-born Hans Tofte, headed one OPC operation in Korea during the period. Tofte was fluent in Chinese, and his World War II experience included running guns into Yugoslavia and working with Jedburgh teams in France (see Chapter 11). After the war, Tofte had remained active in the Army Reserve, and he was on summer duty when the Korean War broke out.

He volunteered for work with the CIA and was put in charge of the OPC office in Japan, where he built a facility at the Atsugi Air Base that eventually included over 1,000 personnel. The variety of ideas and schemes put in place gave a foretaste of some of the methods the CIA would employ in later years.

## Operations Bluebell and Stole

Operation Bluebell was a method of getting intelligence from behind enemy lines. Thousands of Korean refugees were recruited and told to go home behind the lines, and then return on their own with as much information as they could remember. It turned out that children were often the best informants in this method.

Operation Stole was a secret operation in which a Norwegian ship, loaded with three field hospitals destined for North Korea, was to be stopped. After plans to sabotage the ship in Hong Kong were foiled when the freighter bypassed that port, Tofte paid the nationalist Chinese in Taiwan to dispatch a patrol gunboat to hijack the ship on the open sea. CIA officers were aboard the patrol boat, but were below decks when the Norwegian ship was simply pirated by the Chinese sailors.

## Operations Paper and Wolfpack

Once the Chinese communist regime came to the aid of North Korea, in the winter of 1950–1951, Operation Paper was a plan to provide aid to a nationalist-sponsored Chinese force to invade China from the Shan states of northern Burma. General Li Mi operated in Burma with several thousand troops, supplied by the CIA's own airline, Civil Air Transport (CAT), more popularly known later during the Vietnam War as Air America (see Chapter 15).

Li Mi's force operated outside of Chinese and American control, growing larger from local recruits, reputedly up to 12,000 troops. The renegade army remained active long after the Korean War was over, reputedly thriving on heroin traffic in the mountains of northern Burma. In later years, America's early support to Li Mi became a major diplomatic embarrassment, as he conducted unsuccessful raids into China and turned against the Burmese government.

Wolfpack was a fairly successful operation that entailed thousands of Korean troops that mounted numerous raids on the North Korean coast, often with naval gun support. Battalions of 800 men made sabotage and commando raids that disrupted North Korean forces and helped hold down troops away from the front lines.

Both the Chinese nationalists for Operation Paper and the Koreans for Operation Wolfpack were trained at special secret bases set up on the South Pacific island of Saipan.

The overall military effect of the CIA's covert operations was probably not very great in Korea, and the operations against the Chinese turned out to be quite ineffective. However, the long-range consequences were important. The CIA had acquired an airline and experience in Southeast Asia that would be important more than a decade later, during the Vietnam conflict. The clandestine training of large numbers of troops for direct insertion into combat set a precedent that would be played out many times over the next decades in operations in Asia, Latin America, the Middle East, and in Africa. As with almost all CIA operations, when the actions were revealed, supporters found success stories and critics found failures.

# Tapping Land Lines

In World War II, listening to radio broadcasts had revealed how important signals intelligence could be, with the Enigma-Ultra system unraveling German plans, and U.S. Navy code-breakers working on the Japanese navy system (as discussed in Chapters 3 and 4). Unfortunately for the CIA, however, the Russians did not need to communicate by radio, as their satellite countries and lands of the far-flung Soviet Union were all geographically contiguous (except for Albania, isolated by the defection of Yugoslavia from the Soviet bloc). Thus the Russians could send telegrams and make telephone calls by landlines. Without some way to tap into those systems, a major portion of Soviet communication would simply be closed to outside listening. Two efforts later became public knowledge, one in Vienna, Austria, and one in Berlin.

## Vienna

Austria remained under joint allied occupation until May 15, 1955, with its capital, Vienna, divided into occupation zones. In Germany, the three western zones, occupied by Britain, France, and the United States, organized into a separate zone, and then into a nation recognized by the Western allies. In May 1955, the Federal Republic of Germany (West Germany) was admitted to NATO, leaving Berlin, the former capital of all of Germany, as an occupied city inside communist-controlled German Democratic Republic (East Germany). However, when the four occupying powers left Austria in 1955, the country was united as a neutral nation in the dispute between the Soviet bloc and the West.

During the period of occupation in Vienna, from 1945 to 1955, the city was a hotbed of espionage. Both the British and the Americans hoped to use it as a listening post to find out exactly what was going on in the Soviet sector of Austria and more generally, in the Soviet bloc.

Both the Americans and the British hit on the same idea independently, but the British took action first, in Operation Silver. The British purchased a house in the Schwechat suburb of Vienna and tunneled 70 feet under a highway to tap into telephone cables, working successfully in 1951. As a cover for their operations, MI-6 opened a men's clothing store in the house selling British tweeds that suddenly proved to be a busy and profitable business.

---

### Techint

Radio technology changed rapidly after World War II. Ultra high-frequency shortwave (UHF) waves traveled in line-of-sight and did not bounce off the electronic Heaviside layer, so they were hard to intercept. Combined with burst transmission and frequency-changing systems, it was difficult to pick up the new radio transmissions. Telephone and telegraph lines were vulnerable to being tapped anywhere on their length, but gaining access to such systems inside the Soviet bloc was nearly impossible, except in locations like Vienna and Berlin, where U.S. and British outposts were only yards from the Soviet bloc lines. The Soviets used cables that combined four telephone channels and one telegraph channel on the same line.

---

When MI-6 learned that the CIA was planning a similar phone tap, the two agencies cooperated, sharing the massive job of recording and transcribing the flood of information they received.

The Vienna tunnel was so successful that the CIA decided to mount its own operation in Berlin, called Operation Gold (apparently a terminology match for the British Operation Silver in Vienna). Operation Gold entailed a much more expensive and longer tunnel. Plans of the cable lines indicated that an important set of phone cables lay buried about 18 inches alongside the Scheonefelder Chaussee, a highway linking East Berlin with Karlshorst.

In 1953, the Army Corps of Engineers was brought in to construct the tunnel, some 1,476 feet long, and about 6 feet, 6 inches in diameter. The starting point was about 100 yards from the border dividing West Berlin from East Berlin. The top of the tunnel was just over 13 feet below the surface. The tunnel was a masterpiece, the CIA believed, and under the guidance of Allen Dulles, now serving as DCI #5, the plans were kept very closely held.

The landline tap into the East German military telegraph and telephone lines revealed plain-text conversations as well as encrypted telegraph messages.

*Allen Dulles served as Director of Central Intelligence and authorized the Berlin Tunnel. Here he meets with his brother, right, John Foster Dulles, secretary of state under President Dwight Eisenhower.*

*(Courtesy of the Library of Congress)*

At full blast, the Operation Gold system required so much magnetic recording tape that whole plane loads of tapes had to be sent each week from Berlin to Washington for analysis. There a team of about 50, working in shifts of two weeks on and one week off, translated the German and Russian materials. In Berlin, a device called "Bumblebee," working on the principles first propounded by Alan Turing, replicated some of the antiquated Soviet encrypting machines (see Chapter 4) and churned out plain-text versions of encrypted messages.

All worked quite well for 11 months, from February 25, 1955, until January 1956. Then apparently by accident, when an East German repair crew was working on the cable, the tunnel was discovered, complete with its taps, air-conditioning vents, and some end-of-tunnel equipment. But it was no accident.

Soviet agent George Blake, who was working with British MI-6, and stationed in Berlin, had kept the KGB informed of the construction of the tunnel from its beginning (see Chapter 9). At the time, however, Blake was still working undercover and undiscovered by the British, and as far as the public and the CIA knew, the tunnel's discovery was an accident.

The CIA was pleased to learn that the public reaction to their foiled plan was generally to view it as a clever success, rather than a failure. Later, the fact that the Soviets knew about the tunnel from George Blake was used by critics of the CIA (and by the KGB) to suggest that the whole affair was just another CIA failure. That the KGB did not tip off the GRU about the tunnel worked to the advantage of the CIA. The fact that Operation Gold yielded some good intelligence about troop emplacements, the order of battle of the Red Army, and other matters, especially through the decoded encrypted materials, suggests that the tunnel was, after all, as a CIA success story.

# Guatemala

One of the most controversial of all the operations of the CIA in the early 1950s was the overthrow of a socialist-leaning government in Guatemala in 1954. Critics depicted the operation as an U.S. government intervention on behalf of an exploitative American corporation, the banana-growing firm of United Fruit Company, known locally as *la pulpa* (the octopus). Supporters of the CIA saw the operation as a brilliant combination of covert action, propaganda, skillful use of disinformation, and direct ops to achieve a foreign policy objective. Depending on the slant of the writer, the Guatemalan operation showed the CIA at its worst or at its best.

## Jacobo Arbenz Guzmán

Jacobo Arbenz Guzmán was elected president of Guatemala in November 1950, with more than 50 percent of the popular vote. In Hispanic custom, he was known by his first surname, Arbenz. Over the next four years, he began to institute land reforms, one of which targeted *la pulpa*. In February 1953, the Arbenz regime expropriated about 400,000 acres of the 550,000 controlled by United Fruit, offering compensation of 25-year bonds at 3 percent interest. United Fruit rejected the offer as worthless. When John Foster Dulles, Eisenhower's secretary of state, pressed Arbenz to take the matter to the International Court of Justice for arbitration, Arbenz refused.

The CIA soon began to plan Operation PBSuccess. An earlier plan for the overthrow of Arbenz in late 1952, code-named PBFortune, had involved providing arms to United Fruit to be passed to anti-Arbenz mercenaries to come from Nicaragua. When Dean Acheson, Truman's secretary of state, heard of the plan, he convinced Truman to cancel Operation PBFortune. The State Department kept United Fruit out of Operation PBSuccess.

## Key Americans and the Rebel Force

The chief architect of the CIA plan was Richard Bissell and a minor player was E. Howard Hunt, who would become famous many years later for conducting an independent operation to break into the Watergate office building in Washington in a private operation for President Richard Nixon. Another CIA officer was David Atlee Phillips, whose job it was to run a propaganda radio station. To lead the military operations, William A. (Rip) Robertson, who had trained Korean and Chinese volunteers in Saipan, was to set up a rebel army.

Operation Success called for a small liberation army fully funded by the CIA, to be trained in nearby Nicaragua. A covert air force contingent would provide support for invasion by the rebel army. The total rebel air force amounted to a handful of aircraft, including three bombers and an assortment of propeller-driven fighters. Meanwhile, the covert radio station was to spread news of victories, hoping to spread panic in the Arbenz government.

*The CIA arranged this drop of propaganda leaflets over Guatemala as part of the 1954 coup.*

*(Courtesy of the Library of Congress)*

There were a few slip-ups, as might be expected. Castillo Armas, a Guatemalan leader who had led a former unsuccessful overthrow attempt, was recruited to represent the rebel force, and Arbenz leaked word of his liaison with the CIA to the press. The invasion had to be mounted from Honduras. That turned out to be an advantage for the operation, since Honduras has a long land border with Guatemala, allowing the troops to simply drive in by truck, rather than struggle through an amphibious landing.

## Bombing the Brits

Arbenz bought a shipload of arms from the communist Czech government, and the ship arrived at a Guatemalan port on May 15, 1954. The liaison of the Arbenz regime with a communist government gave support to President Dwight Eisenhower's claim that the Arbenz regime represented an attempt to plant communism in the Western Hemisphere, although the weapons were not particularly useful to the Guatemalans.

After an intensive propaganda campaign on the clandestine radio station, and through publications released throughout Latin America, the invasion was launched June 18, 1954, with a force of 200 men. President Anastasio Samoza Garcia of Nicaragua provided two aircraft to replace two of the rebel aircraft put out of action, when promised that the U.S. would replace Samoza's airplanes. In another mix-up, one of the rebel planes bombed and sank a British cargo ship, the *Springfjord*, on the assumption it carried fuel for Arbenz forces. No one was killed or injured, and the ship turned out to be carrying cotton. Later, the CIA quietly paid the insurance loss of the ship.

## Arbenz Out, Armas In

With the bombing of the *Springfjord*, and possibly influenced by false radio announcements of the fall of several outlying cities to the advancing rebel soldiers, the Guatemalan army gave Arbenz an ultimatum to resign. He left office, took refuge in the Mexican embassy, and then the Army, after pressure from the United States, selected Armas as the new president.

**Spy Words**

Inside the CIA, those who planned and executed some risky operations on the ground came to be known as **cowboys**. Even for those inside the agency who believed in and supported direct operations, the term suggested unnecessary risk-taking and violation of the chain of command.

The CIA success in ousting Arbenz, while resulting from a series of accidents, had several unintended consequences. Within the agency, the CIA decided that it needed better control over such plans. It seemed there had been some *cowboys* on the ground. More careful arrangements and better funding would be required in the future. However, the success of the operation, its total cost of some $20 million, and its reliance on only a handful of troops, some phony radio broadcasts, and several outmoded aircraft, suggested that direct operation to overthrow a leftist government was not very difficult.

One long-range consequence of the coup was that Guatemala remained governed by oppressive military regimes over the next decades. The United States may have ousted a left-wing reform government, but it certainly did not achieve the establishment of democracy in the small Central American nation.

## The Least You Need to Know

- The CIA found it difficult to share information with existing American intelligence agencies.

- Some of the first direct operations of the CIA against the Soviet bloc were failures because of effective KGB sources of information.

- The Berlin Tunnel to tap Soviet telephone lines, known as Operation Gold, was widely perceived as a CIA success, despite its 11-month operation and the fact that the KGB knew of the tunnel from the beginning.

- The CIA gained experience, resources, and confidence from operations in Korea and Guatemala in the years 1952 to 1954.

# Chapter 12

# The Politics of Paranoia

## In This Chapter

- ◆ McCarthy and "McCarthyism"
- ◆ The case of J. Robert Oppenheimer
- ◆ National security and individual rights
- ◆ Cointelpro and Chaos

During the 1950s, the revelations of actual cases of espionage, motivated by the ideology of communism, gave what a popular writer, Jessica West, called "The New Meaning of Treason." The conflict between loyalty and the principles of free speech, which had surfaced many times in American life, took an ugly turn in this period. In this chapter, we look at how politicians on both sides of the issue converted the hunt for spies and the identification of disloyalty into a chapter of political paranoia in American history.

## Loyalty and Freedom: An American Issue

The conflict between loyalty and the rights of free speech, free press, and free association was nothing new in American history. It had arisen as early as the administration of John Adams. Under the Sedition Act, passed in 1798, 10 newspaper editors who criticized President Adams were imprisoned, only to be pardoned by Thomas Jefferson when he became president in 1801. During the American Civil War, democratic Congressman Clement Vallandigham pushed the limits of free speech and free press by proclaiming the war goals of the Union illegal. He was arrested and tried by a military commission in 1863, imprisoned for the duration of the war and refused a writ of habeas corpus. During World War I, the socialist candidate for the presidency, Eugene V. Debs, was imprisoned for advocating resistance to the draft. In World War II, the imprisonment in relocation camps of about 40,000 Japanese citizens resident in the United States and about 80,000 American citizens of Japanese ancestry, on grounds of suspicion of their loyalty, fit into the same pattern of conflict between national security and personal freedom.

Although episodes of conflict between individual freedom and loyalty to the state have occurred in many societies, in the United States the issue is brought into focus by protections of basic rights built into the Constitution, the Bill of Rights, and the American judicial system. These famous cases and hundreds of other incidents demonstrate that, when American governmental officials believe national security is at stake, they often override the protections of rights in the Constitution.

In each of the episodes mentioned previously, and in many others, individual court cases and imprisonment of Americans suspected of disloyalty have become nationwide controversies. Frequently, politicians and journalists seized on one side or the other, each claiming that their side was more properly dedicated to the preservation of the nation and its principles. Those who saw the nation in danger believed that opposition to authority and the military played into the hands of the enemy who would destroy America. The protestors saw the abuse of authority itself as violating the principles of freedom on which the nation was founded.

## The Loyalty Issue and Communism

War always reawakened the conflict over loyalty and the effort to enforce it. Wars like the undeclared Naval War with France, the Civil War, and the two World Wars of the twentieth century all saw a replay of the conflict between government power and individual rights. The cold war reawakened that conflict in a particularly ugly fashion.

Most of the convicted or confessed American and British spies for the Soviet Union in the period up to the mid-1950s were motivated by ideological commitment. Although a few, like Congressman Samuel Dickstein, spied for money (see Chapter 10), almost all the others, including the Cambridge Five, Klaus Fuchs, the Rosenbergs, Elizabeth Bentley, and Whittaker Chambers, had been ideological converts to the communist cause.

In cases where the accused spies did not confess and in which there was good evidence they had spied, as in the case of the Rosenbergs and Alger Hiss, defenders of free speech suspected that they were victims of an overzealous government, abusing its power to suppress individuals because of their political beliefs. In the Rosenberg case, defenders of the Rosenbergs blamed the Justice Department and J. Edgar Hoover.

> **Spy Bios**
>
> J. Edgar Hoover (1895–1972) was appointed to head the Bureau of Investigation of the Justice Department in 1924, renamed the Federal Bureau of Investigation in 1935. Hoover apparently was able to keep his post through eight presidents because he maintained confidential files about them that they feared he would expose. His administration of the bureau was characterized by two goals that sometimes came in conflict: On the one hand he insisted that the bureau earn and maintain popular and official respect as a crime-investingating agency; on the other he sought to use the bureau to harass radicals, dissidents, civil rights advocates, and the journalists who spoke in their defense. Increasingly eccentric after 1960, Hoover continued to head the bureau until his death in 1972.

Hoover was well-known for his crusading attitude against communists, summarized in a 1958 book that was a curious mix of informed historical evidence and unfounded assertions, *Masters of Deceit: The Story of Communism in America and How to Fight It.* Defenders of Alger Hiss believed his conviction was a result of a carefully constructed conspiracy between an FBI headed by a paranoid Hoover and the ambitious and crafty Republican congressman Richard Nixon. Rumors and stories about both personalities, avidly spread by their critics, supported the conspiracy theory.

## The Cases That Lived On

Neither the Rosenberg case nor the Hiss case died from public memory very quickly. When researchers published information pointing to the guilt of the Rosenbergs, their two sons, adults by the 1970s, came to their defense and went on speaking tours pointing out the flaws in the legal proceedings against their parents.

Hiss continued to proclaim his innocence until his death in 1993. When Richard Nixon revealed his capacity for hounding political enemies and his obsessive fear of them during the cover-up of the Watergate burglaries, which eventually forced his resignation as president in 1974, supporters of Alger Hiss revived charges that Nixon had colluded with J. Edgar Hoover to frame Hiss. For a generation, conservatives predictably defended both the Hiss and Rosenberg convictions, while liberals predictably criticized them.

The success of Richard Nixon in making the House Committee on Un-American Activities a springboard for his political ambitions was one of the inspirations for a "johnny-come-lately" to the politics of spy-hunting and disloyalty-exposure, Senator Joseph McCarthy.

# McCarthy: The Man

Joseph McCarthy, junior Republican senator from Wisconsin, was virtually unknown outside his own state early in 1950. On February 9, 1950, he gave a speech in Wheeling, West Virginia, claiming that the U.S. State Department was a hotbed of communists. Newspaper accounts varied regarding the number of communists he said worked in the department.

In retrospect, the spectacle of McCarthy waving a piece of paper with his so-called list of communists has often been ridiculed. In fact, it was not so much a wild charge, but one that was just a little late, as the espionage and influence rings identified by Bentley and Chambers in the State Department and other governmental departments and agencies had long before been eliminated through dismissals and resignations.

## McCarthy: The Ism

McCarthy's first speech on the hot-button issue of communism and loyalty came two weeks after the conviction of Alger Hiss for perjury. Compared to the investigative work of Nixon and the carefully presented evidence that had entrapped Hiss in a series of lies, McCarthy simply made assertions. In the world of politics, however, the baseless charge and the flamboyant speech may attract more attention than the lawyer's approach. On the other side, the fact that McCarthy had no evidence to go on made him a much more valuable target for criticism than the better-established red-hunters.

Less than a month after Joseph McCarthy made his West Virginia speech, Herblock, the cartoonist for the *Washington Post*, drew a cartoon that showed a pile of barrels of mud, topped with a bucket of mud ready to fall, with the pile labeled *McCarthyism*. The label caught on. Herblock, who remained a courageous critic of McCarthy and his insults and charges against loyal Americans, may have done a lot to earn Senator Joe his place in history, with a name for an *ism*, and later a name for the whole era, characterized by unfounded charges.

Between 1950 and 1954, McCarthy served as a member of a Senate subcommittee on conduct of the government. Television and radio broadcast his performances live, with his methods of rudely interrupting witnesses, presenting unfounded allegations, and making speeches from a committee chair. His super-serious, booming voice, laden with sarcasm, concern, and allusion to conspiracy, simplified the complex issue for both sides of the debate.

*Senator Joe McCarthy was a "johnny-come-lately" to the spy-hunting business in Congress, but he made lots of enemies and friends with his flamboyant charges, radio speeches, and bullying tactics.*

*(Courtesy of the Library of Congress)*

Although McCarthy never uncovered a genuine communist conspiracy or identified any agents, those who had been shocked by the disloyalty of Americans supporting the Soviet Union were glad to see a well-publicized crusade underway to root them out. Those who feared that anyone who had stood for social reform in the past would be smeared as a communist or fellow-traveler had a perfect symbol in Senator McCarthy of the irresponsible attack on civil liberties. His politics clicked, for both supporters and opponents.

## McCarthy: The Era

After McCarthy claimed that the U.S. Army protected communists and attempted to persecute his own aides, and then, when he attacked a Senate committee investigating his own behavior as doing the work of the Communist Party, he offended the wrong people. The U.S. Senate passed a measure censuring him by a vote of 67 to 22 on December 2, 1954. The Senate ruled that McCarthy "tended to bring the Senate into dishonor and disrepute, to obstruct the constitutional processes of the Senate, and to impair its dignity; and such conduct is hereby condemned."

When later students of the subject wrote of the McCarthy era, they usually meant to imply a much longer period than the 4 year, 10-month career of Senator McCarthy. Bowing to pressure from exposés, President Truman had begun to require loyalty oaths and to demand dismissals as early as 1947. Under J. Edgar Hoover, the FBI continued to track radicals and dissidents, using techniques including telephone taps and mail-opening, throughout the 1960s.

---

### Techint

The technology of tapping telephones underwent continual improvement. Frequently during the 1950s, a tapped telephone line experienced a power drop when tape recording equipment was turned on. Harry Bridges, an Australian-born American labor leader in the International Longshoremen and Warehousemen's Union on the Pacific coast, often knew exactly when his phone was being tapped. The FBI hoped to establish evidence of his affiliation with the Communist Party in order to justify a deportation order. Bridges, in a later memoir entitled *"Having Fun with the FBI,"* recounted how he would harass the listening agents with remarks about their faulty equipment.

---

The hunt for spies of the Soviet Union in the United States led to pressures on civil liberties for a period spanning about 20 years, from the late 1940s through the late 1960s, not just the five years during which McCarthy was active.

# The Oppenheimer Case

The case of J. Robert Oppenheimer became a national scandal in 1953 and 1954, a decade after Oppenheimer had begun work on the atomic bomb.

Oppenheimer was the brilliant young nuclear physicist chosen by General Leslie Groves in 1942 to serve as the civilian technical director of the Manhattan Engineer District (MED) to build the atomic bomb. When Groves recruited him, he knew very well that Oppenheimer was known throughout the physics community for his political leftism and his support for a variety of social causes that had nothing to do with physics.

Nevertheless, Oppenheimer was also known to his fellow scientists as brilliant, personable, energetic, creative, and as a visionary. The fact that he was a bit anti-establishment was probably an asset, as the scientific community of the 1930s and early 1940s tended to include a lot of mavericks who made a point of disliking the authority of the Army, the federal government, or the procedures and ethics of big business. Known to his friends and to the nuclear physics community as "Oppy," he turned out to be a good leader and an able administrator.

*Brilliant, energetic, and well-known for his self-admitted fellow-traveler politics, J. Robert Oppenheimer was the father of the atomic bomb. He later lost his security clearance for his politics and his opposition to developing the hydrogen bomb.*

*(Courtesy of the National Archives and Records Administration)*

## Op-Sec at the MED

As discussed in Chapter 8, the project to build the atomic bomb was surrounded by secrecy, not only to protect the technical details of weapon development, but to conceal the fact that the project even existed. When the Army took over the atomic weapons work from the Office of Scientific Research and Development, it inherited contracts with many academic scientists, including refugees from fascism and Nazism like Enrico Fermi, Leo Szilard, Eugene Wigner, and others of lesser repute like Klaus Fuchs. The Army security officers, and Groves himself, were suspicious of many of the foreign-born scientists, and even took steps to control the amount of information made available to the British and Canadian participants in the project.

### Tradecraft

The Army immediately instituted close operational security at the nuclear research laboratories, and American scientists at places like Los Alamos found themselves in an environment they had never before experienced. The laboratories were surrounded by chain-link fences, with badge-control access, background checks, and a policy that required researchers to clear their desks each night and lock their notes in a safe. Some rebelled, but most went along grudgingly. They understood the prohibition against talking about the project outside the confines of Los Alamos, Hanford, Oak Ridge, or one of the many contract laboratories.

Used to the atmosphere of universities, in which ideas were discussed openly, many of the scientists resisted the Army-imposed concept of compartmentation. When Oppenheimer insisted on weekly seminars for the free exchange of information between different divisions, they saw the move as a case of intellectual freedom winning out over pettifogging bureaucracy.

## Suspicions About Oppenheimer

Boris Pash and other Army security officers were suspicious of some of Oppenheimer's contacts, especially when he made visits to Berkeley and San Francisco or elsewhere in the United States. The fact that Oppenheimer's wife, Kitty, and a former fiancée and girlfriend, Jean Tatlock, had both been members of the Communist Party worried security. Robert's brother, Frank Oppenheimer, was also a member of the party, and Robert himself had been active in organizing a faculty union at the University of California in Berkeley that was known to include many of the faculty members who were communists.

## From MED to AEC and GAC

In 1946, the work of the Army's Manhattan Engineer District was turned over to a new agency, the Atomic Energy Commission (AEC). Two committees were formed to provide advice: the Military Liaison Committee, representing the Army, Navy, and later, Air Force offices concerned with the weapons; and the General Advisory Committee (GAC), involving civilian scientists and administrators with technical knowledge of the bomb and of the facilities inherited by the AEC. Oppenheimer, former technical director of the MED, took an appointment at Princeton University to head the Institute for Advanced Study, and at the same time, he served in a consulting capacity on the GAC. Of course, to serve on the GAC, he and the other members had the highest security clearance, so that they could read and comment on the latest developments in the still-secret areas of nuclear research.

Despite the suspicions that had once surrounded Oppenheimer, he was, by 1946, known throughout the world as the *Father of the Atomic Bomb*. The moniker was a bit of an exaggeration, because several thousand people contributed to the design. Even so, he was widely respected both for his work on the bomb and for his outspoken advocacy of world peace.

Now and then, Oppenheimer tended to offend conservative politicians, either with his views on topics of the day, or because they sensed he thought they were pretty stupid. On at least one occasion, when he was being questioned by a congressman on the joint committee of the House and Senate that had the responsibility to oversee the AEC, he came across as a bit arrogant. The congressman was worried that nuclear isotopes for research purposes had been exported to Norway, and he implied that the United States should not be giving away atomic secrets to a country that was so socialist and so politically unreliable. Oppenheimer pointed out that anyone who knew anything about atomic energy would not worry that research isotopes would represent a threat to American national security. Although of course Oppenheimer was correct, he had not made a friend.

## Oppy on the H-Bomb

After the Soviet Union detonated an atomic bomb in August 1949, President Truman put pressure on the AEC to speed up the production of atomic bombs, and to accelerate work on a more powerful weapon, based on hydrogen fusion, the thermo-nuclear weapon, or hydrogen bomb. The atomic bombs dropped on Hiroshima and Nagasaki were equivalent in explosive power to nearly 20,000 tons of high explosive. An H-bomb, as the hydrogen bomb was known, had the potential of a detonation in the range of five million tons or more of high explosive. With the Soviet Union's detonation of an atomic bomb in 1949, the nuclear arms race was underway.

However, when Truman asked the AEC to proceed with H-bomb research, they asked the opinion of the GAC, chaired by Oppenheimer. Oppenheimer pointed out that while a thermonuclear weapon or H-bomb was possible, it was a bad idea as it would lead to an escalated arms race. The GAC opposed the H-bomb, and Truman was furious. Work continued on the thermonuclear weapon, but Truman and advocates of the new weapon like physicist Edward Teller feared that Oppenheimer's opposition might dissuade other scientists from participating. Some believed that a whole generation of young scientists had emerged from the Manhattan Project as convinced pacifists due to Oppenheimer's influence.

With the election of Republican Dwight Eisenhower to the presidency in 1952, the appointees to the AEC shifted a bit. Conservatives who had opposed Oppenheimer for his position on the H-bomb, and others who had been offended by his manner, now began to listen to the rumors that he had been a security risk during the war. Their concerns were given new impetus by the conviction of Klaus Fuchs, and the revelation that the Rosenberg case had exposed outright espionage at Los Alamos and elsewhere in the MED.

## The Security Hearing

Early in 1954, the AEC appointed a special security review board to consider whether to renew Oppenheimer's security clearance. Although the hearing was held behind closed doors, a transcript of the hearing was published, and because of the drama of the hearing, the transcript was written up as a play, *In the Matter of J. Robert Oppenheimer*. On June 28, 1954, the security review board denied Oppenheimer his clearance.

The case, the transcript, and the dramatized version of the transcript touched on numerous sensitive issues. While no one charged Oppenheimer with espionage, the issues of atomic espionage, operational security, and loyalty were central to the case. Testifying about episodes that occurred a decade before, Oppenheimer did not come across very well. His opposition to the hydrogen bomb and the collection of individuals whom he had offended in one way or another probably caught up with him as well.

One episode that had long ago surfaced as an op-sec matter involved one of Oppenheimer's visits to Berkeley during the war. He reported to security that several people told him that a man by the name of George Eltenton had approached them with the suggestion that he could provide a channel if they wished to get information to the Soviet Union. Later, in 1946, he changed the story and claimed that he had been approached by a fellow faculty union member, and personal friend, Haakon Chevalier, who had told him of the Eltenton approach. The two stories did not quite jibe, and Oppenheimer admitted to the security review panel that he had in 1943 invented a "cock and bull story" to protect Chevalier.

The whole story had been gone over and over with Boris Pash at Los Alamos during and after World War II, and its contradictions left unresolved. But the revival of the story at the 1954 hearing showed that Oppenheimer, at the least, had been careless of the details of operational security. Any approach, direct or indirect, by a foreign agent was supposed to be reported immediately so that steps could be taken to intercept possible leaks. Oppenheimer had waited months to report the episode, and he gave a couple of versions of it, representing clear violations of operational security rules. General Groves suspected that Eltenton had really approached Robert Oppenheimer's brother, Frank, and that Robert had created not one, but two fabricated stories to identify Eltenton without implicating his own brother.

While revoking Oppenheimer's security clearance was no great punishment, it certainly was a slap in the face for someone regarded by the scientific community and the general public as a kind of national hero. One motive behind revoking Oppenheimer's clearance appeared to be his argument against building an H-bomb. The operational security issues appeared to have been introduced as an excuse. Oppy's friends and defenders saw the case as a form of persecution for holding a political view that did not sit well in the era of a nuclear arms race. Oppenheimer's political views gave the hearing the tone of a political witch-hunt.

# Counterespionage or Big Brother

There had been numerous real spies and agents, motivated by ideology, and the ideology of the Communist Party had held wide appeal for more than a decade. So there was evidence to support conspiracy theories by the red-hunters, and a legitimate basis for fears of subversion.

On the other hand there were numerous false charges and cases of character assassination by politicians like Joe McCarthy. Many who had seen communism as a vigorous opponent of fascism or who had been attracted by other parts of the party's doctrine now had reason to fear that their careers would be ruined. If someone looked too closely at their prior political affiliations that they had thought were protected by the First Amendment to the Constitution, they might be exposed at a hearing and then fired. Numerous Hollywood writers with prior communist affiliation were blacklisted, and the studios refused to hire them. So fear on both sides was founded in fact.

In the novel *1984* by George Orwell (published in 1949), the author presented a satirical view of a totalitarian society in which every citizen was subject to surveillance in the name of security, with posters everywhere pronouncing, "Big Brother is Watching." Americans grew concerned that the new technologies of electronic surveillance and an unchecked bureaucracy would lead to a gradual evolution from counterintelligence to an Orwellian society. With the investigations, surveillance, and efforts at *thought control*, it seemed in 1950 that 1984 was just around the corner.

In the atmosphere of political paranoia, officials of the government were not immune, and many of the actions of agencies concerned with national security in the period pushed the limits of appropriate response. When exposed to public view in later years, the counterespionage efforts of the FBI and CIA in the 1950s and 1960s came under intense criticism for too closely emulating the "Big Brother" surveillance warned of in Orwell's work. When the agencies of the federal government spied on the political activities of U.S. citizens, they moved into the grey area between concern with national security and a Big Brother system that violated constitutional protections. (The reaction of Congress and the public when the actions were exposed is discussed further in Chapter 15.)

# Surveillance

Between 1942 and 1968, it was later learned, the FBI conducted over 200 break-ins without judicial authorization, as well as thousands of telephone taps. In Operations Mudhen, Celotex I, and Celotex II, wiretaps and surveillance were established on American journalists, including the popular syndicated columnist Jack Anderson.

Beginning in 1954, in project HTLingual, the CIA began a project of opening the mail of U.S. citizens that lasted nearly 20 years and resulted in opening over 215,000 pieces of mail. Project SRPointer was directed at the interception and opening of incoming and outgoing mail from and to the Soviet Union, Cuba, and China.

# Cointelpro

Sometime in 1956, J. Edgar Hoover established *Cointelpro*, the counterintelligence program. He hoped to use FBI informants within the Communist Party to spread rumors and false stories among party members to fuel dissention, jealousy, and factionalism. A program of anonymous charges, threats against people who did business with communists, and other nonviolent means would be employed to disrupt the party. The operation was conducted in great secrecy, because Hoover and others recognized that it could be viewed as crossing the line into government intervention in political affairs. The use of illegal break-ins and wiretaps also represented a venture across the line of propriety in Cointelpro.

Documents that related to Cointelpro were regularly marked "Do not file," meaning that they were kept out of the regular FBI filing system. According to some reports, the documents were never subjected to the FBI system of numbering as a further means to cover up the activities, and to prevent numerical file gaps in the document sequence.

Some of the agents involved in the work later told reporters that they thought the activities were a waste of time, with harassment of an aging minority of Troskyites, Socialist Workers Party members, and others who represented no threat whatsoever. By the early 1960s, the Communist Party, weakened by exposés of the disloyalty and espionage work of many of its leaders, and by the heightened tensions of the cold war, declined to a mere shadow of its former strength. Hoover and others within the agency quietly took credit for success as the party withered.

Hoover went further with another operation, dubbed *Cominfil*, which was designed to determine whether communists had infiltrated other organizations. Hoover became convinced that black civil rights organizations were engaged in subversive activities, and in 1961, he ordered a full investigation into Martin Luther King Jr. through the Cominfil program.

Altogether, Cointelpro and Cominfil included over 300,000 investigations. None of the investigations uncovered any illegal activity, and the net result was only to damage the reputation of the FBI when word of the programs was released in the 1970s.

*Harry Truman (center) met with the director of the FBI, J. Edgar Hoover (left), and with his attorney General J. Howard McGrath. Hoover began to step up counter-intelligence activities in the mid-1950s*

*(Courtesy of the Library of Congress)*

## Project MKChaos

Project MKChaos, begun by the CIA in 1967, during the Vietnam War on the orders of President Lyndon Johnson, was directed at the infiltration and disruption of anti-war and dissident groups. Like the FBI's Cominfil program, this CIA operation was conducted quietly, and word only became public in later years. In the case of Operation Chaos, it was not the agency that initiated the surveillance program, but the president himself.

Richard Helms, reporting to President Johnson's successor, Richard Nixon, in 1969 that Operation Chaos had uncovered no connection between the antiwar movement and international communism, incurred the displeasure of the president. Like Johnson, Nixon was convinced that the Soviet Union was behind American antiwar demonstrations. Helms noted that the antiwar youth movement, although international in nature, resulted not from any conspiracy, but from the policies themselves and from the antagonism of the younger generation to the policies. Helms never showed any enthusiasm for the CIA's Operation Chaos, unlike Hoover, who initiated and pushed the FBI's Cointelpro.

## From Cointelpro and Chaos to Plumbers

When Richard Nixon was inaugurated in 1969, he believed that neither the FBI nor the CIA was doing enough to uncover domestic subversive activities. He sent a special assistant, Tom Huston, to coordinate the activities of the two agencies and to increase

**Spy Words**

The term **black bag jobs** referred to illegal and warrantless break-ins either to obtain copies of materials or to plant listening devices and telephone taps. Both E. Howard Hunt and G. Gordon Liddy had experience in such work and organized several break-ins in attempts to discredit political enemies of the president as well as domestic critics of U.S. policy.

domestic surveillance. Huston, apparently unfamiliar with both Chaos and Cointelpro, urged a concerted plan to penetrate dissident organizations. However, Hoover at the FBI resisted this plan to extend what his agency was already doing on a quiet scale. He believed that the risk of exposure of Chaos and Cointelpro outweighed the few results that they were obtaining, and he was able to dissuade the president from ordering more intensive programs.

Nixon created a special operation reporting directly to him, headed by a former CIA officer, E. Howard Hunt, and a former FBI agent, G. Gordon Liddy. Informally known as the plumbers, whose job it was to track down and find the leaks, the small organization was established to conduct domestic surveillance and *black bag jobs*.

When the work of the plumbers was exposed, along with the earlier Chaos and Cointelpro, the press and the public had clear evidence that domestic surveillance could indeed cross the line, violating constitutional protections and the laws of the land. In the meantime, however, several major U.S. covert actions had resulted in quite spectacular failures.

## The Least You Need to Know

- The conflict between domestic security and civil liberties has always existed in American history.

- Although Senator Joe McCarthy became the symbol for irresponsible charges of subversion, his five-year career came in the middle of a 20-year period of political misuse of the disloyalty issue.

- J. Robert Oppenheimer had been careless with operational security in the Manhattan Project, but his clearance was not revoked until 1954, when his advice was no longer wanted.

- The FBI and the CIA created extensive programs of domestic surveillance in the 1950s and 1960s, but by 1969, J. Edgar Hoover balked at extending the systems.

# Part 4

## Espionage in Retreat

In this part we look at some of the major failures in intelligence operations. When Gary Powers was shot down over Russia while flying a spy plane, and when a CIA-financed invasion of Cuba at the Bay of Pigs fell through, it seemed American intelligence was discredited.

During and after the Vietnam War, the public began to suspect that the intelligence establishment was out of control. Congress investigated the CIA and the FBI and placed some restrictions on their activities. The U.S. agencies began to rely more on technical and signal intelligence, the gathering of information by satellites and other mechanical means. But, in "the year of the spy," 1985, news came of disloyal Americans with access to technical intelligence who sold out to the Soviet Union. We check the careers of a few of the worst ones, including John Walker and Christopher Boyce.

# Espionage—The Cold War Battleground

The *cold war* was an extended conflict between Soviet bloc countries and the democracies of the West that lasted from 1947 to 1988. At one level, it was not a war at all. The armies of the Soviet Union and its allies never fought the armies of the United States and its allies. The fact that, after 1949, both the Soviet Union and the United States possessed nuclear weapons may have prevented a military confrontation between the two.

However, there were many armed conflicts between other countries in which the Soviet Union supported one side, and the United States supported the other. The two major wars in which U.S. troops were engaged were in Korea (1950–1953) and Vietnam (1964–1973), and during both, the Soviet Union and Communist China provided financial and military support to the regimes the United States fought. The Soviet Union sent troops into Afghanistan (1979–1989), where the United States provided aid to the rebels fighting against the communist government. In addition, over the four decades of the cold war the world saw numerous civil wars and rebellions, fought by *surrogates*. The Soviet Union and communist China supported rebel groups in Colombia and Peru, and clashes in Africa often produced civil wars between pro-Soviet and pro-American sides. For the hundreds of thousands of troops in all these wars, the cold war was quite hot.

## Intelligence in the Cold War

Even though the United States and the Soviet Union did not directly confront each other in battle, the war of spies continued to be fought by thousands of agents. For the spies, surveillance pilots and aircrews, the cold war was frequently a shooting war.

The state of world tension, with the cold war and the nuclear arms race as background, meant that both sides sought to know as much as possible about the other's capabilities. When the Soviet Union built a new missile, the United States wanted to know its range, payload, accuracy, factory locations, and potential weaknesses. When the United States developed a new aircraft, ship, or submarine, the Soviet Union sought the same type of information.

In general it was easier for the Soviet Union to find out about American developments, as a great deal of military information was published in defense magazines and other forms of open literature. Even so, there were whole technologies and sciences in the United States that were kept behind a veil of secrecy: nuclear arms design, missile development, underwater acoustics for the protection and detection of submarines, high-altitude photography, computer encryption methods, and mind-controlling drugs.

---

| Techint |
| --- |

The secret sciences in the United States sometimes involved complete laboratories that were off-limits to outsiders. Classified journals were published, and closed conferences were held to keep those with a need to know posted on developments. Underwater acoustics, for example, involved not only techniques of listening for enemy submarines, but methods of silencing machinery aboard U.S. submarines, cushioning the floor, and reducing the noise of water flow. When underwater listening stations in Britain reported that they could pick up the sounds of a submarine departing from Newport, Rhode Island, and identify, by its unique signature of sounds, *which* submarine was departing, American researchers redoubled their efforts at silencing.

The Soviet Union not only surrounded its weapons technology with operational security, but kept all sorts of ordinary information closely held, such as the quantities of cement and steel produced in different locations. Even the Moscow telephone book was a classified document, and all data that was published was scrutinized for its possible effect on security.

# Human Sources

The Soviet Union continued to rely on agents as it had before and during World War II. The KGB and GRU still recruited informants and accepted walk-ins. Both agencies continued to send both legals who worked for embassies, consulates, and trade missions, and illegals who surreptitiously entered foreign countries with false identities. By contrast, the United States and Britain had to rely increasingly on refugees or defectors from the Soviet Union for information. Once in a while, the West would be fortunate enough to get a *defector in place*, a citizen of the Soviet Union who would stay on the job in a sensitive position and relay information out.

 **Spy Words**

The West got some valuable information from **defectors in place**. Although some may have been able to operate without being detected or exposed, and later lived happily in quiet retirement, a few famous ones who were caught provided the United States and Britain with solid information. Oleg Penkovsky, a Soviet missile officer, decided to provide information to both the United States and Britain, and in 1959–1960 he smuggled out detailed missile plans and even operating instructions and manuals. He was caught, interrogated, tried, and executed for treason in 1960.

## The Techint Choice

It was difficult for the United States and Britain to penetrate Soviet society with spies, and the opportunities to use defectors tended to be limited. Because of compartmentation, most defectors knew only a portion of the information the West desired. So in the 1950s, the United States began a program of aerial photography, using high-flying aircraft to photograph wide swaths of the USSR. A great incentive to develop Earth-circling satellites was the photographic equipment they might be able to carry. When the Soviet Union launched its first satellite in 1957, the American public and the press were shocked that the country had beaten the United States into space. In intelligence circles, the potential of the satellite for spying was seen as even more serious.

Other forms of technical intelligence gathering remained part of the arsenal of the cold war: telephone and cable tapping, interception, and decoding of radio transmissions, radioactive cloud sampling, underwater listening stations to monitor ship and submarine traffic, and clandestine recovery of lost equipment, ranging from test missiles to full-scale submarines. (See Chapter 16 for a few of America's technical intelligence developments during the cold war.)

| Techint |
| --- |
| The Soviet Union, despite its reputation for relying on human intelligence, did not neglect opportunities for electronic surveillance. In a famous incident, the U.S. embassy in Moscow discovered that a microphone had been planted behind a large wooden great seal of the United States in a conference room—the *bug in the seal*. After the device, known as "The Thing" was discovered, it was removed intact and presented at the United Nations by an irate U.S. ambassador Adlai Stevenson in May 1960. A replica of the bugged seal remains on display at the National Cryptologic Museum, maintained by the National Security Agency near its headquarters on the Baltimore-Washington Parkway. |

# A Persian Gamble

In 1953, the United States helped ensure that the Shah of Iran remained in power when his prime minister, Mohammad Mossadegh, moved against the British-owned Anglo-Iranian Oil Company (AIOC). For more than 26 years the interference in the political affairs of another country seemed a U.S. success story. But in later years, as the population turned against the Shah's regime, success looked more like failure.

## The Oil Issue

In 1950, by order of the Iranian parliament, the concession that granted all oil exploitation in Iran to the British-owned AIOC came up for review. The British offered only minor changes to the agreement, and in 1951, a new prime minister, Mohammad Mossadegh, with a strong popular following as a nationalist, proposed complete nationalization of AIOC holdings. The parliament passed the new law May 2, 1951. The British reaction was to evacuate British nationals and put the Royal Navy on alert. After the Truman administration urged the British not to resort to military intervention, the British began to organize a worldwide boycott of Iranian oil. The AIOC filed suit to stop Iranian oil ships in dozens of ports.

## Shah vs. Prime Minister

Through 1951 and 1952, British MI-6 encouraged the CIA to plan a joint operation to overthrow Mossadegh. When the Shah attempted to remove Mossadegh, he failed, and Mossadegh won from the Iranian parliament the power to rule by decree. Although the Shah wanted to work with the British and Americans to retain power, it was clear that with the oil issue, Mossadegh had reduced the Shah to a figurehead and that the real power was in the prime minister's hands.

## Operation Ajax

With the change in administration in the United States and the appointment of Allen Dulles to head the CIA in February 1953, Dulles was more receptive to the MI-6 plan, presented by Kermit (Kim) Roosevelt (nephew of Franklin Roosevelt, and a CIA officer). Dulles approved the plan, dubbed Operation Ajax, and put Kim Roosevelt, the CIA's chief of station in Tehran, in charge. Roosevelt met with the Shah, and promised U.S. support.

In August 1953, when the Shah sent an order dismissing Mossadegh a second time, Mossadegh had the messenger arrested. The CIA recruited 6,000 demonstrators to support the Shah. After a standoff, with street demonstrations on both sides, a unit of pro-Shah tank forces overcame resistance at the prime minister's house, and the military switched its allegiance to the Shah. According to unofficial reports, the United States had spent less than $20 million to assist the Shah.

*After helping to arrange a coup that installed the Shah of Iran, Kermit Roosevelt warned against overconfidence in the method.*

*(Courtesy of the Library of Congress)*

## Winners and Losers

The Shah gained full powers and the Eisenhower administration began channeling aid to Iran. Mossadegh was caught and put on trial. The AIOC went back into oil production, but on much reduced terms.

Iran, it seemed, had been shifted from being a client state of Britain to owing its support to the United States. The Shah remained in power for 26 years, with the aid of a tough secret police trained by the United States. In 1979, he was thrown out of office by a religious nationalist revolution that was decidedly anti-American.

Operation Ajax had succeeded—sort of. Although Kermit Roosevelt received a medal for his role, he was not enthusiastic about the chancy operation that could have resulted in a major embarrassment to the United States. In a debriefing to the White House, he said, "If we, the CIA are ever going to try something like this again, we must be absolutely sure that the people and the army want what we want. If not, you had better call in the marines."

Success or failure? The United States gained a good ally for 26 years, but the price was a deep-seated resentment among Iranian citizens. Critics of the CIA viewed the Iranian affair as a case of the agency overthrowing an elected government; supporters of the agency ranked the Shah's victory right up there with Operation Success in Guatemala (see Chapter 11).

# The U-2: Caught in the Act

On July 21, 1955 President Eisenhower made a revolutionary proposal to diminish tensions between the United States and the Soviet Union. He proposed that each nation allow the other to enter its air space and take pictures of all installations, to preclude a secret buildup of weaponry and to reduce the dread of a surprise attack. He also suggested that each side give the other blueprints of all military establishments.

The *open skies* proposal was treated by American leaders as a daring concept, and by Nikita Khrushchev, the Soviet leader, as "pure fantasy." Neutral observers wondered why the president had made the suggestion, since it was known that the secretive society of the USSR would find such a proposal impossible. Thirty-five years later, after the end of the cold war, a different pair of leaders, George H. W. Bush and Mikhail Gorbachev, implemented exactly the kind of information exchange Eisenhower had proposed, but at the height of the cold war, no such exchange could be achieved.

## U-2: The Aircraft

Six months after the open skies proposal, the United States began to implement a secret program of overflights, skirting the borders of the Soviet Union. A special unit of the CIA recruited pilots from the Air Force and trained them, beginning in early 1956, in the operation of the U-2.

The U-2 aircraft, designed in secret at a Lockheed Aircraft plant known as the Skunkworks, was remarkable. It was capable of extremely high altitude flying, for long distance. In order to fly in the rarefied upper atmosphere, the plane had an 80-foot wingspan, twice the length of the fuselage. The highly flexible wings had to be propped up by disposable pogo sticks at each end during takeoff. The flight ceiling of the aircraft was reported in unauthorized sources as exceeding 70,000 feet, assumed in the late 1950s to be far above the ceiling of Soviet aircraft and beyond the accurate range of the highest-altitude surface-to-air missile (SAM) developed by the Soviet Union. The plane carried automatic cameras that would photograph the ground in wide strips to either side of the airplane's pathway.

## Information from the U-2s

Many of the flights penetrated only along the borders of the Soviet Union, using angular photography capable of picking up ground images at a great distance. The thousands of photographs required large teams of analysts who compared pictures taken at different dates to detect construction, to locate facilities, and to build a more accurate target list of military installations and production facilities in case of war.

Although the planes flew at extremely high altitudes, it became clear that Soviet radar sites were picking up the overflights. When the aircraft were not fired upon, the Americans assumed the U-2 was safe from SAM attack because the missiles were inaccurate at that altitude. And since the Soviet Union didn't announce the incursions, American analysts assumed the Russians didn't want to be embarrassed by their inability to stop the overflights.

## The May 1 Overflight

On May 1, 1960, a U-2 took an extraordinary flight across the Soviet Union. It was unusual for several reasons. First, the flight would originate in Peshawar in northern Pakistan, fly across much of the western section of the Soviet Union, and land in Bodö, Norway, rather than simply skirting along the Soviet borders. Second, the flight was scheduled before the opening of a major summit conference set to begin in Paris on May 16, at which Eisenhower was to meet with Khrushchev. Third, May 1 was a national holiday for the Soviet Union, the international labor day celebrated by communists and socialists around the world.

The reasons for the flight have been debated, but it is clear that the CIA pushed the flights and that President Eisenhower was reluctant to authorize them. Some have suggested the choice of date was intended to embarrass Khrushchev. If so, the scheme backfired.

## Shootdown, Capture, Trial

The pilot selected for the May 1 flight was Francis Gary Powers, a former Air Force pilot.

Powers was four hours into his flight, about 400 miles inside the Soviet Union, a bit south of the city of Sverdlosk, when he heard what he later described as a dull thud. As the plane went out of control and spun toward the ground, he was thrown forward under the instrument panel and realized the plane was breaking apart, apparently from a near miss by a Soviet missile. In his position he could not fire the ejection seat release, but instead, wiggled out of the plane. His parachute, set to open at 15,000 feet, immediately deployed. He came down safely in a field, spotted by farm workers. He surrendered and was taken into Sverdlosk for questioning by the KGB.

If Powers had initiated the ejection sequence, after an interval of 70 seconds—enough time to clear the aircraft—explosive devices would have demolished the plane, leaving only widely scattered scraps. As it was, Soviet teams recovered not only the body and tail section of the plane, but cameras and other equipment, together with Powers' survival kit.

---

### Spy Bios

Francis Gary Powers was born in Kentucky, in 1929, the son of a coal miner. His family put him through Milligan College, and on graduation in 1950, he joined the Air Force. He qualified as a fighter pilot with the rank of lieutenant in 1952. In 1956, he was offered a flying job at higher pay with the CIA, and trained on the new U-2 aircraft. He was stationed in Incerlik, Turkey, with detachment 1010, making shallow penetrations of the border of the Soviet Union. In April 1960, he was transferred to Peshawar, Pakistan, and conducted his ill fated flight over the Soviet Union on May 1, 1960. After his capture, trial, and conviction for espionage, he was exchanged for Colonel Rudolf Abel (William Fischer) in February 1962. After his return to the United States, he finally secured a position as a traffic-reporter pilot over Los Angeles. He was killed in an accident on the job in 1977.

---

At first, the Soviets announced only that an American spy plane had been shot down, but didn't mention Powers' capture, or the fact that much of the airplane had been recovered. The first American reaction was to use the CIA cover story that a weather observation plane might have strayed off course. A few days later, once the president of the United States had committed to the false cover story, Khrushchev announced that the pilot had been captured, and that the spy plane would be put on public display in Gorky Park in Moscow. The United States, said Khrushchev, was not only guilty of spying, but of issuing official lies.

*With a flair for the dramatic, Nikita Khrushchev put the wreckage of the U-2 on display in Gorky Park and then held an "impromptu news conference" at the exhibit.*

*(Courtesy of the Library of Congress)*

Confronted with the evidence, Eisenhower admitted that the United States had conducted the flights and that in the modern world, no nation could live in fear of a surprise nuclear attack. The flights had been a precaution and a measure of self-defense. He also agreed the flights would stop.

By his own admission, Powers was treated well. The KGB realized that the shootdown and capture was a propaganda victory, and exploited it professionally. After questioning, Powers was scheduled for a public trial, at which he was provided with a defense attorney, Mikhail Grinev. Powers didn't think Grinev put up much of a fight, but he did give Powers some advice. He suggested that if Powers confessed, apologized, and admitted his act of espionage, his life might be spared. Powers more or less followed the advice, admitting only to being a pilot, not a spy, but still apologizing. He was convicted and sentenced to 10 years in prison.

## Aftermath

Using the U-2 incident and Eisenhower's refusal to offer an official apology as his reason, Khrushchev walked out of the Paris summit conference, further emphasizing the failed espionage mission. Powers served a total of 18 months, when he was exchanged for Rudolph Abel. (See Chapter 7 for the mysterious Colonel Abel.)

Some unanswered questions surrounding the U-2 incident were not clarified for years. Only much later did researchers learn that Eisenhower specifically authorized the flight on May 1, despite the fact that his memoirs implied he only learned of the flight later.

As in many other exposed operations, both sides sought to gain some propaganda advantages. The Soviets, by treating Powers well, putting him on trial for a capital crime, then sentencing him to a term in prison, were able to appear as the innocent victims of a botched American espionage effort. On the other hand, President Eisenhower admitted that the United States had developed the U-2, and that it had already conducted overflights of the Soviet Union, showing American ingenuity at work in the design of the airplane.

Several controversies surrounded Powers himself. Americans were shocked to see television coverage of his public confession and apology. Many wondered whether he had refused to eject from the aircraft because he suspected it would have blown him up as well. Powers was sure that a particular piece of disinformation was spread by the Russians, and noted that the destruct device would only destroy the cameras, not the aircraft. He had a poison needle he never used, and some thought he should have. On his return to the United States, he was distressed at the negative reaction he received, and published in 1970 a book describing his ordeal, *Operation Overflight*.

Some commentators claimed in retrospect that the U-2 incident represented a kind of change in American public perception of the government and its intelligence agencies. The fact that Eisenhower at first denied the flights, and then admitted he had lied, came as a shock. Possibly that shock contributed to the gradual public disillusionment in government that took place over the 1960s.

# Castro and Cuba

In January 1959, a group of rebels marched into Havana, Cuba, followed a few days later by their leader, Fidel Castro. Castro's bearded ones, or *barbudos*, who had spent years gathering support in the mountains of eastern Cuba, overthrew the corrupt regime of Fulgencio Batista, noted for his brutal secret police. At first the American press treated Castro and his troops as genuine agrarian rebels, liberating the country from a mean-spirited and greedy dictatorship. However, it soon became obvious that Castro worked closely with communist leaders, and as the government began to expropriate businesses and execute hundreds of low-level members of the former government, the press and the U.S. government recognized that the regime was on the way to becoming a pro-Soviet outpost in the Western Hemisphere.

## CIA Planning

On March 17, 1960, on orders from President Eisenhower, the CIA began training Cuban exiles for possible military action against Castro. In August 1960, Eisenhower approved a budget of $13 million for training small guerrilla groups. Apparently inspired by the success of the CIA operation in Guatemala in 1954, the CIA began planning in 1961 a larger operation that would use the Cuban refugees to constitute the core of a rebel army to overthrow Castro. A small air force was assembled, together with a group of cargo ships to transport the invasion brigade from Central America to Cuba.

## Bay of Pigs

On April 17,1961, a CIA-funded force of 1,400 men attempted a landing on the southern coast of Cuba at the *Bahia de Cochinos* or Bay of Pigs. A whole series of mistakes and errors in planning contributed to the failure of their mission. There was no extensive underground movement or rebel group within Cuba willing to rise in support of the invaders. The Cuban army and small air force were loyal to Castro, and Cuban troops surrounded the beachhead. The spot chosen for the invasion was poor, as underwater reefs and rocks made large landing craft impossible to use and stranded some of the invaders' small boats.

The new president, John F. Kennedy, ordered the invasion to take place at night, but no such landing had ever been attempted before. Efforts to set up a program of disinformation over radio, similar to that employed in Guatemala seven years earlier, had no effect. The list of tactical and strategic errors in what the CIA called Operation Pluto, all exposed in hindsight, could go on for several pages.

As a result of the poor planning and lack of an anti-Castro force in Cuba, the invaders were all either killed or captured. After they ran out of ammunition, more than 1,200 were rounded up by Castro's troops. The fact that they had trained in Guatemala and in Nicaragua under CIA officers, and that the CIA had funded the operation, soon became public knowledge. Some of the story had even leaked out *before* the operation.

*Castro, dressed in his characteristic fatigue uniform, read the news of the Bay of Pigs fiasco with some degree of satisfaction.*

*(Courtesy of the Library of Congress)*

As a failure of special operations, it was spectacular. The Bay of Pigs fiasco revealed lapses in intelligence, planning, and operational security. The failure at the Bay of Pigs showed in hindsight that those in charge of setting up the operation simply did not have enough good information about the state of affairs in Cuba and about local conditions to mount such an operation.

## Passing the Buck, and Some Lessons Learned

The press and politicians spent months, and later writers spent years, trying to fix blame for the failure, as did an official investigating commission. President John F.

Kennedy, following the example of Dwight Eisenhower, was quick to admit that the decision to go ahead with the operation was his. Many of Kennedy's supporters, however, spread the word that the original idea had been conceived several months before, under the Republican administration. Some suggested that the CIA itself was to blame, and that it had become a rogue agency. The principle of *plausible deniability*, the harshest critics claimed, had led to the agency making its own decisions without full presidential knowledge.

**Spy Words**

**Plausible deniability** began under CIA director Allen Dulles (1953–1961). According to this doctrine, there would be no paper trail of presidential authorization of a CIA action. The concept would allow the president and his closest advisors to escape blame for failure or any unethical aspects of the operation. When there was a really big episode, such as the U-2 incident or the Bay of Pigs invasion, deniability made it appear the president was not in charge of his own government. Both Eisenhower and Kennedy partially rejected plausible deniability, each in his own way.

Defenders of the agency and defenders of the Cuban refugees blamed Kennedy for a loss of nerve at a crucial point, while others blamed the State Department and some of Kennedy's advisers for not providing stronger support. If he had ordered the U.S. Navy to provide air cover, they claimed, the rebels might have succeeded.

The Bay of Pigs was such a disaster in special operations and in intelligence, that the blame game continued for years. One outcome was that Kennedy asked for the retirement in November 1961 of DCI #5, Allen Dulles, under whom the plans had developed, and the resignation of Richard Bissell, the officer who had been most directly in charge. Another consequence was that President Kennedy was reluctant to work closely with the CIA during the rest of his administration. Operation Pluto had cost more than $100 million. The unfortunate exile members of the invasion brigade were held in prison, then released to the United States in exchange for a multimillion dollar shipment of medical supplies.

## The Least You Need to Know

- ◆ Assessments of failure and success of intelligence agencies are often politically motivated.

- ◆ The CIA supported the Shah of Iran in 1953, and helped ensure his remaining in power over the next 26 years.

◆ The American U-2 was shot down over Russia on May Day, 1960, and pilot Gary Powers was tried and convicted of espionage.

◆ The 1961 Bay of Pigs invasion by CIA-trained and supported Cuban exiles failed because of poor intelligence, poor op-sec, and poor support.

# Great Moles and Mole Hunters

## In this Chapter

- ◆ Penkovsky and Goleniewski
- ◆ The tale behind Topaz
- ◆ James Jesus Angleton: mole hunter
- ◆ Defectors: real or planted
- ◆ The Oswald connection

In this chapter, we'll look at a few of the most spectacular spies who provided information to the West during the early cold war. For MI-6 and the CIA it became difficult to know whom to trust, since the Soviet Union was very good at planting false information. When a defector came to the West with data about the Soviet system, was the KGB using him, either with or without his knowledge, to transmit disinformation? When one defector claimed another was giving false information, which one did you believe? It became what some observers called "a wilderness of mirrors." But in a few cases, particularly the defection of Oleg Penkovsky, the West gained valuable views into the inner working of the military and intelligence systems of the Soviet Union, at least for a short time.

# Penkovsky

Oleg Penkovsky, a colonel in the Soviet GRU, may have been the best human intelligence source within the Soviet Union ever available to the West. One biography of him is titled *The Spy Who Saved the World* (Jerrold Scheckter, 1994). For a period of about 18 months he remained at work in the Soviet Union, smuggling out reports, espionage training manuals, technical information about missiles, his own estimates of espionage strengths and weakness, and literally volumes of material, including the names of hundreds of Soviet agents in the West. His personality remained a mystery to his American and British friends, and finally, to the Soviet prosecutor and so-called defense attorney at his trial.

## A Defection in Place

Penkovsky had been stationed in Ankara, Turkey, in 1955, and MI-6 had spotted him then as a possible defector, according to Greville Wynne, the British agent who finally established contact with Penkovsky in 1960. Visiting Moscow on a technical trade mission, Wynne got to know Penkovsky, who after a few nervous starts provided Wynne with a thick envelope of documents and films.

Once the contact was established, Wynne was able to make arrangements for Penkovsky to head a trade and technical delegation to visit Britain. In April and May 1961, Penkovsky visited London, where it became clear that he chose to remain in the Soviet Union and continue to provide fresh materials, rather than defecting with what he knew. He made further trips to London in the summer of 1961, and to Paris in September and October 1961, when he met with both British and American intelligence officers.

### Tradecraft

When Penkovsky wanted to get materials to American officers in Moscow, he used a system of dead drops. There was a dark green radiator to the right of the door in the lobby to an ordinary apartment house on Pushkin Street. Penkovsky would place a film in a matchbox, wrap the box in paper, seal it with cellophane tape, wind it with wire, and hang it on a hook behind the radiator. Unfortunately for Penkovsky, the KGB spotted the location.

Even though the CIA paid Penkovsky some $300 a month into a Swiss bank account, he never collected it. He seemed to be a rather unique person, ideologically motivated to support democracy and willing to fight the communist system from inside the Soviet Union.

## Penkovsky's Personality

Penkovsky wanted recognition in the West for what he was doing. At one point, on a visit to England as part of a trade delegation, he was standing with Wynne on the street and they both spotted the Queen. Penkovsky wanted to rush right up and explain that he was spying for Britain, but Wynne dissuaded him. At his next debriefing session with MI-6 and the CIA, he insisted on meeting the Queen. Finally a CIA officer suggested he might meet President Kennedy instead, and Penkovsky jumped at the alternative. Quickly, he was flown to Washington and had a half-hour meeting with the president, who praised his work very warmly.

Unfortunately, Wynne noted, after the meeting with Kennedy, Penkovsky was even more determined to meet the Queen. Although he never did get to meet the Queen, MI-6 arranged a meeting between Penkovsky and the Queen's cousin, Earl Mountbatten.

As a way to reward him with some of the recognition that he craved, Penkovsky was offered an appointment as a colonel in the British army. The CIA agreed he could also be appointed to the same rank in the U.S. Army. Commissioning papers were provided, as well as uniforms. At a small reception in his honor, he changed into each uniform and was photographed. He was so touched by this event that he kept the photos, and the KGB later found them in his apartment. The photos were used as evidence against him, along with his mini-cameras, film, documents, and other equipment.

## Penkovsky's Information

Penkovsky provided hundreds of pages of documents, including personally written reports on the structure and operation of the GRU. He pointed out that although there had been a temporary ban on recruiting spies through the local communist parties in foreign countries, that ban had been lifted in 1960. He described in detail the relationship between the KGB and the GRU, the process of spotting talent, the operation of the *rezidentura*, and a complete lecture on how spies should behave in the United States.

Penkovsky supplied a running account of Soviet military preparations for war in Germany, as well as technical details of missiles, missile transporter-erector-launchers, missile deployment sites, and their capabilities. In 1965, after Penkovsky had been caught and executed, the CIA released many of his reports, which were collected, translated, and published as *The Penkovskiy Papers*. The book itself was controversial, as critics wondered how much of it was genuine. The editor, Frank Gibney, offered a convincing explanation for how he got the documents and their basic credibility in a re-edition in 1982.

**Spy Words**

A legal *resident* was a consular or embassy official, a correspondent for the Soviet Press agency, TASS, or a member of a trade mission. The office of **resident** was the post, while the *resident* was the individual. In prior years, the military attaché had automatically been the GRU *resident* but in January 1961 it had been decided that that was too obvious, and the new *residents* tended to operate under civilian cover as ambassador, counselor, or first or second secretary. The GRU was always irritated that more of the posts in the embassies and consulates were given to the KGB than to the GRU.

## Penkovsky and the Cuban Missile Crisis

During the period when Penkovsky provided so much information, the United States learned that the Soviet Union was installing medium-range missiles, capable of hitting most U.S. cities, in Cuba. During the standoff between President John F. Kennedy and Premier Nikita Khrushchev in August 1962, the United States had several sources of information. One was photography from high-flying U-2 aircraft over Cuba. Daring low-level flights to photograph the installations provided another source. A few individuals on the ground relayed sightings of trucks and harbor unloading, but the locations were so well guarded that little local information could be obtained.

Penkovsky's reports were another source, providing details that suggested that Khrushchev was not ready for a true nuclear confrontation. Other details showed exactly the capabilities and specifications of the missiles being installed. The CIA asked Penkovsky for more current information, but he did not reply. It turned out he was already under close surveillance and could not make contact.

Even though Penkovsky mysteriously went silent during the crisis, the details he had already provided helped Kennedy and his policy advisors to call the bluff of Khrushchev during the eyeball-to-eyeball confrontation.

*President Kennedy and Premier Khrushchev, cold war rivals, depended on the latest intelligence from multiple sources as they sparred over Berlin and Cuba.*

*(Courtesy of the Library of Congress)*

# Trial

Both Wynne and Penkovsky were arrested in November 1962, and they were both tried for espionage, beginning May 7, 1963, after extensive browbeating and interrogation. Wynne was arrested in Budapest and flown from Hungary to Moscow, where he was held in Lubyanka. At the trial, both men confessed, as the evidence was overwhelming. However, Penkovsky's testimony made it appear that he had contacted Wynne and that Wynne was not an official agent of the British. The trial was intended, not as trials in democracies, to try to ensure justice, but simply to provide a public forum for the confession of crime and the exposure of the individuals as an object lesson.

One of the most difficult issues for the Soviets was how to explain that such a highly placed individual in the communist state could have turned against the system. They decided to portray him as depraved and greedy, an interpretation hardly supported by the fact that he did not spend the money provided him and contradicted by his many statements critical of the Soviet system and favorable to the West. In his own statement, Penkovsky declared that he provided information to the West out of loyalty to the Russian people, who, he claimed, deserved better than the regime governing them. That particular statement, however, was excluded from the public record of the trial.

Wynne's year in prison was quite rugged, and he was a haggard, worn man when exchanged at Checkpoint Heerstrasse in Berlin on April 24, 1964, for Gordon Lonsdale (see Chapter 9). Penkovsky was, according to Soviet sources, shot a few days after his trial. However, Wynne and others hesitated to publish details of Penkovsky's help to the West out of fear he might still be alive and that their information would lead to further reprisals against him if he were alive in prison.

# Real and Fake Defectors

When Penkovsky started to provide information, some in the CIA doubted that he was genuine. His sometimes casual attitude about operational security, his insistence on working from within the Soviet Union, and the sometimes odd quality of his intelligence, ranging from photos of classified documents, to rambling reports that he wrote, all suggested he might be a *dangle*.

**Spy Words**

A **dangle** is a person who approaches an intelligence agency in order to be recruited as an intelligence source. A basic rule of thumb, official CIA sources note, is to avoid or suspect anyone who takes the initiative in approaching an intelligence officer, because he or she may be planted in order to provide disinformation.

As it turned out, Penkovsky was a strange character, but most of his information was accurate and valuable. He was no *dangle*, but a genuine defector in place. Nevertheless, among the many refugees fleeing the Soviet Union and the Soviet bloc countries were a number of individuals who claimed to have worked for either Soviet intelligence or one of the agencies of the satellite nations, such as the Polish *SB* or the East German *HVA*. Finding out whether their information was genuine turned into a nightmare through the 1960s.

**Spy Words**

The intelligence services of several satellite countries worked closely with the KGB. They were usually designated by two or three letter acronyms, as follows:

Poland Security Service: *Sluzba Bezpieczentwa*—SB

Hungary State Security Authority: *Allavedelmi Hatosag*—AVH

Czechoslovakia Main Directorate of Intelligence: *Hlavni Sprava Rozvedky*—HSR

State Secret Security: *Statni tajna Bezpecnost*—StB

Bulgaria State Security: *Durzhavna Sigurnost*—DS

East Germany Main Department for Intelligence: *Hauptverwaltung Afklärung*—HVA

State Security: *Staatssicherheitsdienst*—SSD or "Stasi"

Yugoslavia stopped cooperating with the KGB in 1948, Albania in 1960, and Rumania in 1964.

## Goleniewski

In 1960, Mikhail Goleniewski defected from the Polish SB to the CIA in West Berlin. He had several pieces of information, including the identification of Gordon Lonsdale, a Russian posing as a Canadian businessman in Britain, who ran a spy ring that included Morris and Lona Cohen (see Chapter 9).

Goleniewski also provided the information that led to the arrest of George Blake, the British mole who had worked for the Soviet Union in Berlin and who had tipped off the KGB about the Berlin Tunnel dug by the CIA (see Chapter 11).

Goleniewski also knew of several other spies, including Heinze Felfe, who spied for the Russians inside the West German Federal Intelligence Service. With such valuable information, it appeared that Goleniewski was genuine.

## Golytsin

Goleniewski's information happened to mesh with a number of pieces of evidence brought forward by another defector, Anatoly Golytsin, who defected a little later, in December 1961. Golytsin had been working for the KGB in Finland. He provided the CIA with a list of more than 100 spies and sources within NATO countries, who had worked for the KGB. Although Golytsin's information appeared to be very good, he warned that the Soviets would be sending out false defectors who would be planting disinformation intended to discredit him.

The problem of who was real and who was fake began to escalate. Some within the CIA believed that Golytsin had been sent to undermine the CIA's faith in other defectors. Some analysts believed that Golytsin was handled incorrectly, and that he needed someone with a firm hand to tell him what he was supposed to do. Instead, he was passed around until he was being questioned by people with little knowledge of Russian culture or psychology. Golytsin began to realize that he would be paid as long as he continued to come up with new information. So, some argued, he started making things up. Others began to trust him, including James Jesus Angleton, the head of the CIA's counterintelligence section. Ever since the exposure of Maclean, Burgess, and Philby, Angleton was ready to believe that there might be more moles within Western agencies.

One of Golytsin's revelations was that Maclean, Burgess, and Philby were only the first three of a Ring of Five in Britain. When suspicion fell on Roger Hollis, many blamed Golytsin for the damage it caused British Intelligence (see Chapter 9). Golytsin's hints corresponded with Angleton's suspicions.

The problem with Golytsin's information about other spies was that, unlike the earlier Goleniewski revelations that led to the arrest of Lonsdale, the Cohens, Blake, and Felfe, his charges could not be proven or disproven. As a consequence, the British, French, West German, and American intelligence agencies spent more than a decade trying to track down the mysterious but unnamed agents that Golytsin said were at work in them.

# The Nosenko/Golytsin Controversy

In 1962, KGB officer Yuri Nosenko contacted the CIA at a meeting in Geneva on disarmament. Like Penkovsky, he offered to stay on in Russia and to spy for the CIA, because, he claimed, his family was in Russia and he could not leave them behind for fear of reprisals. Finally, in early 1964, Nosenko showed up again in Geneva, and this time, he said he was willing to defect.

A startling piece of information made Nosenko very interesting. He said that he had been involved in monitoring the KGB's relationship with Lee Harvey Oswald, the man believed to have assassinated President Kennedy two months before. Nosenko said that the KGB had feared that in some way Oswald had worked for a low-level KGB agent and they had fully investigated until they were satisfied he had no connection with their agency. Nosenko knew everything about Oswald's stay in Russia and his contacts with the agency, and he could provide all the details.

At the time Nosenko defected, in early 1964, the Warren Commission was investigating the Kennedy assassination, and Richard Helms, then Deputy Director of Plans at the CIA, realized that Nosenko's evidence would be important to the commission. The FBI questioned Nosenko and trusted his statements, because they seemed to coincide with one of their own sources, code-named Fedora. Meanwhile, Helms and Angleton at the CIA remained suspicious of Nosenko.

## Holes in Nosenko's Story

It seemed strange that a man who two years earlier had said he did not want to defect had defected two months after the Kennedy assassination, and then claimed that the KGB had made sure that it had nothing to do with Oswald. The CIA thought it too much a coincidence that Nosenko, the only recent source they had from the Soviet Union, had been supervising the Oswald connection in Russia. The Oswald information, and its detailed quality, seemed almost tacked on to the rest of the data provided by Nosenko.

Other aspects of Nosenko's defection seemed suspicious. Some of the information he provided seemed to be give-away information, pieces of knowledge that the KGB could have assumed the CIA already had. Secondly, there were aspects of Nosenko's background that sounded more like a legend than a real life story. There seemed to be gaps in his biography that made no sense. Golytsin was convinced that Nosenko was providing KGB disinformation.

Helms told Chief Justice Warren on the commission investigating the assassination, that the CIA could not vouch for the comments of Nosenko. Peter Bagley, a CIA interrogator who questioned Nosenko, was convinced he had originally been set up to discredit some of Golytsin's information, and that the mission to suggest that Oswald had nothing to do with the KGB had been tacked on at the last minute.

## Will the Real Defector Please Stand Up?

Nosenko was kept in an isolated Virginia CIA property from 1964 to 1967 and questioned daily for months at a time. He was in solitary confinement, given nothing to read, and not brought before a judge. Although not as harsh as Lubyanka, the conditions were not those usually extended to a genuine defector, nor even those as good as provided to accused criminals in the United States. In fact, the CIA treated Nosenko as if he were a disinformation agent from the KGB, either witting or unwitting. With growing disagreement in the CIA about Nosenko and Golytsin, different specialists came up with different views.

Perhaps both Goleniewski and Golytsin were plants, and Nosenko was genuine. Perhaps the flaws in Nosenko's life story derived from poor translation rather than fabricated legend. Perhaps Goleniewski was a genuine defector whose real information had been manipulated and supplemented by the KGB without his knowledge. Perhaps Nosenko was genuine, and Golytsin was the plant, or was simply trying to gain credit by discrediting others. The possibilities went on and on. In general, Angleton, the head of counterintelligence within the CIA, and those who followed him believed in Golytsin.

After more than four years in what amounted to prison conditions, Nosenko was released and reputedly settled down in the Washington area. Years later, it was learned that the KGB regarded him as a genuine defector, and put him on their list of defectors to be assassinated. As far as is known, they never caught up with him.

The *great molehunt*, some observers felt, had the effect of shattering the CIA, raising suspicions where there should have been none. According to one story, Golytsin claimed there was an agent named (or code-named) Sasha in the agency. Finally suspicion settled on one CIA officer whose real name *was* Sasha. After months of harassment and investigation, the CIA employee was cleared.

In addition to the painful hunt for the *fifth man* in Britain that reached as high as the director of MI-5 and the prime minister, as detailed in Chapter 9, the French intelligence service was wracked by the Golytsin accusations. For several years through the 1960s, the CIA refused to cooperate or share information with the French agency because, it was feared, the KGB was so well entrenched there.

# The Tale Behind Topaz

In 1967, the novelist Leon Uris published a spy novel, *Topaz*, loosely based on the life story of a French agent for the *Service de Documentation Extérieur et de Contre-Espionage* (SDECE), the French equivalent of the CIA. In the novel, a French espionage officer finds that his own agency harbors some KGB agents at the highest level, and when he tries to report on them, he finds his life in danger. The real story behind Uris's novel is just as bizarre.

## De Vosjoli: Truth Stranger Than Fiction

Philippe Thyraud de Vosjoli had, like the Americans, become quite concerned about the evidence provided by Golytsin. In 1962, the CIA allowed de Vosjoli to cooperate in the questioning of Golytsin. De Vosjoli knew Golytsin by the French code name Martel. Among Golytsin's other revelations was information that the KGB had agents within the SDECE, in a spy ring code-named Sapphire, suggesting a whole string of jewels.

According to Golytsin, the agents were long-hidden moles, including one at the near ministerial level since 1944. Furthermore, according to Golytsin, the Sapphire ring was relaying back to the KGB information about the United States that had been gathered by the SDECE.

In December 1962, de Vosjoli was ordered back to Paris, where his boss reprimanded him for relaying information gathered on the ground from his own network to the CIA during the Cuban Missile Crisis without first clearing it through SDECE. De Vosjoli had done so because he believed that if he had told his own headquarters about what he learned in Cuba, it would get back through Sapphire to the KGB. When he was ordered to continue supplying information about the United States, he suspected that it would also go via Sapphire to the KGB.

Wracked by doubts from what he learned from Martel (Golytsin), de Vosjoli followed the unfolding saga of events through early 1963. The SDECE tracked down three

KGB agents working within the agency, two of whom committed suicide. The third, Georges Pâques, was arrested. Even after these elements of the Sapphire ring were wrapped up, de Vosjoli resisted gathering information about the United States, fearing it could still leak to the Soviet Union.

In October 1963, de Vosjoli resigned from the SDECE, and then quietly moved to Mexico where he spent the winter living in an obscure squatter community in Acapulco. He feared that someone from either the KGB's *SMERSH* or from the *wet work* group in the SDECE would get him. Later, the CIA provided him a house in Miami, and he settled down to a more comfortable life.

### Spy Words

The KGB maintained a unit known as **SMERSH**, whose job it was to track down important defectors and kill them. Despite the fact that SMERSH had quite a list of targets, including Igor Gouzenko and Yuri Nosenko, they had very few successes. When Reino Hayhanen, the defector who turned in Rudolf Able, died in an automobile accident, the KGB put out the word that his death was a SMERSH operation. Most observers regarded that story as disinformation. The KGB term for killing someone was **wet work**.

On a later visit to Acapulco, de Vosjoli was introduced by a mutual friend to the novelist Leon Uris, who liked his story so much that he entered into a financial agreement to share royalties on a novel based on the tale. Displeased at the fictionalized aspects of the novel, de Vosjoli published his own version of his life story in a work entitled *Lamia*. The title derived from the code name he had used as a member of the French Resistance during World War II.

The novel *Topaz* sold well, but de Vosjoli had to sue to get a settlement on the royalties, as Uris believed de Vosjoli had broken the agreement by publishing his own competing version. Although *Lamia* had a good press run in the United States and was translated into French and Spanish, it never reached a fraction of the sales of the sensationalized version written by the novelist.

## The Least You Need to Know

- Oleg Penkovsky's information turned out to be extremely valuable to Kennedy during the 1962 Cuban Missile Crisis.
- The defection of Mikhail Goleniewski from Poland helped identify KGB spies Gordon Lonsdale, George Blake, and Lona and Morris Cohen.

♦ The defection of Anatoly Golytsin led to extreme disruption of MI-5 and MI-6 in Britain, the CIA in the United States, and the SDECE in France, as each searched for the moles he reported.

♦ Yuri Nosenko was questioned in solitary confinement for four years, because it seemed his claim that the KGB had no connection with Lee Harvey Oswald was planted information and because Golytsin had warned of false defectors.

♦ The novel and movie *Topaz* was based on the exposure of a real spy ring code-named Sapphire, within the French SDECE.

# Chapter 15

# The CIA and the Church Committee Revelations

- ◆ The CIA and Vietnam
- ◆ Value shift in the 1970s
- ◆ Letting out the family jewels
- ◆ Chile: the elusive truth

The mid-1970s saw changes in American public attitudes toward intelligence and toward the government in general. Many journalists, politicians, and opinion-makers and a few former intelligence officers criticized the CIA, the FBI, and other intelligence agencies. The criticisms focused on several issues: abuse of power, invasion of civil liberties, and engagement in unethical or criminal behavior. The public gained the impression that the CIA and perhaps other agencies had acted as *rogue agencies* outside of the control of Congress, the law, public opinion, and even the president.

In this chapter, we look at the evidence for such charges that came out of the congressional and journalistic investigations of the 1970s, at the events that created an atmosphere of public suspicion of intelligence work, and at the changes that resulted. Some critics welcomed reforms as necessary to prevent abuses, but a few defenders of the agencies worried that the exposés and investigations would weaken the government's ability to gather and interpret intelligence and hence weaken national security.

# The Value Shift

Many social commentators have pointed to a change in American political values and attitudes that took place between the mid-1960s and the mid-1970s. To an extent, the changes were a worldwide phenomenon, as the baby-boom generation born after World War II, raised in prosperity and nurtured by new mass media, came to maturity. It was true that by 1975, more Americans were receptive to news articles, editorials, and political appeals that criticized the government.

The popular faith in government that had characterized the World War II generation had been replaced, it seemed, with suspicion that those in authority no longer acted in the best interests of the nation. Some commentators traced the sources for this growing suspicion of authority, not only to the generation shift, but also to specific shocking events.

## Shocks to Confidence

When Sputnik was launched in 1957, American public faith in the technical lead of the United States over the Soviet Union was shaken. When Khrushchev concealed the fact that U-2 pilot Gary Powers was captured alive, he backed President Eisenhower into a publicly admitted lie. The event was seen by some as a watershed event in history. Presidents might have lied to the American people many times before, but they had never been caught so badly that they had to publicly admit the lie two days after making it.

The Bay of Pigs fiasco was another such event (see Chapter 13). Although President Kennedy admitted responsibility for the invasion, it was clear from its timing and from remarks from his inner circle of advisers that they and he blamed the CIA for the failure. The Bay of Pigs incident had certainly contributed to weakened trust in the agency and in the honesty of the U.S. government.

On November 22, 1963, President Kennedy was assassinated, and three days later, his accused assassin, Lee Harvey Oswald, was himself shot to death while being moved from a jail cell in the Dallas police station. His killer was a nightclub owner, Jack Ruby, with mob connections. The fact that Oswald never confessed to the crime, and that he was silenced before his version of events was publicly known, left the assassination as an unsolved crime in the minds of the public.

Lyndon Johnson, Kennedy's vice president and successor, appointed a commission headed by Chief Justice Earl Warren to investigate the assassination. The Warren report concluded Oswald had acted alone. Following its publication, a shelf-full of books, hundreds of articles, and a continuing media barrage of stories reflected distrust in that conclusion. A few of the *conspiracy theorists* speculated, without any credible evidence, that Kennedy's assassination had been planned and carried out by disaffected members of the CIA.

**Spy Words**

Historians and responsible journalists usually reject a **conspiracy theory.** Such a theory relies on the notion that the absence of evidence only proves how well the conspirators covered it up. However, in the world of espionage and covert action, government agencies go to great lengths to prevent disclosure of their work. It is this aspect of intelligence and espionage that leads to the proliferation of conspiracy theories, as well as a rich body of fictional espionage and techno-thriller literature, by such authors as Somerset Maugham, Eric Ambler, Ian Fleming, John Le Carre, and Tom Clancy.

Each of these events in different ways planted suspicions about America's intelligence establishment, particularly the CIA. Thus, when President Johnson began to order increases in U.S. military forces to intervene in Vietnam in 1964, public support for the intelligence services had already begun to ebb.

## Vietnam

In many ways, the American war in Vietnam developed as an extension of early cold war policies and an expanding covert intelligence role. American actions intended to prevent the spread of communism in the former French Indo-China were largely covert from the late 1950s through 1964. Between 1964 and 1972, American participation in the war came into the open. Many aspects of the war contributed to the mounting criticism of America's intelligence establishment.

When the French withdrew from Vietnam in 1954, the country was divided between a communist-ruled northern regime, and a nominal monarchy in the south that was in fact dominated by the military. President Eisenhower and, later, President Kennedy worked to support the anti-communist regime in Southern Vietnam, ignoring the terms of the French withdrawal that had called for a nationwide election to unify the country by 1958. In such an election, the more organized communist forces were sure to win.

Unfortunately, the southern regime was controlled by a small Catholic minority that used troops and police to suppress the practice of religion by the majority Buddhists, angering many in the population. Through the CIA, the United States funded the regime, on the assumption that if it did not do so, the government would quickly fall to rebels supported by the North Vietnamese. Meanwhile, in neighboring Laos, the United States, again operating through the CIA and other covert forces, provided funds to support an anti-communist regime that collapsed, giving way to a neutralist government that virtually conceded the frontier regions with Vietnam. A stretch of Laotian territory, up to 50 miles wide and almost 400 hundred miles long, came to be known as the *Ho Chi Minh Trail*.

**Spy Words**

The **Ho Chi Minh Trail** was a series of paths and roads through the forested regions inside Laos, used by the North Vietnamese to transport arms, supplies, and personnel to the anti-government forces in South Vietnam. Since the North Vietnamese used bicycles and backpacking to transport much of their supplies, bombing could not destroy the "trail" itself. If sections of a pathway were destroyed from the air, the Vietnamese would simply walk or bike around the bomb craters the next day.

As a means of fighting back against the North Vietnamese, the CIA funded many operations. One in particular, Operation Plan 34A, was based on the experience in Korea.

# Oplan 34A

Using small patrol boats, groups of commandos from South Vietnam would land along the coast in the north, conduct sabotage and raids, and withdraw. Like the similar effort in Korea, Operation Wolfpack (see Chapter 11), Operation Plan 34A or Oplan 34A, approved in January 1964, had only a harassing effect. For the raids, the CIA acquired Swift boats, built in Norway.

However, in 1964, North Vietnamese actions with patrol boats against the Oplan 34A infiltration led to an exchange of fire between the North Vietnamese patrol boats and American naval ships in the Gulf of Tonkin. In this fashion, the covert operations, intended to provide support for the South Vietnamese, escalated into a major conflict.

When four small craft belonging to Oplan 34A returned after a raid on the north in early August 1964, they were pursued by North Vietnamese patrol craft that encountered the U.S. destroyer *Maddox*. The ship was on a patrol for Naval

Intelligence. After an exchange of fire between *Maddox* and the North Vietnamese patrol boats on the first night, President Johnson ordered the destroyer *C. Turner Joy* to assist *Maddox*, and then ordered air strikes on North Vietnam. Reports were unclear as to the number of shots fired and received by the ships on the second night. Based on the assumption that North Vietnamese boats fired on American naval vessels in international waters, President Johnson presented to Congress on August 7, 1964, the Gulf of Tonkin Resolution, which authorized further use of force, including combat troops, in Vietnam.

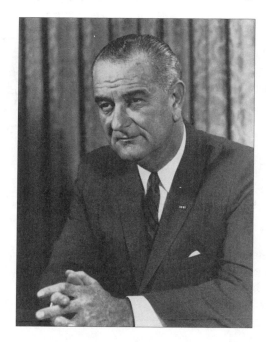

*As a result of the Gulf of Tonkin incident, President Lyndon Johnson obtained support from Congress for commitment of U.S. forces in Vietnam.*

*(Courtesy of the Library of Congress)*

The United States had for several years been providing covert support with the CIA, ONI, Navy Seals, and Special Forces troops. The Gulf of Tonkin incident and congressional resolution shifted the war from a relatively small and low-profile set of undercover operations to a major military commitment over the next eight years. In the light of later criticisms, it's important to remember that Oplan 34A and the other covert operations mentioned here went forward only on the approval of the U.S. secretary of defense and the president. Some later critics of the CIA and of covert action tried to suggest that the war in Vietnam was the result of independent or rogue CIA policies and operations, which was simply not the case.

## The CIA in Vietnam

Only later did the extent of CIA operations before and after the Gulf of Tonkin incident become public. In several operations, the CIA began an action or operation, and then once it was up and running, the agency would turn over the organization to the Army Special Forces—the Green Berets—or to another *special ops* military unit, such as the Navy Seals or Delta Force.

One such early effort had begun about 1961, in which the CIA provided funding and assistance to tribal minority groups in the highlands, collectively known as montagnards. There were several dozen linguistic groups living in the mountains bordering Vietnam and Laos, ethnically more related to Polynesian-Malayan populations than to the Vietnamese. The CIA set up a system of about 80 fortified base camps among the montagnards, known as Civilian Irregular Defense Groups (CIDGs), running the system until November 1962, when the CIA began to turn over the whole CIDG operation to the Green Berets. Between 1962 and 1968, the Green Beret forces involved with the CIDGs numbered nearly 3,500 men. The changeover from CIA to Green Beret control was officially known as Operation Switchback.

### Spy Words

When military operations need to be conducted covertly, but require large numbers of highly trained troops, the work is best carried on by the military services rather than by an intelligence agency, and the activities are known as **special operations** or **special ops**. During World War II, the Office of Strategic Services (OSS) carried on several different kinds of activities, including not only intelligence work but clandestine training and support for resistance groups, as well as some commando and sabotage raids. By the 1960s, however, most special operations by the military were conducted by highly trained elite units of the Army, Navy, and Marine Corps.

This initiation of an action by the CIA and then its transfer to regular military control seemed to represent a lesson learned from the Bay of Pigs and to reflect the advice of Kermit Roosevelt from the Iranian affair (Chapter 13). Although the CIA might be capable of developing and funding a sophisticated covert action, carrying forward the operation on a continuing basis was best given over to the military, with its apparatus of logistic support, communications, command structure, training, and experienced operational personnel.

In addition to the montagnard operations, the CIA ran many other facilities and operations in Vietnam, some of which are still classified. The headquarters in Saigon was said to number 400 officers, surpassing even the Miami office by 1965.

## Air America

The civilian airline owned by the CIA, a proprietary air force, Air America, operated extensively in Laos and Vietnam in support of the montagnard operations. As the war level increased in the late 1960s, the size of the Air America operation increased as well. By 1965, Air America moved 1,650 tons of cargo a month in South Vietnam, with a fleet of more than 50 aircraft. Air America maintained facilities in Bangkok, Takhil, and Udorn in Thailand, with a major maintenance base at Vientiane in Laos. Equipped with helicopters, Air America often rescued downed Air Force bomber pilots inside North Vietnam. By 1968, Air America operated a fleet of almost 200 aircraft, and had some 8,000 employees. The operation was entirely run by CIA officers and contract workers, rather than by the military.

So many people were involved in the Air America operations that even though it was covert, word of the scale of the effort inevitably leaked out. Even so, the many heroic actions of Air America pilots and crews in support of montagnard tribes in Laos and Vietnam and in rescue of downed pilots could not be officially publicized. A few stories became legendary, like that of Tony Po, an Air America pilot who, despite orders to the contrary, engaged in many battles.

---

### Spy Bios

Tony Po (Anthony Poshepny) was a CIA Air America pilot who disobeyed orders regularly to engage in firefights with the enemy. According to legends, he suffered more than a dozen wounds, and once carried a wounded native comrade 30 miles to safety. He led Yao tribesmen in raids into Burma, and according to some sources, even into communist China. Balding, heavy-set, and with little regard for the rules, he was regarded by many as the real-life parallel for the character Colonel William E. Kurtz in the film *Apocalypse Now*. Unlike the character in that story, however, Po survived the war and continued to attend Air America reunions for many years.

---

## Operation Phoenix

Later, the most notorious of the CIA operations in Vietnam, and one that appeared to be the most morally repugnant, was a planned campaign directed at communist *cadres* and village leaders. Funded by the CIA, Operation Phoenix was not officially an assassination campaign. It began as the Intelligence Coordination and Exploitation (ICEX) program in 1968, and its name was changed to Phoenix the next year. Specially trained South Vietnamese strike forces, with more than 500 military advisers and some 20 to 40 CIA agents, actually carried out the work.

By 1971, CIA officer William Colby reported to the U.S. Senate that more than 20,000 Viet Cong leaders had been killed, nearly 29,000 imprisoned, and another 17,000 converted to support the South Vietnamese regime.

One issue with Phoenix was that it operated on tips and accusations, many of which derived from family feuds, personal animosity, and even criminal protection rackets. The Vietnamese military courts extracted confessions under stiff interrogation, and the sentences no doubt included many that were innocent of any support for the communist cause. However, William Colby reported that by 1972, the program, now run by the military, had been so successful in wide areas that all the leadership had retreated into neighboring Cambodia and Laos, forcing the Viet Cong to resort to regular military operations.

However, by 1972, President Nixon had announced a program of Vietnamization, in which U.S. troops would be withdrawn and the military operations would be taken over by South Vietnamese troops. With this plan beginning to have effect, the Viet Cong had every incentive to wait to resume attacks until the American withdrawal was completed and until after a peace agreement was signed in Paris. The 1972 quiet in some parts of the countryside may have been partially due to Phoenix, as Colby believed, but it may also have been a result of a strategic decision on the part of the North Vietnamese and Viet Cong to wait for improved conditions.

## Nixon and Watergate

During the 1972 election campaign, a group of burglars broke into the headquarters of the Democratic National Committee in the Watergate building in Washington, D.C. A night watchman spotted their activities and they were arrested. It was found that the burglars had a list of phone numbers, including those of former CIA officer Howard Hunt, who had been active in both the Guatemala operation and the Bay of Pigs. One of the burglars, Eugenio Martinez, had worked with Hunt, and was still on retainer with the CIA.

CIA Director Richard Helms investigated the connections and soon realized that the current and former CIA men had been operating on assignment from someone in the White House. During the investigation, Helms made sure that there had been no CIA involvement in the break-in, and as evidence began to mount that the funding and planning had come from the Committee to Re-elect the President (known as "CREEP"), Helms and the agency kept at arms-length from contact with CREEP officials. The CIA also refused to help concoct a cover story that would get the FBI to back off from its investigation. Nevertheless, it was clear that Hunt had used equipment, methods, experts, and some personnel from the CIA to organize and carry out the burglary. The investigation went quietly at first and Richard Nixon was re-elected in November 1972.

Over the next two years, as the FBI, Congress, and journalists investigated the burglary, it became clear that the White House engaged in covering up the connection of CREEP and the burglars. Faced with impeachment, President Nixon resigned, and Gerald Ford became president on August 9, 1974.

The extended Watergate scandal and the lengthy and inconclusive Vietnam War further contributed to the growing suspicion of the executive branch, of intelligence, and of the military.

# Investigations and Revelations

By late 1974, suspicions surrounding the CIA had mounted. Not only had the connection of former CIA personnel with the Watergate burglary damaged the agency's reputation, but rumors of the so-called secret war in Laos and about other agency involvement in Vietnam mounted. American popular support for the Vietnamese war had never been strong, and it weakened as the number of casualties climbed and no clear moral justification for the war emerged. Popular antagonism to the war itself often focused unfairly on the troops and the civilians who had risked their lives in the war's conduct.

On Sunday, December 22, 1974, Seymour Hersh, a *New York Times* reporter, published a report about the domestic activities of the CIA that had been directed against anti-war individuals and other political dissidents in the 1960s. Until then, the public knew nothing of Operation Chaos and Operation MKUltra (discussed in Chapter 12). The news was a shock, although congressional committees knew some of the information already.

The media went into a feeding frenzy, as reporters tried to find out more about the operations. In one sense, the scandals derived from a simple issue. There had always been a lack of clarity as to the dividing line between domestic and foreign intelligence, and a lack of clear reporting authority for the CIA to Congress. Presidents from Truman through Nixon preferred to leave the issue ill defined, because it left them with considerable freedom of action. President Eisenhower had opposed legislation that would have established a joint committee on intelligence to oversee both foreign espionage and domestic intelligence. Infrequent briefings by the Director of Central Intelligence to the Senate Armed Services Committee and other committees were never designed to exercise control, but only to receive the information the directors chose to give Congress.

For these reasons, the agency could make its own recommendations as to domestic and foreign activities, get presidential approval for them, and then continue the activities. Maintaining the concept of plausible deniability (as discussed in Chapter 13) had tended to insulate some of the presidents from many of the details. Nevertheless, Eisenhower, Kennedy, Johnson, and Nixon had all been well aware of the major CIA programs. Johnson had enthusiastically endorsed many of them, although Nixon had sought to supplement CIA domestic programs with groups such as the plumbers directed by White House staff.

When the journalistic exposés began in late 1974 and early 1975, the long-standing lack of congressional oversight over intelligence became newsworthy. The ill-defined overlap between domestic and foreign intelligence also suddenly emerged as a politically sensitive issue.

## Church and Pike Committees

In 1975, a Senate committee headed by Frank Church and a House committee chaired by Otis Pike both investigated the CIA, then directed by William Colby, and the broader intelligence community. They called Richard Helms to testify. Helms, who had served as DCI in the period 1966 to 1973, was asked about operations during the Johnson and Nixon years.

Richard Helms found the questions difficult. He was not always frank in answering, resenting what he believed was the committee hypocrisy in asking certain questions. In particular, it appeared that Senator Church sought to place the blame for many CIA clandestine operations that had not gone well, or whose nature was morally dubious, on the agency itself, rather than on the president. When he asked why there was no paper trail or documentation for certain actions, Helms knew that Church should have known that the president would only give an oral approval for many clandestine actions.

In particular, a number of failed efforts to assassinate Fidel Castro in 1962, apparently approved by presidents Kennedy and Eisenhower were portrayed during the hearings as if they were agency decisions. Again, plausible deniability, intended to protect the president, had come back to haunt the agency.

## Helms vs. Colby

William Colby became DCI #10 in 1973, and served through January 1976. Thus, while Helms was testifying about earlier CIA activities on his watch, Colby was the Director of Central Intelligence.

The style of the two men in dealing with Congress was quite different. Helms resented the tone of the questioning and his frustration with the committees showed. Colby, by contrast, had decided to cooperate with Congress from the beginning.

In fact, on the advice of Arthur Schlesinger Jr., Colby prepared a list of dozens of operations that could be construed as damaging to the CIA, a so-called family jewels list. As part of his confirmation hearings in 1973, during the Watergate scandals, he shared the jewels list with Congress. The document was nearly 700 pages long, detailing such issues as CIA contact with those involved in Watergate. It detailed Project Mudhen, the surveillance of journalist Jack Anderson. The list also included Project SRPointer, the surreptitious opening of Russian mail, and Project Merrimac, the monitoring of dissident personnel. Colby listed the assassination plots against Patrice Lumumba in the Congo, Rafael Trujillo in the Dominican Republic, and Fidel Castro in Cuba, and explained what the CIA had done in Chile to oppose the election of Salvador Allende.

*Senator Frank Church of Idaho led investigations into CIA operations, leading to the exposure of the "family jewels list."*

*(Courtesy of the Library of Congress)*

During the 1975 congressional investigations, the agency tended to divide between those who supported Colby's plan of being quite open with Congress and Helms's method of revealing the minimum. Colby protected a few secrets, such as the identity of specific individuals and some of the technical information, but he did not try to stonewall Congress on the nature of plans and activities. He believed the agency would be healthier if the question of what was legal and what was illegal were finally clarified. Helms, by contrast, was "the man who kept the secrets."

Internally, Colby conducted a housecleaning. Disturbed over the expense and resources spent in looking for moles, and convinced that J. J. Angleton had mistreated Nosenko, he obtained Angleton's resignation. (For details on Angleton's suspicions, see Chapter 14.)

For some in the Counterintelligence Staff of the CIA, Colby's methods of being upfront with Congress, revealing the family jewels, and getting the resignation of Angleton added to their discontent. In the paranoid atmosphere of mole hunting, some even accused Colby of being a Soviet plant! The mole hunting sounded very much like the problems confronting the British agency MI-5 and fictionalized by John Le Carre in the novel *Smiley's People*.

# The Case of Chile

One of the CIA operations revealed by Colby during the mid-1970s was the earlier effort under Helms to affect the outcome of the election in Chile. Helms had testified in open session in 1973, when being nominated to serve as ambassador to Iran, that the CIA had not sought to overthrow the Chilean government, that it had not given money to candidates opposed to Salvador Allende, and that it had not cooperated with International Telephone and Telegraph in either activity.

## Colby Contradicts

Although Helms had presented this information to a congressional committee, Colby provided a more forthcoming story before the House Foreign Affairs Committee. While the CIA had not tried to overthrow the Chilean government, it had tried to prevent Allende from becoming president in 1970. Although it did not give money to individual candidates, it did provide funds to Chilean political parties and organizations. Furthermore, the CIA had worked with International Telephone and Telegraph (ITT) to prevent Allende from becoming president. Thus, what Helms had said was certainly not the full story.

After Allende was elected in 1970, despite CIA activities to prevent the vote going in his favor, a group of Chilean army officers conducted a coup that resulted in the 1973 murder of Allende. The CIA was not involved in the coup, but its prior involvement in the election process, kept from Congress by Helms and revealed by Colby, further defined the break in style between the two.

When the two versions of the truth came out, President Ford announced that Helms would resign as ambassador to Iran in 1977. Helms had tried to protect the agency from the dangers that could come out of publicity, and by 1977 he was well aware that the CIA station chief in Athens, Greece, Richard Welch, had been assassinated because of publicity about his role.

### Tradecraft

Philip Agee, a former CIA officer who revealed many details of CIA activities in the book *Inside the Company: CIA Diary*, published an article in an anti-CIA magazine, *CounterSpy*, suggesting that such publicity would bring the CIA's secret activities to an end, urging the world's people "to decide what to do to rid themselves of the CIA." The same issue of the magazine gave the street address of the CIA station chief, Richard Welch. The *Athens News* reprinted Welch's address, and a month later, Welch was shot dead on his doorstep. Although Agee denied it, many in the agency believed that Agee's publicity and that of *CounterSpy* had directly led to the killing of Welch. Later, the public learned that Agee had been actively assisting the KGB with some of his revelations.

The operation in Chile had been conducted during the period 1958 to 1970, including the Nixon administration. In the general anti-Nixon atmosphere of the mid-1970s, Helms was seen as having participated in another Nixon coverup. The charges were not entirely fair. Helms explained why he had been less than forthcoming. He noted that it was extremely difficult to know which congressmen and congressional staffers could be trusted to keep information closely held.

Helms had not been open with Congress in public session because he believed that to do so would have exposed operations that should not be exposed. Even so, Helms was brought to trial on charges of giving misleading testimony before Congress, and he pleaded no contest or *nolo contendere* to the misdemeanor charges.

# Long-Term Consequences

As a result of the journalistic and congressional exposures, and as a result of Colby's change in style at the agency, several basic changes in America's intelligence agencies took place. Some of the changes were embodied in the 1974 Hughes-Ryan Amendment to the 1961 Foreign Assistance Act. The CIA could not engage in covert activities without first informing the appropriate congressional committee and providing a presidential finding.

The idea that the agency would operate covertly, even protected from congressional scrutiny and with a pretense of insulation from the president, was over. Henceforth, the agency would only take actions that were legal, and if Congress sought to find out about them, it would.

## No Assassinations

On February 18, 1976, President Gerald Ford, Nixon's successor, issued Executive Order 11905 that forbade any employee of the United States to engage in political assassination. This restriction applied to military forces in special operations as well as to employees of the intelligence agencies. As a further demonstration that he was distancing himself from the scandals of the past, President Ford dismissed Colby and appointed George H. W. Bush as Director of Central Intelligence.

## Techint and Firewall

Ford's successor, Jimmy Carter, inaugurated January 20, 1977, also sought to make it clear that he was not closely associated with the CIA and its capabilities. As a consequence, the agency profoundly changed between 1972, under Helms, and 1979, under Carter's appointee, Admiral Stansfield Turner. Before the changes of the 1970s, the agency had undertaken a wide range of covert actions, often leaving the full Congress uninformed and only getting verbal approval from the president. By 1979, the agency's independence of action was strictly limited.

The scandals surrounding the CIA's domestic surveillance operations had a further effect. Henceforth, the agency was scrupulous not to engage in following, checking, or investigating American citizens living in the United States, leaving such work to other agencies, principally the FBI. The "firewall" that already existed between the two agencies was now even firmer, with a clearer distinction between foreign and domestic responsibilities.

## The Least You Need to Know

- Although the CIA was not involved in either the Kennedy assassination nor in the Watergate burglary, both events contributed to public suspicion of the agency.

- Richard Helms, who had served as Director of Central Intelligence under both Lyndon Johnson and Richard Nixon, tried to protect the agency from exposure of information.

- William Colby, appointed as Director of Central Intelligence by Richard Nixon before his resignation, did much to reform the agency and to help bring the agency under closer congressional control.

- By Executive Order, the CIA and other government agencies were prohibited in 1975 from engaging in assassination.

- By the end of the 1970s, the agency shifted in the direction of more reliance on technical intelligence and stayed out of the area of domestic surveillance.

# Chapter 16

# American Techint

## In This Chapter

- ◆ Techint vs. Humint
- ◆ Satellite surveillance
- ◆ CIA, Navy, and Air Force
- ◆ Project Jennifer
- ◆ Submarines and secrets

By the 1980s, the United States increasingly relied on technical intelligence. Aerial surveillance could trace its history back to artillery spotting from Civil War balloons and to photographs taken from airplanes in World War I. American expertise in intercepting and breaking the codes of other nations derived in a direct line from the work of Herbert Yardley and William Friedman. Signals intelligence improved vastly with the improvement in computers, and reached into new areas, such as the capture of raw technical data from Soviet missile tests.

During the cold war, American technical innovation in the secret technologies of deep-water submergence, high-altitude flight, satellite imaging of the land, and computer cracking of codes all provided new tools. Technologies that developed in the 1950s and 1960s became major sources for intelligence by the late 1960s. For good reason, many of the specifics have never been released. The account in this chapter is derived from often-incomplete public reports and includes some details that have never been confirmed nor denied by official sources.

# Techint and Humint

Specialists in intelligence and espionage debate the virtues of human intelligence as compared to technical intelligence. Each has its strengths and weaknesses. A human spy can be turned to work as a double agent. He or she may decide to make up information in order to increase importance or to get better payments. The spy can be captured, tortured, or killed. If questioned, the spy can reveal knowledge about the home agency or network. By contrast, a camera or microphone, even when discovered, will teach the other side only that it has been spied upon. Although some false information can be transmitted by deceptive methods through technical sources, such efforts are quite limited. (See Chapter 5 for deceptions that helped convince the Germans that the D-Day invasion was headed for Calais, not Normandy.)

On the other hand, an image from a satellite or aircraft or a recording from a tapped telephone line lacks flexibility. The camera or tape recorder cannot ask questions or evaluate sources, cannot make friends or contacts, cannot identify and recruit supporters, or spread rumors. The agent on the ground who works in the local language can build networks, generate sources, and seek out special information and clarifications. No camera or signals intercept could have supplied the rich information provided by Oleg Penkovsky, and the reports from spies like Klaus Fuchs could never have been obtained by even the best-hidden microphones.

The limitations and virtues of each method of intelligence gathering are illustrated over and over throughout the history of espionage. Anecdotes from that history are often presented to support one or the other side of the continuing debate.

## Why America Shifted to Techint

The increasing reliance on technical intelligence by the United States in the late 1960s and later has been traced to several broad sets of causes. The shift was wise politically. Technical methods continued to improve, making the material produced richer and more reliable. The Soviets were more susceptible to technical penetration than human spying operations. Some have claimed that American reliance on technology reflects deep trends in the culture and history of the United States (see Chapter 18).

As noted in Chapter 15, some of the change in emphasis came at the instigation of the new DCI, Admiral Stansfield Turner, appointed by President Jimmy Carter in 1979. Perhaps in an effort to distance themselves from the scandals that had surrounded the CIA, Carter and Turner supported an approach that relied less on agency personnel and more on equipment. With members of Congress and the press blaming CIA agents and directors for a wide variety of moral lapses ranging from violations of the civil liberties of Americans to support for murder and assassination programs abroad, the amoral character of machines and mechanical systems was a welcome contrast.

As technology systems pushed into the two frontiers of outer space and the deep ocean, those systems could tap rich new sources of data. Technologies that had been promoted and advanced since the 1960s had made great progress, particularly satellite photography, satellite gathering of signals intelligence, and underwater recovery of equipment and information. By the 1970s, the equipment began to get so good it yielded much higher quality and volume of information than earlier efforts. The *product* was often so superior that high-level policymakers began to prefer it. President Jimmy Carter was particularly impressed by detailed photographs from satellites that could be put on his desk within hours of being taken.

**Spy Words**

Intelligence data comes from many sources, and after the data is analyzed, the result is known as **product**. Before product is shared outside an agency, it is usually sanitized so as to disguise its precise source.

Another factor explaining the U.S. shift to techint was the fact that the Soviet Union was extremely difficult to penetrate with human agents. The extensive internal security of the KGB, supported by the secret police agencies of the Eastern European satellite nations, had repeatedly foiled efforts to infiltrate agents behind the Iron Curtain.

For every defector who left the Soviet Union and who might supply good information, others came forward who claimed the first was a liar. The process of separating disinformation from truth and spotting the phonies among the genuine defectors was so complex that it tied Western agencies in knots for years. (See Chapter 14 for the problem of unraveling the truth surrounding the defector Yuri Nosenko.)

## Techint Vulnerability

Although American technical intelligence capability increased many-fold during the 1970s and 1980s, it had a serious vulnerability that became obvious. The Soviet Union continued to recruit human agents, shifting their tactics slightly to look for Americans who would sell secrets for cash, rather than those who would be attracted by communist ideology. As discussed in Chapter 17, just a handful of American traitors with knowledge of the new high technology systems, who decided to betray their country for money, provided detailed information about several of the technical systems. Some technical systems could only succeed as long as the other side knew nothing about them, requiring extreme measures of operational security. When breached or revealed to the Soviets, some systems could be emulated, foiled, or deceived.

In some cases, the Soviet Union was able to take protective measures or to adopt deceptive practices, and in a few cases, Soviet engineers were able to imitate American technical improvements. Some of the damage done by U.S. traitors is outlined in Chapter 17. The cold war battleground pitted the technical experts of the United States against the Soviet manipulators of human espionage.

## Spies in the Sky

Although many advances in U.S. espionage technology remained classified, over the years, the public learned of some of the systems from news stories, trials of American traitors like Christopher Boyce and John Walker (see Chapter 17), from congressional investigations, and from publicly released information. Some air and space experts outside the government published speculative articles in magazines that later turned out to include correct guesses about classified material. From such sources, journalists and others writing in open literature pieced together the story of progress.

**Spy Words**

Telemetry intelligence refers to information gathered from weapons test radio signals sent by a foreign power for their own purposes of monitoring the performance of a missile or other weapons system. From such information, it was possible for the United States to learn some of the characteristics of long-range Soviet missiles, such as range and accuracy.

The U-2 aircraft of the type flown by Gary Powers in 1960 (see Chapter 13), was supplanted by the improved *Blackbird* or SR71 that flew far faster and higher. The lower-flying and slower EC-135s and RC-135s were signals-gathering versions of the Boeing 707 that operated off the coast of the Soviet Union and China. Early photography satellites included Corona and the Samos series.

Air force and CIA imaging satellites were designated as *Keyhole* satellites, with *Keyhole* or KH numbers: such as KH-5, KH-6, KH-7, KH-8, KH-9, KH-ll, and KH-12. Satellites in the *Rhyolite* series gathered *telemetry intelligence*, primarily from Soviet missile tests, ferret satellites detected radar installations, and still other satellites gathered signals intelligence. In 1961, all CIA and Air Force aircraft satellite-imaging programs were consolidated in a new agency, the National Reconnaissance Office (NRO), whose existence was kept classified for several years.

Even while much of the technology remained classified, government sources regularly leaked, often intentionally, photographic and other satellite product during the 1970s and 1980s. From the leaks, the leaders of the Soviet Union soon realized that American intelligence agencies could track the number and location of all of their large weapons systems, such as surface ships, short- and long-range missiles, and aircraft. The leaks made it clear to Soviet leadership exactly how readily the United States could detect the production, development, and movement of Soviet military equipment. Any threatening move could be immediately identified. Furthermore, the leaks made it clear that if the Soviet Union agreed to arms limitation, the United States had an independent means of verifying compliance with the agreement.

| Techint |
| --- |

Glossary of some U.S. Satellite Terminology:

*Corona Satellites:* CIA, then NRO program 1961–1972

*Samos:* Satellite and Missile Observation System—Air Force satellites including weather satellites 1960

*Talent:* Aircraft-borne imaging: U-2 and SR71

*Keyhole:* After 1963, NRO imaging satellites

*Rhyolite:* Satellites for telemetry gathering

*7000 series:* Satellites for signals intelligence gathering

*Jumpseat:* A *ferret* satellite—to locate radar facilities

# Undersea: Spies in the Deep

With the development of nuclear-powered submarines in the mid-1950s, the United States possessed a powerful instrument in the quiet war of espionage. Nuclear-powered submarines were usually divided into two categories: attack submarines outfitted with torpedoes, with the mission of hunting down enemy submarines or surface ships; and after 1960, missile submarines carrying Submarine Launched Ballistic Missiles (SLBMs). In the 1960s, the SLBMs were the Polaris design, capable of being launched underwater. However, a third mission for a small number of nuclear submarines was that of gathering intelligence.

The U.S. Navy utilized submarines in numerous ways to gather information. During World War II, submarines were often used to transport infiltration agents who would row ashore at night from surfaced subs. In the early cold war in the 1940s and 1950s, a risky intelligence technique was to penetrate close to Soviet waters, come to periscope depth, and to visually and acoustically observe the coming and going of ships. A somewhat safer method was to cruise submerged along the course of Soviet submarines and ships, listening and recording the sounds they emitted.

American submariners developed a technique of tracking behind a Soviet submarine. The sounds given off by the U.S. submarine would be masked by the turbulence of the Soviet submarine's own underwater wake. Operation Holystone, the tracking of Soviet submarines, was revealed by *New York Times* journalist Seymour Hersh in 1975. By the 1980s, the location of nearly every Soviet submarine was known in this manner, and if a nuclear war had begun, most, if not all of the Soviet missile submarines would have been targeted for destruction in the first minutes of the war. Such close tracking involved its own risks, resulting in dozens of collisions between Soviet and American submarines. Many tense encounters held the potential for initiating an armed conflict.

Other capabilities remained classified, and some were not widely revealed to the public until the 1998 publication of *Blind Man's Bluff* by Sherry Sontag and Christopher Drew. Based on dozens of interviews with intelligence officers and submariners, the book brought to light a portion of the 50-year history of the silent intelligence war beneath the sea. Some of the stories presented in the book have never been officially confirmed, and some may have been fabricated or exaggerated for dramatic effect by the submariners the authors interviewed.

According to Sontag and Drew, deep-diving submarines carried cameras capable of spotting debris on the ocean floor, including wreckage from Soviet tests of long-range missiles over the open ocean as well as lost ships. In one case, a U.S. sub spotted a diesel-powered Golf II missile-carrying Soviet submarine that had gone down with all hands in the central Pacific Ocean. Several U.S. submarines carried small deep-submergence vehicles that allowed for retrieval of debris from the ocean floor. The greatest intelligence coup from submarine work alleged by Sontag and Drew was the ability to tap undersea telephone lines operated by the Soviet Union in at least two remote regions: the Sea of Okhotsk in the Soviet Far East, and the Berents Sea, northeast of Finland.

One undersea intelligence operation, that sprang from discoveries by the Navy and was then conducted by the CIA, accidentally became public in February 1975. Operation Jennifer was the code-name for the secret effort to recover the lost Soviet Golf II submarine from the ocean floor.

Criticized by agency opponents as a wasteful expenditure of money and as at least a partial failure, Operation Jennifer was exposed to the press just as the CIA was suffering from the public criticism from the investigations headed by Senator Church and Congressman Pike. Pike and his staff conducted a probing and critical investigation of Project Jennifer.

| Techint |
| --- |
| In the Sea of Okhotsk and in the Berents Sea, the Soviets ran telephone cables from one territorial shore to another, across the seabed under international waters. Assuming this to be the case, American submariners reputedly tracked down the underwater cables, traced them out to sea, and then planted special pods on the lines. The pods would pick up messages by electrical induction, not requiring any physical penetration of the cable itself. The pods contained long-running tape recorders, and the submarine would return after several weeks or months to pick up the tapes. Since the Soviet author ities assumed the cables were secure, they used direct voice communication and very low-level telegraphy codes, providing details of conditions, equipment, supply needs, logistics, and force strengths at these remote locations. |

# From U-2 to Corona to *Rhyolite*

Technical intelligence derived from the spies in the sky played a crucial role in several episodes in the early cold war. In the 1960s, when John F. Kennedy ran for president, he charged the Eisenhower administration with allowing a missile gap to develop. With the U-2 overflights suspended after the May 1, 1960 shootdown of Gary Powers (see Chapter 13), and before the *Corona* satellites were yielding information, there was indeed an information gap, but no missile gap.

Soon after Kennedy took office in January 1961, Corona imagery projected that the Soviet Union had at most five or six Intercontinental Ballistic Missiles (ICBMs), while the United States had some 200. That knowledge emboldened Kennedy to challenge Khrushchev in 1961 over the issue of Berlin, and to take a strong line during the Cuban missile crisis of 1962. Kennedy used photographs from U-2 overflights to estimate the exact nature of the missile installations in Cuba in 1962, and concluded that the Soviet troops on the island were unprepared to defend the island in case of a major invasion.

Like other intelligence data, the material gathered from satellites could be used to support either military confrontations or to provide tools for arms control verification. Whether the intelligence would be used for war or peace would depend on the decisions and policies of the president and his advisors.

## Some Satellite Product

Early KH satellites were programmed to drop buckets with film capsules by parachute over a stretch of the Pacific Ocean, where they were snatched from the air by specially outfitted aircraft trailing a cable and hook arrangement that would snag the parachute lines.

During the Nixon administration, KH satellites closely observed the Soviet missile test program. Tests of the long-range surface-to-surface (SS) missiles of the SS-16, SS-17, and SS-18 classes revealed key information. American observers learned that the SS-16 did not go beyond the development stage, that there were problems with the SS-17, and that the later SS-18 and SS-19 were successful. In fact, the 1974 inaugural shot of the SS-19 was watched in Washington, not only from satellites, but also by observers on U.S. Navy ships. At the same time, an American *Rhyolite* satellite picked up the unencoded telemetry data from the missile.

In 1976, the KH-9 series satellites noted that the Soviet Union had begun to modify missiles to make them capable of carrying multiple independently targeted reentry vehicles, or MIRVs. The precise number of ICBMs could be counted, the locations of the silos containing them could be spotted, and the national intelligence estimates of Soviet strength could be accurate, rather than approximate.

## Satellite Product from Carter Through Reagan

President Jimmy Carter used KH-derived intelligence to verify the number of missiles held by the Soviet Union, and as discussions began on the never-ratified second Strategic Arms Limitation Treaty (SALT-II), the information allowed Carter's negotiators to keep a check on the truthfulness of Soviet claims.

Carter used data from a KH-11 satellite to locate the Americans held hostage in the embassy in Teheran in April 1980. The information was provided to help plan the rescue mission that failed for reasons unconnected with the satellite information. In the early 1980s, many keyhole satellites were launched to gather information about trouble spots including Libya, Nicaragua, and Afghanistan.

A series of major accidental explosions at a Soviet missile installation in May 1984 were captured on KH-8 film. Regularly orbiting between 77 and 215 miles out in space, the KH-8 could be controlled from the ground to drop to an altitude as low as 69 miles, allowing resolution of pictures showing articles as small as 3 or 4 inches across. Detailed photos of the explosions at Severomorsk provided the Reagan administration with a complete inventory of what had been lost in the accident.

In April 1986, a KH-11 satellite provided detailed information used in the raid on Libya in Operation El Dorado Canyon and later provided photos used to assess the damage. One month later, the same KH-11 yielded pictures showing the damage to the Chernobyl nuclear reactor.

## Some Tech Specs: *Hexagon* and *Kennan*

The KH satellites were given code-names. The improved, KH-9, developed in 1968, was designated the *Hexagon* satellite. Unofficially, the KH-9 satellite was known as Big Bird. The KH-10 program was scrapped, and KH-11, known for a while as KH-X, became known as *Kennan*. Aerospace writers have described some of the assumed specifications for these satellites.

Although the first cameras for *Corona* satellites had been designed by the ITEK Company, owned by the Rockefeller interests, the Perkin-Elmer Company developed later cameras. The Big Bird camera was a Perkin-Elmer design, including a compact telescope of the Cassegrain design, a telescope that uses a primary and secondary mirror to fold the incoming light beams back on themselves. The original design, developed in the late seventeenth century, allowed astronomers to achieve the magnification of a long telescope in a short lens and mirror housing, making it suitable for the confined space of a twentieth-century satellite. Even so, the KH-9 was huge by 1960s and 1970s satellite standards, with the primary mirror about 6 feet in diameter.

In addition, Big Bird had an array of other sensors, including infrared. By remotely controlling the angle of the mirrors inside the satellite, operators based on the ground could direct the incoming beams to the appropriate sensor.

Over the period 1971 to 1977, the number of days per year of full satellite coverage of the Soviet Union increased. In 1971, satellites scanned the Soviet territory 158 days, and in 1976 coverage was 248 days. Full 365-day coverage began in 1977.

One of the problems with the KH-8 and KH-9 satellites was that they relied on dropping film in buckets by parachute. Once all the film had been used, the satellites were nearly useless. The KH-11 *Kennan* design improved on that. KH-11 used an electro-optical system with a charge-coupled device or CCD invented at Bell Laboratories in 1970. The CCD produced images that could be digitally converted to electronic signals that could be encrypted, sent to a ground station at Fort Belvoir, Virginia, decrypted, and resolved into pictures. At first the quality and resolution of the *Kennan* KH-11 images did not match that of the film-dropped system of the KH-9 and earlier designs, but later designs improved the quality.

In theory, the KH-11 CCD system allowed for real-time capture of information. However, the mass of information and the delays involved in photo-interpretation and in transmitting pertinent information to those with a need to know at first delayed delivery by hours or days.

## Photo-Interpretation

The mass of information flowing from the *Hexagon* and *Kennan* satellites was so vast that systems of sorting the information and determining what was important had to be developed. Some methods became well known. For example, the Soviet Union made a practice of setting up at least three perimeter fences around important military installations such as missile bases. Thus, in sorting through the volume of images, interpreters looked for concentric rings of fences, often finding that at the center of the rings there was something worth looking at.

Another well-known interpretative method was to look for roads that had broad curved corners when making a right-angle turn, rather than a sharp 90-degree angle. Missile transporter trucks could not turn sharply, but required the broad turn, and such roads often led directly to a missile silo. Techniques developed by interpretation of photos from the U-2 and SR-71, such as following railroad tracks to their destinations, and looking for signs of new construction, helped interpreters wade through the millions of images.

Although the degree of resolution of the various satellites remained classified, outside experts calculated that it would be possible to read a license plate or a newspaper headline from outer space. Objects or patterns of 3 or 4 inches could be readily spotted, such as the painted lines in a parking lot. According to the memoirs of some CIA officials, even the earliest Corona images from 1961 allowed interpreters to determine the makes of different cars parked in Red Square.

Because of this degree of accuracy or resolution, when the SALT-II treaty was negotiated, it included a provision that the missiles enumerated in the treaty could not be altered by more than 5 percent. The verification that the missiles would not be altered beyond that amount was left to national technical means, that is, to verification by satellite observation. The National Photographic Interpretation Center established by the CIA assured the State Department that any change, even to the small SS-11, beyond 5 percent could in fact be detected readily by satellite observation. Such a change would represent about 3 or 4 inches.

## Techint Product from Under the Sea

Nuclear submarines are ideal platforms for intelligence gathering, with their ability to operate undetected and silently beneath the sea. But a nuclear submarine equipped for attack or for missile launching needed to be modified to carry out special intelligence missions. According to Sontag and Drew, several submarines were modified especially for intelligence work, including *Halibut*, *Parche*, *Richard P. Russell*, *Sea Wolf*, and *Swordfish*. All of the crews took on risky assignments, and the crews of *Halibut*, *Parche*, and *Richard P. Russell* won the Presidential Unit Citation for their actions.

Among the dozens of daring missions and accomplishments of these submarines were the location of the lost Soviet Golf II submarine in 1968 by the crew of *Halibut*. *Parche* made seven trips to the Barents Sea, to gather recorded messages taped in underwater pods attached to Soviet phone cables.

| Techint |
| --- |
| *Sound Surveillance Systems* (SOSUS) were another form of intelligence gathering from beneath the sea. These devices, dropped to the ocean floor, could detect passing subs and ships, and as the data collected grew, each submarine could be identified by its characteristic sound patterns from motor noise, propeller wash, and acoustic flow noises. A string of SOSUS sensors was established across the gap between Greenland, Iceland, and the United Kingdom (known as the GIUK gap) through which Soviet submarines had to pass to enter the Atlantic Ocean. Other SOSUS nets at other choke points, and off the shores of the United States, helped track the voyages of the Soviet fleet, and to warn of approaches of vessels to the continental shelf of North America. |

# Project Jennifer

When President Richard Nixon was inaugurated, he was presented with the photographs that showed *Halibut* had located the sunken Golf II submarine in the Pacific. Over the next several years, the CIA worked to recover the Russian submarine through a newly created joint Navy-CIA office, the National Underwater Reconnaissance Office (NURO) that matched the NRO, the joint Air Force-Navy-CIA office for satellite intelligence. However, the Navy recognized that because of limitations on its own funding, the CIA would dominate NURO.

Many naval intelligence experts argued that it would be much easier to cut a hole in the outer skin of the sunken submarine and to extract any useful information, than it would be to try to raise the entire Russian sub. Ship structural experts explained that a submarine that had fallen below crush depth and had lain on the ocean floor for years would be too brittle to stand the stresses in raising it. Nevertheless, with the CIA directing the operation, the effort was made to recover the whole submarine.

Operation Jennifer, which eventually cost more than $500 million, was used to support the development of the ship *Glomar Explorer*. Rigged with a giant claw on a barge contained within the ship and nicknamed *Clementine*, the assemblage would be lowered several miles to the sea floor to try to pick up the submarine. After years of preparatory work, the effort was mounted in 1974, only to fail when one of the branches of the claw broke, with only a small section of the submarine retrieved.

Remains of six Russian submariners were found in the retrieved wreckage, and they were given a formal burial at sea, which was videotaped. Later, the video was provided to the Soviet Union. There was very little intelligence take or product, however. A waterlogged journal kept by one of the Soviet seamen was carefully treated and dried, and the CIA later claimed it yielded good information. No one in the intelligence community, however, thought the journal was worth $500 million. Critics charged that the information that would have been obtained even if the entire submarine had been recovered was so outdated that it was no longer useful.

## Jennifer Exposed

Although Seymour Hersh and other journalists got wind of the story, they knew few details and agreed to remain quiet about what they had learned. But the press began to piece together more accurate details. The story began to make headlines because it was too good to pass up.

On the one hand, the wasted money, lack of good intelligence product, excessive secrecy, and effort to suppress the news all added to the mid-1970s criticisms of the CIA. On the other hand, the daring magnitude of the effort and the technological feat of trying to raise a wreck from the ocean floor may have enhanced the admiration for technological innovation in intelligence work. Like the Berlin Tunnel more than 20 years earlier, Project Jennifer caught public attention as a fascinating case of techint.

## The Least You Need to Know

- While technical intelligence is more reliable than human intelligence, it has its limitations, including inflexibility and the need for extreme operational security.

- American satellite surveillance programs began in 1961 and continued to yield good intelligence, at first with parachute-dropped film capsules and later with near-real time images broadcast to Earth.

- One of the richest sources of information during the cold war came from the U.S. Navy's submarines.

- In the 1970s and 1980s, American satellites provided the national technical means for verifying Soviet compliance with arms control agreements.

- The volume of information gathered by technical methods tended to outrun the ability to analyze and make use of it.

# Walk-In American Traitors

- ◆ The changing meaning of treason
- ◆ Andrew Lee and Christopher Boyce
- ◆ A family of spies
- ◆ Spying for Israel

The motivations for Americans working in sensitive positions to betray their nation and turn over information to the Soviet Union or other foreign powers were quite different by the 1970s. In the 1930s and 1940s, the Soviet spy apparatus in the United States had built on pro-Soviet and pro-communist sympathies among many Americans. Some of the most important, like the Rosenbergs and Elizabeth Bentley, had been attracted by the communist ideology, although a few, like Congressman Samuel Dickstein, had seen an opportunity to make some easy money. However, the motivation for treason seemed to be shifting by the 1970s. In this chapter, we review the motives of several of the new generation of traitors and spies, some of the legal difficulties in the cases, and try to assess the damage.

## The *Newer* Meaning of Treason

In 1945, writer Jessica West published a bestseller, *The New Meaning of Treason*, in which she showed that a host of traitors had been captivated by communist or fascist ideology. She expanded her work in 1965 in a new edition. She examined British, Canadian, and American traitors who had given their loyalty either to Nazi Germany or to the Soviet Union. Some were amateurs, and others professionals. Their motives were ideological, psychological, and wrapped up in their strange personalities. Some had been blackmailed, but most she described had become caught up in the attractions of ideology and had escaped being caught in the act or prevented from stealing and passing on secret information through lax operational security.

But by the 1970s, the package of motives that led to espionage by Americans against their nation seemed to have changed again. There was a *newer* meaning of treason. Most of the important later spies saw espionage as a business opportunity, and frankly decided to sell what they knew in an attempt to grow rich. As Jessica West might have put it, their ideology was "self-help."

Some spies were enticed by methods that the KGB knew well—sex and romance, the lure of adventure, blackmail, personal disappointment in life, or disillusionment with American ideals. However, the deeper one examines the personalities of these traitors, the more conflicts and complexities show up. Their defenders tried to depict these people as victims of personal misfortune or social factors, but like other criminals, the crimes they committed were nobody's fault but their own.

## The Justice Dilemma

Holding a fair trial under the American system of justice and at the same time protecting national security had proven difficult in the Rosenberg case (see Chapter 8). In the Alger Hiss case, the FBI and NSA did not want to give details of the Venona code-breaking that might have helped convict him of perjury (see Chapter 10). In other cases, the American government had assets inside the Soviet Union that helped point to the American traitor, but to bring forward the evidence supplied by the American agent or informant in the Soviet Union would put that source at risk. The same sorts of dilemmas recurred over and over in later cases.

The trials of some of the traitors were made more difficult by the fact that the government did not want to disclose the exact nature of what the spy had taken. In some of the cases, it was not clear exactly how much had been passed to the foreign agencies, and by listing significant losses the government would only be revealing what was most important. If the prosecution in a trial opened a topic, the defense would have a right to explore it and that could lead to further revelations. Some of the spies, when caught, even refused to confess in front of FBI agents, because the agents were not cleared to know certain CIA information!

## Limits to What We Know

In many of the cases, therefore, what the public learned and what has appeared in print so far, is only the tip of the iceberg. But even so, that part of the story reveals that ideology no longer had much appeal to traitors in the 1970s and later. While some of the newer generation of traitors reflected the psychological turmoil or arrogant disregard for national interest described by Jessica West in the spies of the earlier era, the most important of them appeared to be just in it for the cash. They chose to ignore the fact that their actions could lead to the death of American servicemen and put others at risk.

## Damage Assessment

The walk-in traitors of the 1970s and 1980s provided access to some of the most closely guarded techint secrets of the era, including details of the satellite and submarine technologies described in Chapter 16. However, exactly what information was transmitted was sometimes difficult to determine, even after the spies were caught. The final damage assessments themselves were usually classified, and the public can only get a rough idea of the harm done, based on guesswork by journalists and outside commentators.

# The Falcon and the Snowman

Two young men from the wealthy Los Angeles suburb of Palos Verdes were the most notorious of the traitors of the mid-1970s. Christopher Boyce and Andrew Daulton Lee knew each other from grammar school days. Boyce had taken up the hobby of falconry (and hence his eventual unofficial code name "Falcon") and Lee became a dealer in drugs, including cocaine (hence, "Snowman"). After dropping out of college, Boyce got a job at the defense-contractor TRW, through a contact of his father, a retired FBI agent.

At TRW, Boyce worked in the "Black Vault," a room locked with a combination lock, where he handled secret communications dealing with TRW projects for the CIA. His correspondence included details of the *Rhyolite* satellite and the planned follow-on system, Argus. He monitored communications between the CIA and the Australian satellite receiving station, and sometimes by accident ran across numerous CIA communications that dealt with matters unrelated to TRW systems. Once, while getting high with Lee, he mentioned that he had information that the Russians would be glad to know about, indicating CIA involvement in Australian politics and labor unions.

# The Mexican Connection

Lee jumped at the opportunity, and took a batch of photocopies provided by Boyce to the Mexico City embassy of the Soviet Union in April 1975. He was literally a "walk-in," much to the horror of the KGB station chief there, who knew the embassy was constantly watched by American and Mexican agents. The materials were valuable, however, and soon the KGB arranged for Lee to make further contacts in Mexico City, using more clandestine means. Learning characteristic KGB tradecraft, Lee would mark utility poles with taped crosses to signal a meeting at prearranged contact points, including a nightclub and a pizza parlor in Mexico City.

Over the next year, Lee made a total of seven delivery trips to Mexico City and in March 1976, a trip to Vienna, where he received some further training in espionage basics from Soviet instructors. Despite instructions to the contrary, Lee always stayed at expensive hotels and flaunted the money he made from the sale of secret material, using it to purchase drugs and to impress his girlfriends and others.

In October 1976, Boyce joined Lee on a trip to Mexico City, where the KGB made him an offer that would involve his return to college to study political science. Apparently the KGB hoped that Boyce, in a career like those of the recruits in Cambridge about 40 years earlier, would become a mole in the American State Department or CIA.

# Caught in the Act

On January 6, 1977, Lee attempted to contact the KGB in Mexico City. Impatient because he sought funds to make a major drug purchase, Lee grew frustrated when his lamppost signals were ignored. Although he had been warned to stay away from the Soviet embassy, he approached it directly, emboldened after smoking a joint. When the guards would not admit him, he wrote the letters "KGB" on the inside cover of a small Spanish-English dictionary he was carrying and threw it over the embassy wall. One amazing aspect of the Lee and Boyce treason was how anyone so spaced-out and careless could have gotten away with acting as an espionage courier for nearly two years.

After he tossed the book, Mexican police, who were guarding the embassy against demonstrators, spotted Lee, and he was immediately detained. At first the police thought he might have been throwing a bomb. When he tried to get rid of a small stash of marijuana he was carrying, it made matters worse. He was also carrying an envelope full of photographed Top Secret documents from TRW, describing Pyramider, a proposed satellite system. After several days of rough questioning by

Mexican police, he cooked up a story that he was working for the CIA to provide disinformation to the KGB.

The Mexican authorities turned him over to the Americans, and he was arrested. As his story unraveled, the FBI arrested Lee and then Boyce, charging both with espionage.

## The Boyce and Lee Trials

In 1977, Boyce and Lee were tried separately. During and after the trials, the writer Robert Lindsey interviewed both of the young traitors and then wrote the best-selling account, *The Falcon and the Snowman*, later made into a movie. During the trials, each concocted a story intended to incriminate the other and to put their own actions in a better light. Boyce claimed that he had provided one set of documents to Lee, and that Lee had later blackmailed him into providing more. Boyce also claimed that most of the material he sent via Lee to the KGB was outdated or superceded information. A key charge against Boyce was that he had transmitted Top Secret TRW proposals for Pyramider, a planned satellite that would be used for secure CIA communication. The technical proposal had not been accepted, and thus, he claimed Pyramider was over-classified.

The judge and jury did not buy any of the defense arguments in the Boyce case, and he was convicted and sentenced to 40 years in prison.

At his separate trial, Lee claimed that Boyce had insisted that the photocopies were disinformation materials, prepared by the CIA to confuse the KGB. His claim, regarded as simply a fabrication by the judge, was that he was convinced he was working indirectly for the CIA, through Boyce. Outstanding warrants for Lee's arrest on drug charges, and numerous statements by Lee when he bragged to friends about his deals with the Russians, worked against him. One of the jurors later claimed she had argued for reasonable doubt, but in the end, Lee was convicted. He was sentenced to life in prison.

Three years later, Boyce escaped from prison, evading capture for more than a year and getting funds by robbing banks at gunpoint. He learned how to fly, apparently planning to fly a small plane from Alaska to the Soviet Union. His escape and capture provided the material for a sequel to Lindsey's first book, entitled *The Flight of the Falcon*.

## Motives: Cash and Disillusionment

The two cases drew lots of public interest and raised many questions. Lax security at both the CIA and at TRW had created an opportunity. The placing of a low-paid college dropout in the Black Vault was an obvious mistake. But many wondered how the two young men, often drunk or stoned, could have carried off the espionage. Boyce and Lee were two of the most important of a much larger group of the *Merchants of Treason.*

---

### Spy Bios

In 1988, the military historians Thomas B. Allen and Norman Polmar published *Merchants of Treason*. They gave details on the U.S. traitors who sold out their country in the 1980s. A partial list:

Marine Sergeant Clayton Lonetree. Gave KGB access to the U.S. embassy in Moscow, 1984-1986. Court-martialed, sentenced to 33 years.

James Durwood Harper. Provided high-technology information to Polish intelligence. Plea-bargained and sentenced to life in prison.

Ronald W. Pelton. Communication specialist at the National Security Agency. Sold interception secrets for more than five years. Sentence: three consecutive life terms.

Brian Horton. Attempted to sell Navy fleet intelligence information to Soviets. After court-martial, given a six-year sentence, later reduced to three years.

Jeffery Pickering. In June 1983, sent secret document to the Soviet embassy, while absent without leave from the Marines. Sentenced to 18 months.

Altogether, Allen and Polmar identified more than 60 Americans who had been caught after attempting to defect or sell classified information to the Soviet bloc between 1953 and 1987.

---

Lee bragged about the money he made from the sale of material, but Boyce's motives appeared more confused than simply making some fast dollars. He may have started copying documents out of a kind of disillusionment in the U.S. government brought on by the Vietnam War, the CIA-Allende scandals, and Watergate. But as Robert Lindsey pointed out, millions of other young people at the time experienced similar disillusionment without turning to treason, and Boyce did not represent a broader trend of ideologically committed agents. Boyce claimed he could see little difference between the KGB and the CIA, and he had no loyalty to the communist cause. Both Lee and Boyce freely spent the funds they received, and Lee had plans to use a big score from espionage to build up to a wholesale drug purchase level.

## Damage

Although it was true that the Pyramider plan had not been implemented, until that time, the CIA had not admitted that the KH satellites in the *Rhyolite* program were used for surveillance of the Soviet Union. Furthermore, information released at the trial damaged U.S.-Australian relations. For months, the Australian press investigated the charges that the CIA had been engaged in Australian party politics and labor affairs, and continued to investigate the use of satellite listening stations for espionage purposes.

Even though such public exposure was embarrassing to the CIA, it was difficult for the public to know exactly how much the Soviets had learned from Lee's photocopies. One apparent consequence was that after 1977, the Soviet Union began to encrypt the telemetry messages from their test missiles, rather than sending the data unencoded. Some writers speculated that Soviet protective measures taken after the Boyce-Lee espionage made it more difficult to rely on national technical means for arms control verification.

# Walker and the Spy Family

While Boyce and Lee were selling secrets about the satellite programs, a petty officer in the U.S. Navy, John Walker, sold vital information on naval codes, ship movements, and war planning to the KGB. He recruited a close friend, his brother, and his own son into the business. For 17 years, between 1967 and 1985, he built up the transmission of secret information into his main source of income. Assessments of what he stole by both the KGB and the U.S. Navy suggest that the so-called Walker Family Ring was the most serious penetration of American military secrets since the atomic espionage of the 1940s.

## Walker's Crimes

John Walker served in the U.S. Navy as a warrant officer and supported his wife and four children on a meager salary. Ambitious to make more money, he had opened a bar near Charleston, South Carolina. Troubled by debts and increasing estrangement from his wife, he decided to supplement his income. In December 1967, he walked into the Soviet embassy in Washington, carrying the current monthly key list for decoding one type of code machine. He had photographed the document while working in the communications vault in Norfolk, Virginia. Like the Enigma machines of the 1940s, the KL-47 machine operated with changed rotor settings. With one of the machines or an operating manual, and with a monthly supply of the settings, it would be possible to read Top Secret messages.

Walker demanded a salary for regular deliveries of secret information. The Soviets agreed, and provided instructions to Walker on how to make deliveries and pick up cash payments at dead drops in the Washington area. At his next meeting, Walker provided the key list to a more advanced KW-7 machine.

---

### Techint

On January 23, 1968, shortly after John Walker's first delivery of material to the Soviet embassy, the USS *Pueblo*, a Navy communications vessel, was captured off the coast of North Korea. The crew of the *Pueblo* were held prisoner for more than a year, and tortured for information. Later observers suspected that the ship was captured because the Soviets wanted to acquire cryptographic equipment to couple it with the key lists provided by Walker. In fact, a KW-7 machine was taken from the ship before it could be destroyed. The National Security Agency was aware the machine had been captured and probably given to the Russians. But since KW-7's were so widely used, the decision was made to simply modify the machine and to rely on new monthly key lists with new settings to maintain security.

---

Walker began to regularly provide not only key lists but also the wiring diagrams and technical modification specs for the KW-7. After the North Korean capture of the *Pueblo*, the Soviet Union had access to a KW-7 encryption machine. As a consequence of the ship capture and the material provided by Walker, over the next 16 years, the Soviet Union had the tools to decrypt an estimated one million Top Secret naval communications, ranging over the whole gamut of information about submarine tracking and SOSUS locations and strategic documents such as war plans, as well as day to day plans of naval operations off Vietnam.

*The KW-7 encryption machine, shown here in closed position, used cards to set up the ciphers. John Walker began revealing key lists to the Soviets in 1967.*

*(Courtesy of Jerry Proc Crypto Machine Photo Collection)*

Walker frankly put the spying operation on a business basis. He earned $725 a month as a warrant officer and the KGB paid him another $4,000 a month for documents, in cash. He moved to a new apartment, bought new furniture, and explained to his Navy friends that his bar business was prospering. They believed him. His wife knew better, but after Walker planted a syringe in the house, she assumed for a while that he was dealing in drugs.

## A Family Affair

Walker's decision to involve others in his espionage began almost accidentally. His wife discovered a metal box in which he had left $2,000 in cash and some details of a dead drop for exchange of documents. When she questioned him about it, he told her he was spying.

| Techint |
|---|
| Through the 1970s and 1980s, the KGB continued to use the same tradecraft methods for leaving signals and arranging dead drops that they had found worked decades before. Both John Walker and Andrew Daulton Lee were instructed to mark certain utility poles when they wanted to make contact. In Walker's case, he then was to leave photographed materials in a bag of trash at a prearranged dead drop spot in the country, identified with a soda can. His cash payment would be at a second dead drop spot, also identified with a soda can, also in a bag of trash. The spots picked were country roads not far out of Washington, D.C. Apparently the KGB counted on Americans to keep littering. |

Barbara Walker wanted to help, she said, and John Walker thought that if she became an accomplice, it might protect him from the risk she might betray him. So he took her on one of his deliveries, following his system of looking for empty soft-drink cans that were used to identify the dead drop spots along rural roads in Maryland.

However, the Walker marriage was terrible. Walker had numerous affairs, spent lots of his money on girlfriends, and made it clear to his wife that he could not stand being with her. Dependent on him, lacking enough self-confidence to leave, she became an alcoholic. The family was clearly dysfunctional, with incidents in which she tried to shoot him, he beat her, she abused the children, and the children took drugs.

Walker was transferred from his job at Norfolk to a less sensitive position in San Diego, and he began to consider how he might bring in others to supply information to the Soviets. He requested sea duty, and in 1971, was assigned as documents officer aboard the Navy supply ship *Niagara Falls*, off Vietnam. Soon he recruited a friend, Jerry Whitworth, his own older brother Arthur Walker, and his son, Michael Walker.

Although the quality of information each provided varied, Walker continued supplying the KGB with cryptographic material from these sources until 1985.

## Walker Caught

In the spring of 1985, Barbara Walker told the FBI of her estranged husband's activities. John Walker had tried to recruit one of his daughters to spy, and when questioned by the FBI, she confirmed what her mother had told them. After testing Barbara with a polygraph lie detector, the FBI obtained permission to tap John Walker's phone. Soon, evidence of his espionage began to mount. However, Walker had retired from the Navy, operated a small private detective business, and had learned a great deal about wiretapping and bugs. The FBI feared he would find out he was being monitored or that his ex-wife would tell him that she had tipped off the authorities. Furthermore, it was difficult to question the others in the ring, because the FBI feared that word would get back to Walker and he would flee before they could collect enough information to arrest him.

Eventually, the FBI decided that the only way to get enough evidence on Walker was to actually follow him to a dead drop and collect evidence of his delivery of information and retrieval of cash. The FBI had never used that method to get evidence or to arrest an espionage suspect, but it seemed the only way to catch Walker and expose his family ring of spies. Following Walker to his dead drop spot near Poolesville, Maryland, was difficult, but the FBI discovered his dropped delivery of documents that included a long note he had written to his KGB handler about future deliveries. Inadvertently, the FBI removed one of the signal soda cans, obviously tipping off the KGB contact from the Soviet embassy, who quickly left the country. With the evidence in hand, the FBI arrested Walker at a motel in Rockville, Maryland.

One by one, Whitworth, Arthur Walker, and Michael Walker were arrested. They were all tried and convicted. John Walker was sentenced to life in prison; Jerry Whitworth was sentenced to 365 years in prison and a $410,000 fine. Arthur Walker was sentenced to life in prison and a $250,000 fine. Michael was sentenced to two 25-year terms and three 10-year terms. He would be eligible for parole in 1993.

At the sentencing hearing, the judge in John Walker's case said, "One is seized with an overwhelming feeling of revulsion that a human being could ever be as unprincipled as you." The feeling was widely shared.

## Damage Assessment

Although the direct impact of Walker's espionage on the Vietnam War was difficult to assess, a later defector from the Soviet Union, Vitaly Yurchenko, told the FBI that the Walker spy ring had been the most important KGB operation in its history. He confirmed that the Soviets had used the Walker information to decipher more than a million messages.

By the mid-1980s, the Soviets began to improve the design of their newest class of submarines to make them more silent and less easily tracked. Some analysts believed that the redesign sprang from what the KGB learned from the Walker ring.

# Jonathan Pollard

In November 1985, Jonathan Jay Pollard was arrested; combined with the arrests of the Walker family of spies and some of the lesser cases, his arrest helped make 1985 "the year of the spy." As with Christopher Boyce and John Walker, the issue of what motivated Pollard became the center of public fascination and continuing controversy.

Pollard was the son of a prominent professor of microbiology, and as a child had accompanied his parents on academic trips to Europe and Japan. Despite a childhood that most would regard as highly privileged, Pollard later claimed that experiences of harassment as a Jew living in a largely non-Jewish community shaped his childhood and teenage years. After graduating from Stanford and taking a two-year course in international affairs at Tufts, Pollard joined the U.S. Naval Intelligence Service as a civilian analyst.

Shortly after beginning work there, he made several efforts to contact Israeli intelligence, and succeeded in 1984. In that year he was assigned by the U.S. Navy to work for the Anti-Terrorist Alert Center, an office within the Naval Investigative Service's Threat Analysis Division. For more than a year he transmitted classified information to a contact with the Israeli Office of Scientific Liaison (LAKAM) in the Defense Ministry. A separate office from Mossad, the main Israeli intelligence unit, and apparently somewhat competitive with Mossad, LAKAM was willing and eager to receive the information, particularly as it dealt with Israel's potential enemies in the Middle East. Pollard's first contact, Aviem Sella, put Pollard in touch with the head of LAKAM, Rafael Eitan.

Israel specifically used information provided by Pollard to conduct a raid on October 1, 1985, on Palestine Liberation Organization headquarters in Tunisia, in retaliation for a terrorist murder of three Israeli tourists vacationing in Cyprus.

## How Pollard Got Caught

Pollard made a practice of ordering documents from a variety of intelligence agencies, taking them home on weekends to copy them. It was against the law to take such documents home, and his supervisor, increasingly suspicious of Pollard's erratic behavior and comments, eventually noted the pattern. He discovered that Pollard routinely checked out documents dealing with Soviet weapons systems and Arab military capabilities, even though his assigned area of research was the Caribbean. He had no "need to know."

When confronted, Pollard at first denied he was spying. During several days of questioning, his wife made contact with his Israeli handlers, who then quickly left the United States. Pollard and his wife were convinced the Israelis would arrange an escape plan for them as well, but no such plan existed.

On November 21, three days after his interrogation began, Pollard had still not been arrested. He drove to the Israeli embassy, assuming he would be given sanctuary. Instead he was turned away and immediately arrested by the FBI.

## Two Possible Motives

Although Pollard agreed with authorities not to reveal anything further while in prison, he invited the journalist Wolf Blitzer to interview him in jail. Blitzer, at that time the Washington correspondent for the *Jerusalem Post*, jumped at the opportunity. Blitzer drew heavily on the tape recorded interviews in news stories and in a later account of the case published as *Territory of Lies—The Exclusive Story of Jonathan Jay Pollard: The American Who Spied on His Country for Israel and How He Was Betrayed*. Israel's lack of support for Pollard when he sought sanctuary accounts for the suggestion in the title that Pollard was "betrayed."

Blitzer relayed in great detail Pollard's account of his motives. According to Pollard's own view, he had felt intense loyalty to Israel from an early age and was dismayed when he discovered that the United States did not fully share its intelligence information with Israel. LAKAM paid Pollard a flat $2,500 a month for his materials, and provided generous subsidies, as much as $10,000, to cover expenses. Blitzer discounted other interpretations of Pollard's actions put forward by other journalists, including assertions that Pollard wanted payments to support his drug habit or that he was psychologically disturbed. Despite the fact that Pollard collected detailed information on U.S. cryptography, and Top Secret material on Soviet weaponry and provided it to the Israelis, he denied that he had ever spied *on* the United States.

Pollard used his clearance to visit other intelligence agencies in the Washington area and to obtain information on order for the Israelis. Of course, revealing the information not only violated the law and his oath, but it revealed details about how American intelligence services gathered information. The distinction Pollard made between spying "on" America and "in" America did not impress his judge.

Anne Pollard pled guilty to the charge of conspiracy to receive embezzled government property. The fact that Pollard had conducted interviews with Blitzer without first disclosing to authorities the content of the interview was a violation of his plea agreement, and that violation came up at his sentencing hearing. Anne Pollard was sentenced to five years in prison. Jay Pollard confessed to the crime of conspiracy to commit espionage and was sentenced to life in prison.

## Aftermath

On the surface, the case made little sense. Why had Israel, a country on friendly terms with the United States, and with many official channels for information, risked the relationship by spying? American officials claimed that covert operations against the United States were entirely unnecessary, since Israel could get almost all the information it wanted simply by asking. Later, American security claimed that the breach of security was severe, but the details of exactly what Pollard had smuggled out were not made public.

The Israeli government, in an effort at damage control, claimed that LAKAM was a "rogue" intelligence activity, unauthorized. According to Pollard's own description of his activities, that seemed unlikely. U.S. intelligence officials continued to worry that information sold by Pollard to Israel could leak in one way or another to other intelligence agencies, either through Soviet spies inside Israel, or by Israel simply trading the information for other information they desired.

In Israel and the United States, the case caused a sensation. Within a decade, democratic President Bill Clinton was deluged with petitions asking that he pardon Pollard, but the petitions were denied. In Israel, the Labor Party supported American efforts to investigate the espionage, while Likud Party members argued for stonewalling the investigation, leading to a continuing controversy there regarding the case.

## The Least You Need to Know

◆ Christopher Boyce and Andrew Daulton Lee spied for the Soviet Union, providing secret techint information from CIA contractor TRW in 1975 and 1976.

◆ John Walker set up a spy ring involving his family and spied on the U.S. Navy for the Soviet Union from 1968 to 1985.

◆ Jonathan (Jay) Pollard spied for Israel, using his position in the Naval Investigative Service to provide a large volume of material from different U.S. agencies on order to his Israeli handlers from 1983 to 1985.

- Each of these traitors seriously damaged U.S. security, each did it for cash payments, and each received a life sentence in prison for his crimes.

- The KGB readily adjusted to the walk-ins and to the new crop of traitors who betrayed their country for money rather than ideology.

# Part **5**

## Retrospects and Prospects

With the end of the Cold War, the story of Soviet espionage against the West was revealed in decoded Venona documents and in the memoirs and notes of former Russian spies. But spying was not dead. In the 1990s, the American defense establishment needed information to ensure that the Russians were keeping up their part of the arms control agreements getting rid of nuclear weapons, and then for the Persian Gulf War. And it turned out, two of the most highly placed spies for Russia were still at work: Aldrich Ames and Robert Hanssen.

Then in 2001 and 2002, the United States faced new challenges. When Islamist terrorists attacked the United States and when intelligence showed Iraq was still making weapons of mass destruction, new kinds of spy work were demanded. The lessons of the twentieth century would apply in the twenty-first, but the intelligence community faced some rapid adjustment.

# Chapter 18

# Cultural Styles and Espionage Motives

## In This Chapter

- ◆ British, American, and Soviet cases compared
- ◆ Soviet tradecraft and American technology
- ◆ Professionals and amateurs
- ◆ Implementing open skies

In this chapter, we look over the espionage of the cold war era to see what patterns can be identified. Over and over, it seems, counterintelligence efforts failed, often for similar reasons. In the United States and Britain, the agencies charged with tracking down spies had a difficult time learning from history or applying the lessons learned to later cases. We can also identify some national traits of character that help explain the successes and failures of British, American, and Soviet espionage operations.

Despite the cultural differences between the three countries, intelligence agencies in all three showed some of the same characteristics. All had problems with operational security, and all the agencies seemed unwilling to cooperate with their sister agencies in the same country.

When the Russians and Americans signed the arms control treaties that ended the cold war, they agreed to a new kind of open exchange of information to verify compliance with the treaties. We take a look at the methods of gathering intelligence spawned by the treaties.

# The Cold War As Spy War

From the 1930s through the 1980s, the major powers of the world maintained active espionage agencies, both in wartime and peacetime. The cold war is usually dated from 1947 to 1988, in which the nations of the Warsaw Pact or Warsaw Treaty Organization (*WTO*) lined up against the countries of the North Atlantic Treaty Organization (*NATO*).

**Spy Words**

NATO and **WTO** made up the two "sides" in the cold war.

In 1949, the United States formalized its alliance with the countries of Western Europe by setting up the North Atlantic Treaty Organization. Under the treaty, each country would treat an attack on any other member as an attack on itself. Original NATO countries included Belgium, Canada, Denmark, France, Greece, Iceland, Italy, Luxembourg, Netherlands, Norway, Portugal, Turkey, United Kingdom, and the United States. In 1955, the Federal Republic of Germany (West Germany) joined. Spain joined in 1982.

Responding to the inclusion of West Germany in NATO in 1955, the Soviet Union formed the Warsaw Treaty Organization (WTO), usually called the *Warsaw Pact*. Joining the Soviet Union in the original WTO were Albania, Bulgaria, Czechoslovakia, German Democratic Republic (East Germany), Hungary, Poland, and Romania. In 1968, Albania withdrew. The WTO disbanded in 1991.

The nature of the cold war led to a rapid expansion of intelligence, creating secret armies that tried to penetrate each others' barriers. There is a reason why the decades of the cold war produced such a proliferation of agencies, agents, spies, traitors, and intelligence collection, unparalleled in any period of peace in history.

The reason has to do with the nature of the cold war itself. While the two alliances, led by the United States and the Soviet Union, faced each other with hostility, both sides sought to avoid direct war, especially after 1949 when each side was armed with nuclear weapons. Yet each side treated the other much as armed belligerent states had faced each other during short lulls in past wars: each sought to learn the strengths and weaknesses of the other, *just as they would have in a period of armed conflict*. And each tried to protect that information from disclosure to the other. The Soviet Union's intelligence establishment officially called the United States the "main adversary" by the early 1980s.

In the United States, knowledge of the Soviet adversary was essential to military budgeting, planning, and organization, and to diplomatic relations with countries inside and outside the two alliances. Although not fought army to army, the cold war was fought by aircraft incursions into airspace, submarines that sometimes pushed into territorial waters, with hundreds of spies illegally operating on each other's territory, and with surrogate armies that clashed in guerrilla actions, rebellions and civil wars in Latin America, Africa, and Asia.

## From Spy Novel to Spy Spoof

Western pop culture soon reflected the fact that espionage dominated the relations between the two superpowers and their allies. Spy novels authored by Eric Ambler, Graham Greene, and John Le Carre were soon followed by lighter-hearted, tongue-in-cheek works by Ian Fleming and others. Fleming, who had worked in British intelligence, drew a few ideas from his own experience, but then took James Bond into a fantasy world of beautiful women, narrow escapes, and adventures that saved the world from a wide variety of villains, some from the Soviet Union.

Other writers and film producers made spoofs of the spoofs. Mel Brooks created Maxwell Smart (Agent 86) of *Get Smart* who would only refer to his wife by her code-number "99." The television show ran for five seasons (1965–1970) but lived on in reruns for decades. The series of five *Pink Panther* movies, starring Peter Sellers, made the incompetent Inspector Jacques Clouseau a household word around the world. The taste for comedy based on reducing espionage to a parody survived into the twenty-first century, with *Austin Powers*, who turned the Bond character into a joke on a joke.

No doubt it helped a bit to laugh at the business that was deadly serious. Although after Hiroshima and Nagasaki, the new weaponry remained unused in the twentieth century, espionage by the superpowers represented a constant war that kept millions of civilians at risk. So when Agent 86 made a phone call on his shoe or Peter Sellers bumbled his way out of an international crisis, the world's population could thank the comedians for letting us lighten up a little.

## Spies in Peace and War

Although espionage is an ancient art, in past centuries it had been mostly practiced in time of war, or in periods immediately preceding war. Thus, early American spies of the period of the American Revolution and the Civil War are remembered, but there are only few stories of American intelligence operations in the long half-century from the American Civil War (1861–1865) until the United States entered World War I in 1917.

When the Comintern, directed from Moscow, began to use Communist Party members and others who were sympathetic to their cause as spies in the 1920s and 1930s, American and British counterintelligence operations were slow to respond. Amateur spy-hunters and enthusiastic officials in Army G-2 and the FBI made little headway against the Soviet professionals and the volunteers they recruited. MI-5, charged with internal security in Britain, also seemed incapable of dealing with the new breed of well-trained spies coming out of Moscow and with the sons of the ruling class they recruited to help them.

# Culture and Espionage

Historians and other analysts who have examined the history of spying in the twentieth century identify some deep-seated patterns in the cultures of Britain, the United States, and the Soviet Union that help explain why the Soviets were able to produce so much valuable intelligence but were unable to make good use of it. Soviet agents including Richard Sorge (Chapter 7), Klaus Fuchs and the other atomic spies in the United States (Chapter 8), the Cambridge Five (Chapter 9), and the spy rings in the U.S. government in the 1940s (Chapter 10) transmitted a rich body of information. But when that information did not fit into the preconceptions of Soviet leadership, it was often ignored or rejected.

British respect for privacy and trust in personal connections were both strengths and weaknesses in British espionage and counterespionage. America's open society and protection of individual civil liberties made the country easy to penetrate for foreign agents.

The Soviet system, which treated the individual as a component in the larger machinery of society and subject to manipulation and control, had its strengths and weaknesses in the realm of intelligence. For Soviet citizens like Igor Gouzenko (Chapter 7) and Oleg Penkovsky (Chapter 14), who got a taste of Western freedoms, the oppression they felt in the Soviet system gave them good reason to defect. But for others, the detailed control of daily actions could lead to excellent tradecraft, so that every move of a courier or an agent was practiced and rehearsed to avoid detection. Rigid and careful following of the rules of op-sec and compartmentation tended to work, and an agent who stuck with the precepts of his training could do fairly well. Of course, if the political winds changed in Moscow, as they often did, a spy who had succeeded in Canada, the United States, or Britain, might return home only to be thrown in prison or executed under suspicion of political deviance.

However, when looking at these broad and general explanations for espionage styles, we have to remember that the public usually only hears about the cases of failure. The spies who get caught, or who defect, or who make big mistakes, or who are exposed for political reasons, are the ones that end up in news stories and history books. For every failure, there were dozens of never-revealed successes. So we have to beware of making too glib generalizations when the facts are only partly known.

Another difficulty in reaching general conclusions is that the KGB and its successor Russian agency, the SVR, very carefully released information in the 1980s and 1990s intended to stress Soviet espionage successes. Cases of Soviet blunders, alcoholic agents, sexual perversion, and the worst of the KGB's dirty tricks were simply not disclosed in these officially released documents. (See Chapter 19 for the story of information control by the SVR.)

## Soviet People-Manipulation

The KGB and GRU became expert at the manipulation of people, through a wide variety of appeals. The spies who worked for them often described Soviet handlers and controllers as charming, friendly, and exuding sincerity and warmth. In a few cases, such as that of Elizabeth Bentley and Jacob Golos, the traitor fell in love with the controller. Whether through training or through careful personnel selection, many KGB and GRU controllers displayed great patience and understanding of the British and American turncoats who worked with them.

Once in a while, however, the KGB employed a bumbler, such as Reino Hayhanen, who betrayed the operation of Rudolf Abel. Kim Philby's contact in the United States lost a whole set of instructions and payments for Philby. In some other cases, the control or handler was rude, bureaucratic, sadistic, or otherwise so unattractive that he or she went down in history as a really unpleasant character.

Furthermore, even though the collection of information by the KGB and GRU was often outstanding, for many decades (and especially in the Stalin era from 1928 to 1953) the Soviet government was so paranoid about conspiracies that good information was often poorly analyzed or simply not analyzed at all. For a period during World War II, the Soviets believed that the Cambridge Five were part of a deception operation, even when they provided top-notch information from Britain. Jealousies among Soviet intelligence officers, denunciations, accusations, and threats constantly marred their work. So we need to beware of getting the impression that the Soviet agencies were always professional or slick in their operation.

## Americans: Hard to Handle

From the Soviet viewpoint, it was easy to penetrate the United States, but it was frustrating working with American traitors. Americans were not good at following rules, thought they could make up their own procedures, and were frequently careless. The very qualities that made it easy to recruit spies in North America seemed to work against keeping them in line. An American or Canadian sailor, soldier, or defense industry worker who was so disloyal and contemptuous of operational security rules that he would provide information to his country's enemies was the kind of person whom the KGB or GRU would find difficult to order around. If the traitor disobeyed the rules of the system in which he or she was raised, it was unlikely that such a person would obey the new rules laid down by a Soviet handler. People like Martha Dodd and Andrew Lee drove their handlers to distraction.

However, even if American traitors made amateurish spies, several of them inflicted serious damage to American security. Some, like Samuel Dickstein (Chapter 10) or John Walker (Chapter 17), went undiscovered for years.

When American traitors were careless about operational security, Soviet handlers tried to train them. Sometimes the Soviet agency would bring the traitor out of the country to Vienna or behind the Iron Curtain for a short course on tradecraft, evasion of surveillance, and operational security. The trip to Austria was taken so often that the CIA began to call the KGB tradecraft methods, "Vienna Rules."

Americans working for the Soviet Union rarely adhered to the detailed control of dead drops and signals, making contact, evading surveillance, or destroying evidence of their treason. Americans like Bentley and Chambers told others of their work. Later spies like Boyce and Walker, when they failed to make a contact, would disobey instructions and flaunt the carefully constructed rules of operational security established by their Soviet handlers. More than one American traitor kept secret documents at home, bragged to friends, and spent the spy revenue carelessly.

## Motives, Money, and Moscow

Psychological studies of American traitors showed a variety of motives and mental aberrations. Some sought adventure and romance. During the 1940s and 1950s, some, like the Rosenbergs, Alger Hiss, Whittaker Chambers, Morton Sobell, Alfred Sarant, Theodore Hall, and others were attracted by communist ideology. When walk-ins like Walker or Lee demanded cash for secrets, the KGB understood and paid up. The Soviet espionage agencies not only tried to enforce day-to-day procedures, they controlled through blackmail, temptation, ideological allegiance, romance, cash, or whatever else would work. And we have to remember that even if the Soviet spies seemed good at what they did, dozens were identified and expelled, through tips, slip-ups, lapses of operational security, and confessions of their sources.

# Knowing the Target

From the Soviet point of view, the target countries of Germany, Britain, and the United States each had certain characteristics. The national traits, if well understood, could be assets for the spies

The Soviet intelligence officers in the field sometimes seemed to understand their target countries pretty well. The Germans stationed in Japan trusted Richard Sorge, relying on his good-fellowship and rich knowledge of Japan to bring him into their confidence. The British class structure, and the reliance there on family connection and social position as qualifications for high position created opportunities for the KGB and GRU. The Soviet handlers understood that the undergraduates at Cambridge in 1934 would represent the leadership class in Britain by the period 1945–1955 and recruited a group of moles. The Cambridge Five took years to put in place, but the effort paid off handsomely with the betrayal of top-level secrets in the 1940s and early 1950s.

On the other hand, the Soviet agencies sometimes displayed a heavy-handed ignorance of life in the United States or Britain. Some of the efforts to plant disinformation or rumors simply fell flat.

**Tradecraft**

The KGB sometimes tried to spread rumors to discredit particular people. The KGB planted rumors about J. Edgar Hoover, suggesting he was a secret cross-dresser, and trying to get people to believe the FBI was full of homosexuals. When the KGB found that Martin Luther King did not endorse revolution, they spread rumors about his sex life as well. Apparently no one paid much attention to the so-called scandals, probably because Americans were so used to being bombarded with stories about public figures from the regular U.S. media that they ignored most of them. Figuring out how Americans would react to such disinformation schemes was really tough for the Soviet agencies.

American political and personal freedom, and the tendency to challenge authority could all make the United States a rich recruiting ground. When the appeals of communist ideology faded by the 1950s and 1960s, Soviet agents had no difficulty emphasizing cash payments when they were presented with a walk-in. In the United States, with so many opportunities to make money, a new car or new apartment, or a flashy roll of folding money would not stand out as they might have in Russia, Poland, or Czechoslovakia.

## American Critiques of Counterintelligence

During the 1970s, in the wake of the Vietnam War and the scandals of Watergate, Americans grew shocked at the revelations of methods employed by the CIA and FBI in counterespionage. The opening of mail, the surveillance of journalists and radicals, the tapping of telephones, and the many other invasions of privacy and civil liberties raised a storm of protest. After the hearings conducted by Senator Frank Church and Congressman Otis Pike, the agencies reformed. Surveillance and wiretapping had to be ordered by a judge, only after credible evidence. Part of the effect of such changes was to make it even more difficult for the Naval Investigative Service, G-2, and the Army's Criminal Investigative Command, the FBI, or the CIA to track down the spies of the 1980s.

Most of the American traitors and spies who were caught in the 1970s and 1980s were trapped because of tips from vengeful relatives (as in the Walker case), or as a result of tips from Soviet defectors, or through their own negligence. That fact suggested that American security procedures were not very effective. In case after case of the spies who were caught, outsiders were shocked that such obvious security risks had been granted clearances and that the traitors had gone undetected.

Thomas Allen and Norman Polmar, in *Merchants of Treason*, put the problem of too-easy granting of access to classified material very succinctly. Some Americans who were granted top secret clearances and certified as having a need to know highly secret information had records of past criminal behavior, drug use, and dubious associations. Some such individuals holding Top Secret clearances could not be hired to work in a convenience store!

## British Issues

The scandals in Britain differed a bit from those in the United States. The social position of some spies, like Anthony Blunt and Kim Philby (Chapter 9), protected them from exposure or punishment. By the mid-1980s, critics like journalist Chapman Pincher and former intelligence officer Peter Wright alleged that the old-boy networks of Britain were protecting moles and traitors who still worked within the government at the highest levels.

Chapman Pincher, in a hard-hitting critique, *Their Trade is Treachery*, suggested (without directly stating) that the former head of MI-5, Richard Hollis, was in Soviet employ, and that he may have been the "Fifth Man" of the Cambridge Five (later named as John Cairncross) or perhaps the spy code-named "ELLI" (who eventually turned out to be a man named Leo Long). Pincher had met former MI-5 intelligence officer Peter Wright at the home of Lord Victor Rothschild in 1980. Pincher agreed with Wright that he would base his exposé on Wright's claims and evidence without revealing Wright as a source. Wright was to get half of the book's royalties. Wright had been MI-5's scientific officer and deputy director of MI-5 before retiring in 1976.

Pincher also revealed in his book that former Prime Minister Harold Wilson had been suspected by MI-5 of being a Soviet plant, and that MI-5 had worked to throw Wilson out of his post. Wright also told Pincher of episodes in which MI-5 had bugged cabinet meetings, and had worked for the resignation of particular government ministers. The charges made the British government appear little better than a Third World regime where secret police plotted the overthrow of petty dictators. Before publication, Pincher had his manuscript reviewed by personnel in MI-5 and MI-6 who did not ask for any deletions.

## The Spycatcher Affair

Prime Minister Margaret Thatcher admitted in Parliament that Pincher's allegations that Hollis had been under suspicion were true. However, he was later cleared, she said. In 1987, Peter Wright published his own version of the events, in *Spycatcher: The Candid Autobiography of a Senior Intelligence Officer.* By this time, Wright was living in Australia and his book was first published there.

In that work, Wright detailed the fact that Prime Minister Harold Wilson, who served from 1964 to 1970 and 1974 to 1976, had been investigated as a possible KGB agent. Wright, then living in Australia, could have been prosecuted under the British Official Secrets Act for revealing secret information, if he had still been living in Britain.

Wright's book was banned in Britain, and the British government made efforts to suppress it in Australia. The attendant publicity made the book something of a bestseller, with a reputed one million copies sold worldwide.

The fact that Chapman Pincher's book based on Wright's information had been reviewed by MI-5 and MI-6 before publication mitigated in court against the British government's case for suppression of Wright's book. Eventually Wright's *Spycatcher* became available in Britain as well as the United States and Australia.

The criticisms brought by Pincher and Wright rocked the British establishment and revealed the extent to which Soviet agents had relied on characteristics of British society for their recruiting efforts. Furthermore, a combination of family connections, respect for privacy, and governmental concern to suppress scandal had protected not only the guilty, but had led to cover-ups even of the investigations of people found innocent.

## Parallels and Differences

There were some similarities in the flaws criticized by Pincher and Wright in Britain and by Allen and Polmar in the United States. In both countries, agencies were not very good at counterintelligence work, and tended to put their energies into intelligence gathering rather than tracking down traitors. Furthermore, in both countries, different intelligence agencies tended not to share information with sister agencies, usually out of a concern to protect sources and methods.

Yet the critics pointed to some different weaknesses in the two countries. The American military services conducted their own investigations and punished spies with courts-martial, rarely sharing their findings with the civilian agencies. In both countries, agencies sought to suppress scandal, but the protection was based more on friendship, family, and personal connection in Britain. In the United States, the different bureaucracies each appeared to avoid scandal, fearing that public scrutiny might lead to congressional budget-cutting or revelation of methods, sources, and other classified information.

# Spying with Machines and People

Given the unreliability of human agents, it is not surprising that by the late 1960s, the United States began relying more heavily on technical intelligence. Satellites, submarine cable tapping, and a variety of decryption and eavesdropping technologies provided a flood of information. Yet it was clear by the mid-1980s that, through the treason of people like Christopher Boyce and John Walker, and the earlier capture of the communications ship *Pueblo*, the Soviet Union and its Warsaw Pact allies could read many of the classified communications of the United States. Furthermore, the Soviet Union had learned a great deal about the technologies, and in a few cases, could imitate them. Many analysts worried that the human card could trump the machine card, that no matter how good the technology, its betrayal by traitors would neutralize its effect.

## Open Skies and Covert Spies

President Eisenhower had proposed the concept of open skies in a speech in 1955. Although the Soviet Union rejected the concept of voluntarily opening its airspace to intelligence gathering, technology soon allowed the U.S. to implement Eisenhower's concept without Soviet permission. The American U-2 flew along the borders of the Soviet Union and, it was thought, above the altitude limit of Soviet surface-to-air missiles.

After Gary Powers' U-2 was shot down May 1, 1960 (Chapter 13), the United States had no eye in the sky over the Soviet Union until the first *Corona* satellite, launched aboard the earliest successful *Discoverer 13* in August 1960. Not until *Discoverer 29*, launched April 30, 1961, did the satellites show conclusively the limited number of Soviet long-range missiles. The Soviet Union understood satellites could be used to gather intelligence and claimed the right to shoot down any passing over their territory, no matter what altitude. As far as is publicly known, they never did. After all, they had set a precedent with the overflight by Sputnik in 1957.

Without agreement from the Soviet Union, the United States had unilaterally implemented a system of open skies. Over the next 25 years, the intelligence gathered would be crucial to the United States in the cold war. It was used both to call Soviet bluffs (as in the Cuban Missile Crisis in 1961), and to detect real Soviet installation of threatening missiles, as in 1978–1979, when the Soviets installed SS-20 missiles threatening Western European targets. The United States responded by planning the installation of medium-range guided missiles in Western Europe.

Although the Soviets learned of American satellite capabilities from Christopher Boyce and the close American tracking of their submarines from John Walker, what they learned made it clear that in the mid-1980s, the United States was quite capable of carrying out the complete devastation of the Soviet Union in any nuclear exchange. American techint allowed the United States to learn details of Soviet armaments; Soviet humint, in turn, allowed the Russians to learn that the United States was well ahead in the technology of warfare as well as the technology of espionage. When, in 1986, Soviet leader Mikhail Gorbachev met with President Ronald Reagan at Reyjavik, Iceland, each side had a pretty clear understanding of the capabilities of the other.

**Spy Words**

The concept that both the United States and the Soviet Union should reduce the total number of nuclear weapons deployed to zero was introduced in 1982 by President Reagan. The idea had been discussed in Germany by nuclear disarmament advocates as the concept of Null Lösing or zero solution. At their meeting in Reykjavik, Iceland, in 1986, Reagan and Gorbachev spoke of a "global zero-zero option." By this term the leaders meant that both countries would work toward the elimination of all nuclear weapons in both the Soviet Union and the United States. The **zero option** concept shaped the Intermediate Range Nuclear Forces Treaty (INF) in 1987, and the Strategic Arms Reduction Treaty (START) in 1991.

In this sense, the unilateral open skies established by the United States and the hidden spies set up by the Soviet Union were able to achieve the goal of shared information outlined 30 years earlier by President Eisenhower. Espionage, which had been the battleground of the cold war, can be seen as the instrument that brought the cold war to an end. Both Gorbachev and Reagan began to consider the *zero option*.

Over the period 1986–1990, the United States and the Soviet Union negotiated a series of treaties and agreements that effectively brought an end to the cold war. The treaties were based on extensive knowledge each side had of the other's terrible weapons capability, gained through espionage, both techint and humint. And the treaties would be monitored, as Eisenhower envisioned, by openly looking down from the sky at each other's compliance with the agreements. What had been technical espionage in the 1970s became national technical means of treaty verification by 1988.

---

### Techint

National technical means, mostly satellite photography, were used to verify compliance with arms control treaties. Both sides agreed to supplement that form of verification with visits by expert teams of intelligence officers on the ground. The On-Site Inspection Agency (OSIA), established in 1988, carried out this open intelligence gathering effort for the United States, using military and civilian weapons intelligence experts.

Arms Control Treaties enforced by techint and OSIA:

INF (Intermediate-range Nuclear Forces), ratified, 1988

CFE (Conventional Forces in Europe), signed, 1990

START I (Strategic Arms Reduction Treaty), ratified 1992

START II (Strategic Arms Reduction Treaty), ratified 1996

---

## Open Intelligence Exchange

While clandestine espionage gathering had been the main battlefield of the cold war, openly admitted intelligence methods became part of the peace agreements that marked the end of the cold war. Instead of secretly trying to assess exactly how many weapons each other had, both sides agreed to allow both satellite observation and on-site inspection.

Former intelligence officers, expert in the technology of weaponry, formed teams that visited each other's countries. In the United States, the On-Site Inspection Agency (OSIA) employed thousands of specialists, sending them to the former Soviet Union, and later to former Warsaw Pact nations and to the former Yugoslavia. The OSIA teams watched the destruction of missiles and weapons, installed cameras and other detectors to monitor weapon manufacture and storage facilities, and exchanged detailed reports with their Russian counterparts.

Similar Russian teams visited the United States and watched as missile silos were decommissioned and bomber aircraft were cut to pieces and scrapped. Information that spies had once risked their lives to learn was now freely traded. However, as we will see in Chapter 19, the open exchange of weapons-treaty verification intelligence did not represent the end of espionage.

## The Least You Need to Know

♦ Both American and British agencies had difficulty identifying and rooting out Soviet spies.

♦ American technical intelligence was highly successful, although the Soviets learned of many of the methods through traitors who sold them information.

♦ The cold war was fought with espionage, and ended with agreements to freely exchange the information once obtained by human spies on the ground and technical eyes in the skies.

♦ The U.S. On-Site Inspection Agency, established in 1988, and Russian counterparts openly sent expert teams to check on the destruction of nuclear weapons, missiles, and conventional weapons under the new treaties.

# Chapter 19

# After the Cold War

## In This Chapter

- ◆ Intelligence in the Gulf War
- ◆ Venona revealed
- ◆ Soviet files opened
- ◆ Spies still at work

In the Gulf War, in which a coalition of nations fought Iraq after that country invaded Kuwait in 1990, wartime and postwar intelligence reflected the impact of some new techniques. With the United States and the countries of the former Soviet Union moving to a new status of peacetime diplomatic relations, several batches of documents were made public. In addition to the decoded Venona files, collections of papers and memoirs of former KGB officials came out.

Historians and intelligence analysts produced a new crop of revised spy history books. But just as the British, Canadian, and American publics began to believe that the era of spying had ended, American officials arrested a highly placed spy in the CIA and then another spy at the FBI. A scientist was arrested at Los Alamos, the birthplace of the atomic bomb, on suspicion of spying for China. In this chapter, we see that the age of the spy had not really passed into history.

# Intelligence and the Gulf War

In August 1990, Iraq invaded Kuwait. President George H. W. Bush, former Director of Central Intelligence, was stunned. Only a week before, his ambassador to Iraq, April Glaspie, had met with Saddam Hussein and told him that the United States did not want to interfere in disputes between Arab states, but that the United States hoped Hussein's claims against Kuwait would be resolved peacefully. The brutal and rapid seizure of Kuwait surprised not only American officials, but all the other major powers as well.

The United Nations condemned the action, and Bush ordered General Norman Schwarzkopf to provide assistance to protect Saudi Arabia and the smaller countries of the Persian Gulf from any further advances by Hussein in Operation Desert Shield. When Hussein refused to obey a UN ultimatum to withdraw from Kuwait in mid-January 1991, the United States and a large coalition (numbering about 34 other countries) began a two-phase Operation Desert Storm.

In the first, air phase, Coalition aircraft destroyed missile sites, airfields and aircraft, military headquarters and troop concentrations, and communication and transportation facilities. Then, in the ground phase, more than 570,000 American and Coalition troops pushed into Kuwait to liberate it, in a lightning strike that took about 100 hours. During this war, intelligence played a crucial part, as it always had during other wars, whether brief or prolonged.

## Tactical and Strategic Intelligence

The Gulf War displayed several consequences of the years of perfection of American technical intelligence and reliance on machines rather than on human sources on the ground. Critics of techint had always claimed that machines could never derive the motives or intentions of an enemy. Although air and satellite surveillance had revealed the massing of Iraqi Republican Guard troops on the Kuwait border, it was impossible to know, even from real-time photographs, what Hussein's next step would be, even two days before his invasion.

On the other hand, such methods provided excellent information when Desert Storm began. Tomahawk missiles from ships and air-launched cruise missiles, controlled in flight, could zero in on particular buildings and even particular floors of buildings that housed Iraqi military and government facilities.

Because Western techint capabilities were so well known, and because the damage was so carefully pinpointed, Iraq adopted several military tactics in response. Hussein knew his aircraft would be vulnerable to attack, and he had many of his airplanes shuttled to Iran, which remained neutral in the conflict. The modified Soviet SS-1 missiles in the Iraqi arsenal known as scuds were mounted on trucks and constantly moved from site to site to prevent their detection and destruction from above. Despite a concentrated effort to eliminate them, Iraq survived the war with a few dozen scuds intact. Because of the Coalition's ability to pinpoint targets, Hussein personally moved his headquarters almost daily, frequently, it was reported, to deeply buried and concealed underground bunkers.

Because of the limits of techint, two days before the ground assault of Desert Storm, American and British commandos penetrated Iraq in small groups of 4 to 10 men, locating on the ground specific targets and then calling in air strikes on targets they identified. Andy McNab, one of the British special forces soldiers, later wrote an account of his behind-the-lines work and his subsequent capture, *Bravo Two Zero*.

**Spy Words**

The British military outfit, the **Special Air Service (SAS)**, like the U.S. Army Rangers, the Navy Seals, and Delta Force, was a highly trained elite group set up for special operations. The 22nd regiment of the SAS sent several teams into Iraq to try to locate Scud launchers.

## Deception and the Hail Mary Strategy

General Schwarzkopf took advantage of surveillance and deception when planning the attack on Hussein's forces. It was clear from aircraft reconnaissance that the major Iraqi forces faced the Saudi border in Kuwait, with a large reserve of several Republican Guard divisions based to the north of Kuwait in Iraq, ready to move forward should the Coalition attack.

Accordingly, Schwarzkopf planned what came to be known as the Hail Mary strategy, moving the main invasion force to the western desert, where the Saudi-Iraqi border was relatively undefended. Schwarzkopf created the impression that the Coalition troops remained massed directly across from Kuwait inside Saudi Arabia. Just as the Germans expected the 1941 attack at Calais, not Normandy, so the Iraqis expected the 1991 attack close to the Persian Gulf coast, rather than inland to the west (see Chapter 5). The massive movement of troops was conducted quietly, swiftly, and with no leakage to the media or to the enemy.

In related deceptions, U.S. marines maneuvered in the Persian Gulf, leaving the impression that a major amphibious landing directly at Kuwait City should be expected. Again, the Iraqis focused on the wrong location.

## Mouthy Media Muzzled

In the modern world of instant media, the world's press corps reacted with ambivalence to the control of information that the Coalition enforced. On the one hand, daily press briefings, many released films from aircraft and even from missiles, photo-opportunities, and good access to the commanders for question and answer sessions all seemed to herald a new kind of openness. America, it seemed, was into Glasnost.

However, more seasoned reporters were frustrated. They were not allowed to take their cameras to the battlefront, and the material they got, although apparently rich, was strictly controlled. The Coalition treated the question of media relations as an aspect of intelligence-control and operational security, and some reporters grumbled that their rights and freedom of the press were endangered. It was the classic conflict between military security and the public's right to know, with security winning out.

## Quick Victory, and Aftermath

Some later analysts concluded that despite the quality of air-surveillance, the Coalition forces had overestimated the ability of the Iraqis to hold their conquered territory and to fight the Coalition army. Again, the photos from the air did not lie, but there was no way such intelligence could reveal very much about Iraqi troop morale, will to fight, training and preparation, or officer quality. It was assumed that the Iraqi army, after about a decade of experience in a prior war with Iran, would be battle-hardened and tough. But without much high-quality humint, there was little reliable intelligence on these topics. As a consequence, the Coalition was unprepared for the flood of surrendering Iraqi troops, or for the headlong retreat of others toward Baghdad. As they fled, they abandoned miles of trucks, armored vehicles, and stolen automobiles, leaving them to be strafed from the air.

The purpose of the whole Gulf War had been to evict Iraq from Kuwait and that objective was rapidly achieved. None of the allies and none of the military advisers recommended pursuit of the Iraqi troops to Baghdad or the capture of Saddam Hussein. Many members of the Coalition, including the United States, assumed that the destruction of the Iraqi regime would destabilize the whole region. When the peace terms were imposed on Iraq, several unique features of the surrender reflected intelligence concerns.

## Weapons Inspection

As part of the surrender terms, Iraq agreed to stop all its programs of development of weapons of mass destruction, including chemical, biological, and nuclear weapons.

Inspectors, appointed by a new UN agency, UNSCOM, would conduct on-site inspections, similar to the on-site inspections conducted under the nuclear arms agreements between Russia and the United States (see Chapter 18). In fact, the U.S. On-Site Inspection Agency (OSIA) established to monitor the compliance of former Soviet and Soviet bloc disarmament, would provide some of the logistics and training for UNSCOM. By the late 1990s, OSIA was merged into a larger Defense Department office, the Defense Threat Reduction Agency.

In another agreement, Iraq agreed not to fly any fixed-wing aircraft in two "no-fly" zones, one north of the thirty-sixth parallel, and the other south of the thirty-third parallel within Iraq. Until the arms inspections were complete, the no-fly zones and an embargo on trade with Iraq would stay in effect. The inspections, no-fly zones, and embargo of trade created continuing crises for the next decade.

## OSIA and UNSCOM Foiled

Over the period 1992–1998, the UNSCOM inspectors discovered not only that Iraq had started an extensive nuclear-weapon construction program, but that the regime had established a special office whose job it was to conceal that and other programs. The arms inspectors soon encountered obvious cover-ups, locked gates, delays, and a list of sites that were entirely off-limits to them. American and British aircraft patrolled the no-fly zones, giving them close aerial surveillance capabilities over the whole country as well as the two zones they patrolled. But only on-site inspectors could locate the laboratories, factories, archives, and weapon-storage bunkers of the Iraqi regime.

With the Coalition members, including the U.S. government, unwilling to enforce the inspection agreement with armed force, the UNSCOM intelligence-gathering mission was finally withdrawn in 1998. President Bill Clinton then ordered Operation Desert Fox, which bombed many of the suspected sites. Despite the no-fly zones and the embargo, Hussein decided he could outwait the patience of the Coalition members. By 2001, it seemed he was winning the war of nerves.

From leaked information, defections, and other sources, U.S. and Coalition intelligence agencies learned that the Iraqi weapons development programs were underway again. This issue would lead the next administration in Washington to consider in 2002 the necessity of an armed invasion of Iraq to eliminate the weapons development work there, especially the nuclear weapons program. The UN followed up with a new resolution and a new inspection team late in 2002.

# Opening the Files

The end of the cold war, it seemed, had established a "New World Order," a phrase used during the first Bush administration to describe the post-cold war world. The rapid construction of the international Coalition to oppose Saddam Hussein's aggression, which involved members of the former Soviet bloc as well as NATO members, provided convincing evidence that the world was moving to a new system of international order. It appeared that the tensions of the cold war and its heritage of espionage were now clearly things of the past. Both the United States and Russia released long-held secrets that gave new insights into the long years of espionage.

## Viewing Venona

One of the most complete revelations by the United States came from a joint CIA/NSA project to declassify and release the Venona transcripts. As noted in Chapter 8, the decoding of these secret messages between Soviet embassies and consulates in the United States and Moscow during World War II had provided leads to Harry Gold, the Rosenbergs, Alger Hiss, and other Soviet spies in the 1940s and the 1950s. The decoded files were known as the Venona documents.

However, the United States had kept the details of Venona classified, and had not used the Venona decrypts as evidence in the Rosenberg or other espionage cases. When the Venona files were published (in both paper version and on the Internet) in 1996, they created quite a stir in the community of historians and espionage specialists. The documents demonstrated even more clearly that both the Rosenbergs and Alger Hiss had been working for the Soviet Union, and also showed the close linkage of the head of the American Communist Party, Earl Browder, with the Soviet espionage apparatus.

## Post-Venona Revisionism

In a number of works that might be called post-Venona revisionism, historians of both espionage and the Communist Party spelled out the detailed connections between the KGB, the GRU, and the Communist Party of the United States of America (CPUSA). The new evidence showed that the Communist Party had operated for most of its history as a recruiting ground for Soviet agents. The American party, despite its claims to the contrary, expected its leadership and members to give their first loyalty to the Soviet Union, not to the United States.

For some students of the history of the left in the United States, this evidence came as quite a jolt. Some had assumed the CPUSA was simply another American political party on the left and that charges of its work for Moscow were part of a reactionary attempt to discredit it. The documents showed conclusively that the CPUSA and other communist parties around the world had usually taken orders directly from Moscow. Countries whose Communist Party refused to follow the Moscow line, such as Yugoslavia, Albania, and China, were treated by the Soviet Union as renegades from the true path.

## Sudoplatov and His Claims

Memoirs of former KGB agents tended to substantiate what was shown in the Venona files, but in particular, two major releases further confirmed the extensive work of the KGB in the United States and elsewhere. One rather sensational memoir was produced by Pavel Sudoplatov, former head of a section of SMERSH (said to be a contraction of *Smert Shpionam*—"Death to Spies," but see the glossary). It was the section within the KGB devoted to "wet work" or "special tasks." Among other operations, Sudoplatov had been instrumental in managing the assassination of Leon Trotsky in Mexico in 1940.

Sudoplatov not only revealed the variety of assassination attempts, successful and unsuccessful, pulled off by the KGB, but he went on to make other claims that some experts regarded as outrageous or not otherwise substantiated. For example, he claimed that the advisor to President Roosevelt during World War II, Harry Hopkins, was an *agent of influence*, and that he worked closely with Alger Hiss. This charge, like some others of Sudoplatov, was based on hearsay or assumptions, rather than evidence, and other experts suggested that he jumped to conclusions. While Hopkins and others were pro-Soviet, there was little evidence of any disloyalty in his case.

Among other claims that Sudoplatov made, were charges that J. Robert Oppenheimer intentionally leaked atomic information to the Soviets. Despite his tendency to sensationalize aspects of his own role and to jump to conclusions, Sudoplatov's revelations, when studied carefully, added to public knowledge of the KGB's years of operations, including its use of murder, torture, blackmail, and mass executions.

**Spy Words**

In addition to informants, the KGB sought to identify friendly figures in Western governments who would influence policy in a pro-Soviet direction. Some of these people would be carefully cultivated with friendly and open official contacts from embassy personnel. In some cases, a contact might move from being an informant to becoming an **agent of influence**. A number of pro-Soviet officials in the Roosevelt administration were remembered as being in this gray area.

# The Mitrokhin Archive

A much more authoritative source became available when Vasili Mitrokhin left the Soviet Union and took his collection of documents to London in 1992. Mitrokhin had worked for years as the archivist of the KGB, and he had carefully copied documents and smuggled the copies out of the headquarters, storing them under the floorboards of his country house. At first he kept them in a butter churn that he buried, and then, as the volume increased, he stored them in metal trunks. After the collapse of the Soviet Union, he made arrangements with British MI-6 to take his massive collection of files and his family out of the former Soviet Union.

Mitrokhin's files were shared with British and American intelligence agencies. Then, working with a leading British scholar on intelligence matters, Christopher Andrew, the two prepared and published in 1999 a comprehensive history of the KGB's operation from the 1930s through the late 1980s. Much of what Andrew and Mitrokhin published was previously unknown, and its rich detail confirmed many of the details of the Venona documents and some of Sudoplatev's claims.

Since Mitrokhin had copied the documents and smuggled them out, there was no absolute proof of their authenticity. The SVR, the Russian successor agency to the KGB, denied some of the stories published in his work, but admitted to others. On the whole, Western experts judged the Mitrokhin files as quite genuine, as so many details explained and fitted into other pieces of evidence. The details of work of the Cambridge Five (see Chapter 9), for example, meshed very well with the accumulated evidence on their cases, and clarified a few facts, such as Philby's false claim that he was appointed as a KGB colonel.

# Western Scholars Gain Access

For a brief time in the early and mid-1990s, some of the KGB official files were selectively opened for use by Western scholars trying to unravel the story of Soviet espionage. The Russian SVR, which had supplanted the KGB, worked with Allen Weinstein, Alexander Vassiliev, John Costello, Timothy Naftali, and David Murphy. They operated through an agreement negotiated by the American publisher Random House. These authors uncovered many details, including some of the stories of high-level spies, such as Martha Dodd, Congressman Samuel Dickstein, and others discussed in Chapters 8, 9, and 10.

Many of the details meshed with the releases from Venona, and fully supported the idea that the international communist movement was a tool of Soviet intelligence. However, none of the scholars were allowed to look at files other than those provided by the SVR, leading them to worry that while what they got was authentic, it wasn't the whole story. However, over and over, a Venona document, laboriously decoded in Washington, matched word for word the KGB copy in the SVR files, helping to confirm that both collections were authentic and not corrupted by disinformation.

# Moles Again: Undercover at the Top

Although a clearer picture of espionage history was emerging in a spirit of friendly cooperation, the spying work of the SVR was not over. Two arrests of American traitors in the 1990s confirmed that the successor agency of the KGB still operated in the United States and elsewhere, using the tried and true methods of dead drops, signals, and cash payments for information. Neither of the two prominent spies for Russia was revealed in the carefully controlled release of documents in Moscow. Both cases required careful investigative work.

The two traitors were highly placed. One was Aldrich Ames, caught in 1994, after nine years of spying from his posts in the CIA for the Soviets and their Russian successors. The other was FBI agent Robert Hanssen, who provided information to the KGB and the SVR for at least 17 years before his arrest in 2001.

## Ames: Motives and Career

Aldrich Ames had joined the CIA in 1962 at the age of 21. His father had been a career analyst in the agency, suggesting that the agency had fallen into the "good old boy network" trap that had proven so dangerous in Britain.

After assignments in Washington and Mexico City, Ames was put in charge of the counterintelligence branch of the Soviet/East European Division in the CIA's Operations Directorate in 1983.

In 1985, he became a paid agent for the Soviets. From assignments in Rome and in Washington, Ames continued to provide the Soviets with names of double agents— Soviet citizens working for the United States. One after another, they were arrested and some of them executed.

## Catching Ames

Ames spent the funds he received quite lavishly, with an expensive sports car, a big house, extensive foreign travel, and many other purchases that his salary could not support. He paid for his Jaguar and his $500,000 house with cash. For some years, these expenses raised no question, as others in the agency assumed that Ames's money was his wife's, Rosario's, who came from a distinguished family in Colombia. No one checked to find out that although the family was prominent, it was not wealthy, and that in fact, Ames provided his in-laws with some funds.

*Rosario and Aldrich Ames were deeply involved in selling out the names of CIA informants to the KGB and the SVR.*

*(Courtesy of the AP/Wide World Photo)*

Counterintelligence officers in the CIA found that Ames had many documents in his office that had no bearing on his current assignment. A check of his bank records revealed large deposits beginning in 1985. For example, in 1992, he deposited 30 payments totaling $187,000. Eventually, the case of Ames was turned over to a joint FBI/CIA investigation. The teams carefully conducted garbage stakeouts to examine his trash. He was put under surveillance, and agents witnessed him dropping off documents, picking up cash payments, chalking mailboxes, and visiting dead drops.

### Tradecraft

After securing a warrant, the FBI was confronted with a puzzle. Although they could plant electronic bugs to listen to Ames's phone calls and conversations, accessing documents in his house might leave traces that would tip him off. Agents instead retrieved his trash cans during the night, sorted through the trash, and then arranged it in the same order in the cans so that if he were to throw something away the next morning, he wouldn't notice any difference. Inside the trash, the agents recovered, among other items, a computer printer ribbon from which the original messages could be retrieved. Dirty work, but somebody had to do it.

## Ames: Damage

As in the Walker case (Chapter 17), it appeared that Ames had spied for the Soviet Union mostly because he wanted the money, and partly because he was frustrated at his own career.

Both he and his wife were arrested in February 1994, and when confronted by evidence, he agreed to plead guilty in exchange for a reduced sentence for his wife. He was sentenced to life in prison, and she was sentenced to five years in prison, but released in 1998. The damage Ames did was difficult to assess, but most analysts agreed that at least 10 Soviet citizens working as agents for the United States were executed after being identified by Ames.

---

### Spy Bios

Some of the American and British agents identified by Aldrich Ames to the KGB:

Agent code-name Fate

Adolf Tokachev GT/Sphere executed 1986

Dimitri Polyakov GT/Accord/Top Hat executed 1988

Oleg Gordievsky GT/Tickle safely exfiltrated by MI-6

Gennadi Varenik GT/Fitness executed 1985

Others identified as betrayed by Ames included GT/Cowl, a Soviet intelligence officer in Moscow; GT/Motorboat, an East European security officer; GT/Million, a lieutenant colonel in the GRU; and others. The total was at least 10 or 11, and may have been greater.

---

Another aspect of the damage was the scandal. Ames may have been the highest-paid spy in history. The fact that he went undetected for so long embarrassed the CIA. He had paid cash for huge expenditures, raising no questions. He had passed a CIA lie-detector test. He was notoriously drunk and inefficient on the job. He had debriefed Oleg Gordievsky, who defected to the West after Ames himself had turned him in to the Soviets. He had worked in the CIA's counterintelligence arm, the most sensitive of positions and the worst to have penetrated.

Congressmen, journalists, and James Woolsey, the new Director of Central Intelligence appointed by President Bill Clinton, all lambasted the agency's record. After reprimanding various officials in the CIA, but firing none (thereby angering both supporters and critics of the agency), Woolsey himself resigned the agency early in 1995.

## Hanssen: Caught Red-Handed

The fact that Ames was tracked and arrested by the FBI briefly left the impression that, in the long-standing rivalry between the FBI and the CIA, the FBI had scored a few points. However, in the year 2001, the discovery of another spy for Russia in the FBI itself brought any such impression to an end.

Robert Hanssen's case, like that of Ames, represented a highly placed intelligence officer with access to information about U.S. efforts to penetrate the Soviet Union. However, Hanssen was a very different type of individual. Religious, careful of spending, and cautious, his espionage went undetected for at least 17 years, perhaps longer. Although he received over $1.4 million in cash and diamonds for his espionage, he tended not to spend it. In fact, his handlers held some $800,000 in an account for him.

Hanssen concealed his identity and the agency he worked for even from his KGB and SVR handlers, communicating entirely through dead drops that he arranged. Because he had access to information about continuing FBI investigations, the bureau had an extremely difficult time gathering evidence against him without his knowledge.

Suspicions that the SVR had an agent in the FBI pointed to a limited number of people with access to the kind of information Hanssen regularly used. Using a court-authorized warrant, the FBI monitored his computer use, put an electronic homing device in his car, and placed him under surveillance in 1997. Agents followed him to one of his dead drop exchange spots, near a bridge in a park in Vienna, Virginia, arresting him in February 2001.

## Hanssen Damage

As in the Ames case, the information that Hanssen provided to the Soviets apparently led to the execution of agents in Russia who worked for the United States. Valeriy Martynov (GT/Gentile) was executed in 1987 and Sergei Motorin (GT/Gauze) in 1986. A third agent, Boriz Yuzhin, received a long prison term. Some accounts of the Ames case included the assumption that Martynov and Motorin had been betrayed by Ames, but apparently the information came from a 1985 letter by Hanssen to Victor Cherkashin, a Soviet agent in the Washington embassy.

Working with Plato Cacheris, the defense attorney who had worked out Ames's plea bargain, Hanssen agreed to submit to debriefing with polygraph tests. In exchange he received a sentence of life in prison rather than a death sentence.

The press and the public had a hard time trying to understand Hanssen. He had befriended a stripper and sometime prostitute, giving her money, but never developed a physical relationship with her. He was a member of Opus Dei, a somewhat secretive organization of devout Catholics. He did not squander his funds, but apparently used some of the proceeds from espionage to pay for private schooling for his children. Not your typical spy, and a very different sort of person from the abusive and flamboyant John Walker, the incompetent Aldrich Ames, and the youthful radical dissenter, Christopher Boyce.

# Wen Ho Lee: Innocent Until Proven Guilty

In December 2000, federal officials arrested a Taiwanese-American researcher at the Los Alamos National Laboratory. Wen Ho Lee was charged with 59 counts of mishandling classified documents. The charges stated that Lee had downloaded 1.4 gigabytes of nuclear weapons data in 1993, 1994, and 1997. The charges were sensational as they came at a time when the U.S. Congress was investigating charges that the Chinese had developed a miniaturized nuclear weapon that corresponded to the American model W-88, and the assumption was that the design had been obtained by espionage.

Wen Ho Lee denied that he had conducted any espionage. He had copied the files, he said, to protect against them being lost in the computer. When he was fired from Los Alamos in March 1999, for security violations, he simply disposed of the tapes, he claimed.

# Holding Wen Ho

Friends, relatives, and eventually, a mass organization began to plea for his release, charging that he was a scapegoat for government embarrassment over the possible leak of information to China. His supporters further charged that he had been imprisoned because, as an ethnic Chinese, he was a convenient target. The fact that he was held in solitary confinement and that he continued to insist that he was innocent added to the public focus on the case.

Colleagues doubted he was guilty, pointing out his enthusiasm for the United States, his regular, middle-class lifestyle, and his devotion to his research. Some suggested that he might have downloaded files and computer programs with the thought that the information would help him if he searched for a job outside the laboratory. Others doubted that story, claiming he was too smart to have misunderstood the consequences of mishandling classified information. Some claimed the information was not at all crucial to the design of the new weapons and that the FBI exaggerated its significance.

Lee was held for nine months in federal prison. Finally, in September 2000, he pled guilty to one charge of mishandling documents in exchange for a pledge to submit to lie-detector tests and to explain everything he knew about the missing tapes.

Although the case created a press furor for nearly a year, its inconclusive end left public and official opinion divided. The judge who released him after months of solitary confinement said that the government owed him an apology. After all, the government had not proven a case of espionage against Wen Ho Lee, and under American law he was innocent until proven guilty.

## The Least You Need to Know

- During the 1990–1991 Gulf War, several classic deceptions kept the Iraqis in the dark about Coalition assault plans, while American techint sources did not give a clue to the failure of morale on the part of Iraqi troops.

- Iraqi resistance to UN inspectors violated their terms of surrender, and Western analysts believed Hussein planned to build weapons of mass destruction.

- In the mid-1990s, the cases of Aldrich Ames and Robert Hanssen showed that espionage by Russia against the United States was a continuing threat.

- In the year 2000, the case of Wen Ho Lee indicated that the FBI still regarded atomic espionage as a danger.

# Chapter 20

# Intelligence in the War on Terror

## In This Chapter

- ◆ September 11: Pearl Harbor again
- ◆ Techint and humint in the War on Terror
- ◆ Classic intelligence dilemmas
- ◆ A different kind of enemy

In this chapter, we look at some of the intelligence issues stemming from the terrorist attacks of September 11, 2001, that claimed 3,000 lives, mostly civilians, in the United States. Some of the questions and dilemmas that resulted from the attacks were classic intelligence problems, familiar to students of the subject. But the nature of the attacks, paid for and organized by a group that did not represent a single state or nation, presented some new intelligence issues. We'll look at how these new questions of spies and espionage may shape the direction of intelligence in the coming decades.

# Another Pearl Harbor

September 11, 2001—the date will echo in history for its tragic events. Four airliners were hijacked and used as missiles. Two destroyed the World Trade Center, a third crashed into the Pentagon, and the fourth crashed in Pennsylvania, foiled in its attempt to strike the U.S. Capitol by passengers who fought the hijackers. As the news shocked the United States and the world, for historians of intelligence, there was a sense of *déjà vu*. Almost 60 years before, on December 7, 1941, the United States had suffered another surprise attack, when Japanese aircraft bombed the U.S. Naval base at Pearl Harbor.

*The attack on the World Trade Center was on the same order of magnitude as the attack 60 years before on Pearl Harbor.*

*(Courtesy of the AP/Wide World Photo)*

## Parallels and Differences

In 1941 and in 2001, the attacks were treated as failures of intelligence. There were many other parallels. The number of deaths was on the same order of magnitude, running just over 2,000 in 1941, and just under 3,000 in 2001. In both cases, the attack was unprovoked and sudden. And in the aftermath of each attack, critics asked what did American intelligence know, and when did they know it? Congress and the press sought to place blame for the failure of intelligence as high as they could in the chain of command.

However, the differences were profound. The attack of 1941 was conducted by Japanese naval aircraft against a military target. In the sanitized language of later generations, it was a pre-emptive strike, intended to destroy the American capacity to wage a naval war in the Pacific. Civilians were not targeted. By contrast, the attacks on the World Trade Center, the Pentagon, and the intended attack on the Capitol were conducted by a group that did not represent a government. The attackers were civilians and the majority of the casualties were civilians as well.

## War or Crime

The attacks of 2001 were treated by the U.S. government as an act of war, rather than a set of criminal acts. Yet there was no evidence that any particular government officially sponsored the attacks. Much evidence pointed to the group known as *Al Qaeda* (also spelled *al-Qa'ida*), funded with money from individuals in Saudi Arabia and elsewhere in the Arabic-speaking nations of the Middle East.

*Al Qaeda* was known to have operated training camps in Sudan and in Afghanistan, but those countries, while hosting the organization and preventing outside authorities from arresting or apprehending members, could not be said to have committed an act of war. It was a new phenomenon, dubbed by Paul Wilkinson, director of the Center for the Study of Terrorism and Political Violence at St. Andrews University in Scotland, as borderless terrorism.

As the investigation proceeded, the Al Qaeda connection became well established, although the hijackers were different from many of the *Arab Afghans* brought by Al Qaeda to support the *Taliban* regime.

 **Spy Words**

**Al Qaeda,** a phrase in Arabic meaning "the base," was a loose organization that supported the **Taliban.** Taliban (meaning "students") referred to the government that took over Afghanistan in 1996, made up of religious students, many of whom had studied in Islamic fundamentalist schools in Pakistan. Al Qaeda funded an international group of young men, all of who were Islamists or radical fundamentalists to provide an armed force to assist the Taliban regime in control of Afghanistan. Since many of those who came to Afghanistan to support the Taliban were from Arab-speaking countries, they became known as Afghan Arabs. The September 11 hijackers, while members of the Al Qaeda network, tended to be well educated and adapted to life in the West, presenting a different image than the volunteer army in Afghanistan.

## War on Terror

As the nation and the world reeled from the horror of the attack, President George W. Bush announced a War on Terror. The United States would use its military force, its police agencies, and its diplomatic contacts around the world, to "bring to justice, or to bring justice to" the perpetrators and organizers of the attacks. The American public, and large sectors of the publics of many other countries, endorsed the effort.

# Classic Issues

As the U.S. War on Terror took shape, it had several aspects, reflecting classic issues in intelligence.

In prior decades, coordinating information between agencies had always been a problem for the American intelligence community. Parallel problems had surfaced in Japan, Russia, Britain, and Germany, as agencies failed to share sources.

As the United States reviewed its information sources, the realization came home that technical intelligence and signals intelligence were inadequate tools for apprehending the sponsors of the attacks. Yet human intelligence soon showed its limits as well.

In prior conflicts, identifying enemy agents who might be in the United States had been difficult. Operational security and counterintelligence required that possible allies of the enemy within the United States be questioned, and if possible, apprehended. Ethnic identity and ethnic origin could define a large group among which enemy sympathizers might be found, but, as in the past, rounding up suspects on the basis of ethnicity alone flew in the face of American values and the legal system that protected the rights of those accused or suspected by the state. Americans still remembered the internment of thousands of Japanese Americans in World War II as a violation of civil rights.

## Connecting the Dots

As in 1941, the attack itself was perceived as a failure of intelligence. In 1941 and 2001, it appeared that various agencies had bits and pieces of information that might have forewarned of a coming attack. Part of the reason for the creation of the CIA in the post-World War II era was precisely to coordinate information from diverse sources (see Chapter 11). The *intelligence community* had not worked as a community, it seemed.

**Spy Words**

By the term **intelligence community,** American analysts meant to include the following 14 agencies in the year 2002:

    Central Intelligence Agency (CIA)
    Department of the Treasury
    Department of Energy
    Department of State
    Defense Intelligence Agency (DIA)
    Federal Bureau of Investigation (FBI)
    National Imagery and Mapping Agency (NIMA)
    National Reconnaissance Office (NRO)
    National Security Agency (NSA)
    U.S. Air Force Intelligence
    U.S. Army Intelligence
    U.S. Navy Intelligence
    U.S. Marine Corps Intelligence
    U.S. Coast Guard Intelligence

In June 2002, part of the reaction of the administration was to put a proposal before Congress to create a new Homeland Security Agency, with the job of coordinating security information. Congress also passed a Patriot Act, which increased the government's investigative powers, and conducted an investigation into why the data hadn't been properly analyzed—or, in the language adopted by congressmen and journalists, why no one had connected the dots.

## Some Unconnected CIA Dots

In 2002, both the CIA and the FBI came under scrutiny for missing signals of the looming attacks. However, much of what the agencies knew was of a generic nature, and offered few clues to a particular plan. *Newsweek* reported that the CIA's Counter Terrorism Center had identified two terrorists, Nawaf Alhazmi and Khalid Almihdhar, based on tips from Malaysia. However, the CIA didn't tip off the Immigration and Naturalization Service or the State Department. The two men were aboard American Airlines Flight 77, which crashed into the Pentagon.

This information was later confirmed in a staff report to a joint Committee on Intelligence. The staff report identified many items of intelligence that, had they been properly considered together or analyzed, might have led to the apprehension of some more of the intended hijackers.

No one could say, however, what might have happened if more of the hijackers had been arrested. The methods of Al Qaeda included great compartmentation and resistance to interrogation, making it possible that a substitute team of hijackers could have been assembled.

## NSA Dots

The National Security Agency intercepted two strange communications originating in Afghanistan on September 10, 2001, referring to a major event scheduled for the following day. Apparently the messages, caught in the flow of massive amounts of information, were not read until September 12. The delay in translating and processing the information was normal. The process could be speeded up in cases where the communications came from known sources, but no one in the agency knew whom the intercepts were from.

The agency intercepted literally millions of conversations a day over phone lines and the Internet. The classic problem of techint and sigint yielding too much information was clearly at work. Furthermore, the warning contained in the messages, even when deciphered and viewed after the event was too vague to suggest a course of action.

## And a Couple of FBI Dots

An FBI agent in Phoenix, Arizona, wrote an e-mail memo in July 2001, about two months before the attacks. The memo expressed concern that Middle Eastern men were training at U.S. flight schools. About a month later, Zacarias Moussaoui, who had sought flying lessons in Minnesota, was arrested on an immigration violation. Later, Minnesota FBI agent Colleen Rowley released a scathing letter criticizing the FBI for ignoring warnings from the field offices.

The failure to connect the dots was a classic dilemma of intelligence. Lots of information got collected, but only after the event could the pattern be seen and the significance of various clues be interpreted.

Although Moussaoui had sought training, the evidence surrounding his case was confusing, as was his erratic performance in court when asked how he would plead: guilty or not guilty. Some evidence suggested he was engaged in the plan for a separate attack, perhaps one to involve the use of crop-dusting aircraft to spread some sort of toxic chemical or biological agent. Yet Moussaoui was said to have received funds from Ramzi bin al Shibh, a Yemeni who provided funds for the September 11 attacks.

## Oops! at the INS

In March 2002, six months *after* the terrorist attack, it was disclosed that a service contractor for the Immigration and Naturalization Service (INS) had mailed visa extensions for two of the hijackers, who had been identified as among those killed in their terrorist act on September 11. The INS was embarrassed, as it appeared that whoever processed the paperwork was too busy to watch television or read the newspapers.

As in the aftermath of Pearl Harbor, the crisis brought to the forefront the inadequacy of existing agencies to deal with the unexpected. Heads would roll. Although in 1942, inquiries were directed at military officers Admiral Husband Kimmel and General Walter C. Short, in 2002, some civilian officials felt the heat. In August 2002, commissioner of the Immigration and Naturalization Service, James W. Ziglar, announced he would resign.

## Humint and Techint in Afghanistan

In November and December 2001, American troops moved into Afghanistan, and soon scored victory after victory against the Taliban regime that had offered sanctuary to the leaders of Al Qaeda. Part of the effort to bring Al Qaeda leaders to justice focused on the capture of specific individuals, including Osama bin Laden, who had used his fortune and his access to the fortunes of others to fund terrorist training camps.

Although allied with an anti-Taliban Afghan force, the Northern Alliance, and supported by President Pervez Musharraf of Pakistan, the effort to use the military as a police force to track down individuals was not very successful. Analysts and commentators soon identified the reasons. The United States had long relied on techint, but techint was not the best way to track individuals. What the CIA and other agencies needed was *ground truth*.

**Spy Words**

Troops and CIA personnel hunting for individual members of the Taliban regime or of the Al Qaeda organization needed detailed information about the whereabouts of specific individuals at a specific moment in time. This information on the ground was known as **ground truth** as distinct from aerial surveillance photographs that were usually not available in real time. Even the use of unmanned aerial vehicles (UAVs) with television cameras, a new type of techint brought to Afghanistan, could not substitute for reliable human testimony about specific people in specific places at a specific moment in time.

## International Agency Cooperation

The military and CIA officials had different views about working with Pakistan's Inter-Services Intelligence agency (ISI). One of the problems was that until the late 1990s, the ISI had cooperated with the Taliban, partly because the rank and file members of the ISI were Islamic fundamentalists.

Finding that the ISI did not provide much information, the CIA and the military tried to work with members of the Northern Alliance. U.S. Secretary of Defense Donald Rumsfeld indicated that if Osama bin Laden were to be caught, it would be because of a scrap of information from some person. The United States put a price of $5 million on Bin Laden's head, but he continued to elude capture. Earlier, it is interesting to note, Osama bin Laden had set a price of $9 million apiece for the assassination of several American leaders.

## Humint Weaknesses

Like many humint sources, especially those operating for pay, some of the Afghan informants colored their stories with exaggeration, good-sounding information, and often, downright lies. Despite complete dossiers routed to American intelligence from Russia, Saudi Arabia, and Yemen, the leadership of Al Qaeda slipped away.

Most analysts believed that, using bribes and contacts, many Al Qaeda leaders moved through Pakistan, finding refuge there. The border, or tribal region of Pakistan was only nominally under control of the Pakistan government, and the last time Pakistan army troops had penetrated all the way to the border with Afghanistan had been in 1973. Through this region, ruled by local warlords, Al Qaeda middle and top leadership cadres could move rather readily.

There were dozens of mountain passes, impossible to watch with the scattering of U.S. troops and Northern Alliance allies. Thus, Al Qaeda members moved into towns, villages, and even into major cities like Karachi, renting apartments and setting up safe houses.

By September 2002, some of the Al Qaeda groups could be traced by cell phone calls, interviews with the media, and other means, leading to a few Pakistani arrests of some of the hunted members. However, it appeared easy for fugitives from Afghanistan who were funded by Al Qaeda, to merge into the Pakistani population in remote towns and in the large cities of the country.

The problem of getting good ground information in Afghanistan was complicated by the language problem. Few Americans spoke any of the numerous languages used in Afghanistan, and simply finding translators and trainers delayed all operations.

Like other subversive and terror organizations before it, Al Qaeda and related terror groups relied on a structure of independent cells and compartmentation. As the FBI began to put together the scraps of information regarding the cell that had planned the attacks of September 11, the picture emerged that the group had been based in Hamburg, Germany.

# A Strange New World

Despite the fact that many classic issues in intelligence, counterintelligence, interpretation and analysis, operational security, and old-fashioned forensic investigation were demonstrated in the War on Terror, the situation was very new in some regards.

Since the attack was organized by an international group with recruits from Arabia, Chechnya, Indonesia, Malaya, and with cells in Europe, North America, and elsewhere, it was a new kind of organization, unrelated to the government of any country. Thus the defeat of a regime in Afghanistan that provided sanctuary did not mean the collapse of the terror organization. The American defense establishment, honed for 50 years to deal with the perceived threat of the Soviet Union, China, and other countries, was not attuned to the challenge of a group that knew no borders, operated through international banking, and was adept at clandestine operations.

## Deterrence No Longer

The lack of a national base for the terrorists led to the more ominous fact that the long-standing strategy or principle of deterrence did not apply. In the old culture of military intelligence, analysts at the Pentagon and in the CIA examined Soviet capabilities, wondering what would happen if the Russians ever attacked.

Developing a second strike capability, allowing the United States to respond with a nuclear strike against the attacking country, led to the uneasy balance of Mutual Assured Destruction. Intelligence assessments focused on finding out what the Soviet (and later, the Chinese) capabilities were, and estimating whether sufficient American weapons would survive a first nuclear strike to deal a devastating attack back. With that second-strike capability, the first strike was deterred.

The principle of deterrence kept a nuclear balance. However, in the suddenly new world of the twenty-first century, there was no way to deter an attack with weapons of mass destruction. Since Al Qaeda did not have a capital city, or any national infrastructure, the threat of retaliatory attack could not be mounted to deter the first strike.

## New Intelligence Culture

The new situation required a completely new intelligence culture. The new system would need to go beyond assessing a national capability, to deciphering such elusive qualities as intention, support networks, financial transfer points, small training facilities that could be moved, and numerous, compartmented cells scattered across several countries.

That new culture required cooperation between disparate agencies, not only in the United States, but between the United States and friendly and supportive regimes in Germany, France, Italy, Spain, Canada, the Philippines, Malaysia, and elsewhere. Evidence mounted that, like the *moles* of a half-century earlier, the terror groups would operate with *sleeper cells*.

 **Spy Words**

American intelligence agencies, as they investigated the links between the September 11 terrorists and others, began to suspect that other small groups, funded from overseas, lived in the United States or Western Europe and planned further terrorist activities. Dubbed **sleeper cells** by the press, these groups presented several problems for law enforcement. As long as they committed no overt act, and as long as no one testified against them, they were difficult to apprehend. In the United States, if the individuals in a suspected cell were U.S. citizens, prosecutors would need solid evidence to get a conviction.

## The Firewall Problem

As a result of the investigations by Senator Frank Church and Congressmen Otis Pike in the mid-1970s, and as a result of the press and public uproar over excesses of domestic surveillance by both the FBI and the CIA, both agencies had reformed (see Chapter 15). The CIA was more scrupulous in avoiding domestic surveillance. The FBI did not conduct wiretaps, searches, or follow individuals without a warrant. President Gerald Ford forbade U.S. government-sponsored assassination.

The two agencies established something of a firewall between themselves. If the CIA identified a foreign agent, it was to transfer information and jurisdiction to the FBI when the agent crossed into the United States, but not before. But in the light of the political uproar when the CIA had been found to operate inside the United States in the 1970s, the cultural style of the agency by the 1990s was to stay out of American domestic affairs. The hand-off of information from overseas to domestic agencies was impaired, not only by formal rules, but also by a long-standing aversion to crossing the firewall between the agencies.

## New Tools and Civil Liberties

The FBI traditionally tended to operate passively, investigating criminal acts after they occurred, with little role in preventing crime. Proactive and preventive tools were increased with the Patriot Act, signed by President Bush in October 2001, which gave the FBI some new powers. The act established a counterterrorism fund, enhanced the power to conduct electronic surveillance, eased restrictions on search warrants, set up tools to trace laundered money in the United States and abroad, strengthened the protection of the borders, stiffened passport and visa requirements, and called for more coordination among intelligence agencies. Even with the enhanced funding and powers, the task confronting the FBI was enormous. According to one report, about half of the Bureau's 11,000 agents worked on tracking down exactly what had already happened in the September 11 conspiracy.

## Ashcroft at Work

Attorney General John Ashcroft urged the new FBI director, Robert Mueller, to conduct massive dragnets and arrest members of possible terror cells before they could strike. The policy created some backlash.

The roundup of several thousand individuals of Middle Eastern citizenships on charges of violation of visa regulations, usually overstaying a student or visitor visa, led to some rumbles in the media. Students of history recalled the Palmer Raids of 1919–1920, when Attorney General A. Mitchell Palmer arrested 2,700 Russian and Eastern European anarchists and socialists for their political affiliations in the wake of domestic bomb threats and attacks. Critics asked if Ashcroft was falling into a similar pattern of indiscriminate arrest.

Yet in 2002, the threat to national security was far greater, and the voices of criticism of the twenty-first century attorney general were far more muted than they had been in the 1920s. Furthermore, Attorney General Ashcroft was scrupulous to remain within established procedures. For example, when the press complained he would not release a list of those detained, he pointed out that the government had always regarded it as the prerogative of the accused to notify the press or others that they were detained, as a matter of privacy. Immigrants with questionable status were always detained until the question of their status was properly cleared up, so detention of immigrants with visa violations was not a new process.

As the visa status problems were reviewed and those detained were either released or deported or charged with crimes, judges tended to support the government's position that national security demanded a vigilant prosecution of suspicious cases. The attorney general's high-profile actions had suddenly put the spotlight on procedures that most Americans had never thought much about.

## Airplanes as Weapons

The central aspect of the terrorist attacks of September 11 was the use of commercial airliners as weapons. Although the public and many authorities believed that no prior hijacking of an aircraft had been staged with that purpose, the intelligence community had learned of several such plans. As later investigators examined the intelligence that had come in, they uncovered quite a few examples of information that indicated the possible use of aircraft as weapons:

◆ In December 1994, a group of Algerian terrorists hijacked an Air France flight and threatened to fly it into the Eiffel Tower. French officials tricked the hijackers into believing the airplane did not have enough fuel to reach Paris and it landed in Marseilles. There, French antiterrorist teams raided the plane and killed all four of the terrorists.

◆ In January 1995, Philippine authorities raided an apartment in Manila and discovered that a group of terrorists there planned to crash an airplane into CIA headquarters. The Philippine National Police passed on information to the U.S. Federal Aviation Administration (FAA), which briefed airline company officials.

◆ In January 1996, American intelligence officials learned of a planned suicide attack by a group associated with Al Qaeda. The group planned to fly a plane from Afghanistan and crash it into the White House.

In addition to these indications, the intelligence community learned of at least nine other plots involving aircraft prior to September 11, 2001. These included a plan to hijack a Japanese airplane over Israel; a use of an unmanned aerial vehicle to attack a U.S. embassy; a 1998 plan to fly a plane loaded with explosives from a foreign country to attack the World Trade Center; and plans to crash airplanes into airports, military targets, government buildings and public gatherings. The CIA had passed on reports of these types of plans to the FBI and to the FAA.

The failure of the intelligence community and especially of the Counter Terrorism Center in the CIA and the FBI to take these threats more seriously was shocking to congressmen, journalists, and the public. However, the failure to "connect the dots" and to properly come up with a strategic analysis of the various pieces of information is easier to understand when put against the broader history of intelligence.

# Predicting the Unpredictable

Over and over in intelligence history, evidence from the field has been ignored, analyzed incorrectly, or collated improperly. And over and over, agencies within the same country have had difficulty cooperating to achieve national security goals. Some examples:

- Despite evidence of mounting Japanese forces, the United States was surprised at Pearl Harbor in 1941 (see Chapter 3).

- Despite warnings from the Roto Kapelle, from Richard Sorge, and from Enigma decrypts passed through back channels, Joseph Stalin could not believe Germany would attack the Soviet Union. In 1942, he was stunned when they did (see Chapter 4).

- Despite thousands of conflicting pieces of evidence, and helped along by British and American deceptions, Germany did not anticipate that the 1944 D-Day attacks would come at Normandy (see Chapter 5).

- The information provided by Cicero to Germany was some of the highest quality intelligence of World War II, but it tended to be ignored (see Chapter 5).

- The United States could not believe the Soviet Union would detonate a nuclear weapon before the early 1950s. The American public was stunned when the Soviets did so in 1949 (see Chapter 8).

## Reasons for Prediction Failure

Almost every chapter of this book includes many such episodes and cases of ignored warnings, misplaced optimism, and successful deceptions based on erroneous preconceptions held by the other side. In every such case, there was an attempt to pin blame for the errors on generals, admirals, intelligence officers, and even chiefs of state.

There were many reasons for such failures of strategic prediction based on intelligence but several themes run through the history of such failures:

- Too much data, too little time
- Outside the paradigm

- ◆ Group-think

- ◆ Interagency failure to cooperate

- ◆ Criticism from hindsight, or "could-have, should-have, would-have" thinking

- ◆ Mirror-imaging

Those who analyze the inner working of intelligence analysis and who teach the subject in training programs focus on just such problems. All of these patterns were found in the failure to "connect the dots" in 2001.

- ◆ **Too much data, too little time.** When there is a flood of information, it is extremely difficult to identify patterns among thousands of data points.

- ◆ **Outside the paradigm.** Some data is faulty or false and when trying to judge what is valid, those items that do not fit the existing understanding, or the existing background culture, tend to be discounted. By its nature, surprising or out-of-character information (such as the idea of Soviet high technical achievement in 1949) is discounted.

- ◆ **Group think.** When an organization has habits, patterns, and expectations based on experience and expectations, the members of the organization tend to go along with the established view, and discount data or ideas that don't fit as aberrations, unpopular, politically incorrect, defeatist, or simply wrongheaded.

- ◆ **Interagency failure to cooperate.** Even when agencies work hard to cooperate, it is difficult. Sources and methods must be protected from disclosure, and hence material tends to be sanitized to conceal its origin. Sometimes one agency will pass on a piece of information with a note that it comes from a usually reliable source, or from an unconfirmed rumor. The receiving agency has difficulty assessing it.

- ◆ **Could-have, should-have, would-have thinking.** Students of history realize how easy it is to see patterns in retrospect that were not obvious at the time. Because something seems obvious after the fact, it is difficult to understand how all the evidence of *what should have been done* was ignored. As bettors at the racetrack often say, "*I could have, should have, would have*" after they fail to bet on the winning horse to take home a fortune.

- ◆ People of one culture often believe they can predict the behavior of those in another culture, expecting them to "mirror" their own patterns. Such thinking can lead to miscalculations and faulty predictions.

## Some American Factors

In 2001, the problem of communication within the U.S. intelligence community may have been made more serious by firewalls between domestic and international intelligence, established in the 1970s to protect civil liberties. Furthermore, the nature of free societies tends to make it relatively easy to cross borders and organize a clandestine operation. The fact that over the period 1940–2000, so many spies and traitors operated in the United States suggests the truth of the concept that the price of freedom is eternal vigilance.

In their defense, the agencies have pointed to the glut of information, the unusual nature of the new threat, and the difficulties of surveillance in a free society.

## From Looking Backward to Looking Ahead

Although intelligence agencies may work hard to protect national security, there are bound to be unpleasant surprises. The only hope for avoiding them is to be sensitive to the unusual, to the odd fact that doesn't fit, and to the pattern that may lie beneath the surface. Sometimes assessing that information correctly requires listening to views that are unpopular, noted in the field but discounted at headquarters, and respecting the minority view within an organization. It was never easy, nor will it be in the future.

## The Least You Need To Know

- ◆ The terrorist attacks of September 11 surprised the intelligence community, although there were pieces of evidence that in retrospect showed such an attack was possible.

- ◆ The threats to U.S. security and to the security of other Western nations posed by Al Qaeda are difficult to oppose or deter because they are not sponsored by a single state.

- ◆ The failure to "connect the dots" and to predict surprise attacks is extremely common in the history of intelligence.

- ◆ Rather than focusing on whom to blame for failure, intelligence agencies need to adjust their style as much as possible to the changing and unpredictable world of the twenty-first century.

# Glossary

**Afghan Arabs**    Since many of those who went to Afghanistan to support the *Taliban* in the 1990s were from Arab-speaking countries, they became known as *Afghan Arabs.*

**agent of influence**    The KGB sought to identify friendly figures in Western governments who would influence policy in a pro-Soviet direction. A number of pro-Soviet officials in the Franklin Roosevelt administration were remembered as in this gray area.

*agent provocateur*    A French term referring to a false agent whose task it is to lure members of an organization into overt, violent, or criminal actions that will expose them to arrest.

*Al Qaeda*    A phrase in Arabic meaning "the base," *Al Qaeda* (also spelled *Al Qai'da*) was originally a loose organization that supported the *Taliban. Al Qaeda* or "The Base" funded an international group of young men, all of whom were Islamists or radical fundamentalists. By 1999, the organization became dedicated to attacking the United States.

**AMTORG**    A Soviet trading company set up in New York in the 1930s, doing several hundred million dollars of legitimate business. However, AMTORG also provided a cover for espionage agents. About half of the American employees of AMTORG were also members of the CPUSA.

**AVH**    *Allavedelmi Hatosag,* Hungarian State Security Authority.

**black bag jobs**   Illegal and warrentless break-ins either to obtain copies of materials or to plant listening devices and telephone taps.

**Black Chamber**   Yardley called his memoir of his work in setting up a decoding system for the U.S. government *The American Black Chamber,* alluding to the prior history of "Black Chambers" for the interception and decoding of messages. The most famous of prior Black Chambers was that in Vienna, Austria in the eighteenth and nineteenth centuries.

**Center**   Both the civilian and military espionage agencies of the Soviet Union referred to their headquarters in Moscow as *Moscow Center.*

**Cheka**   Cheka was the Soviet Union's first secret police (1917–1922), under Lenin. Later agents were called "Chekists" even when working under the NKVD or KGB.

**clandestine activity**   A broad term that covers spying, sabotage, and the planting of false or skewed information or propaganda.

**Comintern**   The international league of communist parties, the Comintern was established in Moscow in 1920 and disbanded in 1943, to be replaced after World War II by a less formal organization, the Cominform. All Comintern parties followed the lead of the Soviet Communist Party. Dedicated members of these overseas parties would sometimes be identified and selected to assist either the KGB or the GRU in their espionage activities by Recruiters.

**compartmentation**   The principle within an organization of keeping information controlled on a need-to-know basis and dividing the organization to limit the chance of secret information being leaked. See *firewall.*

**conspiracy theory**   Such a theory relies on the notion that the absence of evidence only proves how well the conspirators covered up the evidence. Because conspiracy theories do not rely on evidence, but only on assumed connections, they are usually rejected by responsible analysts, but they make for plausible espionage explanations, often the core of fictional tales.

**control**   The supervisor of an intelligence agent.

**counterintelligence**   The process and agencies devoted to tracking down spies and traitors within a nation.

**cover** (n.)   A false identity adopted by an agent.

**cowboys**   Inside the CIA, those who planned and executed some risky operations on the ground came to be known as cowboys.

**CPUSA**   Communist Party of the United States of America. From its inception in the early 1920s, the CPUSA provided a recruiting ground for informants and agents for the Soviet spy organizations including *GRU* and the *KGB* and its predecessor organizations.

**cryptanalysis**   The art of cracking the codes of other countries.

**cryptography**   The field of creating codes.

**cutout** (n.)   In building a network, controls sometimes contact agents through a third party, known as a cutout, to protect compartmentation. In a block cutout, the contact person knew the name of all the agents working in a particular operation or cell. In a chain cutout, the contact knew only one agent, linking only the person below and the person above him in the chain of information flow.

**dangle** (n.)   A dangle is a person who approaches an intelligence agency in order to be recruited as an intelligence source, but who is a walk-in planted in order to provide disinformation.

**dead drop**   A dead drop is a spot at which an informant or agent can leave a message to be picked up by a contact, often in a public spot such as a park or roadside.

**defectors in place**   The term was used to define informants in Soviet bloc countries who stayed on the job to provide information. Oleg Penkovsky was the most famous of them. From the Soviet viewpoint a defector in place was a traitor and when caught, was subject to capital punishment.

**disinformation**   Planted stories and false information designed to confuse an enemy intelligence organization or to undermine public confidence in an enemy regime.

**double agent**   One who works simultaneously for two enemy agencies. Some historical double agents were loyal only to one side, while others became confused and alternated their loyalties.

**DS**   *Durzhavna Sigurnost*, Bulgarian State Security. This agency was reputed to carry out some assassinations and other direct operations at the request of the KGB during the cold war.

**espionage**   The act of spying. Espionage refers to a wide range of secret activities, including gathering intelligence through such means as interviews and reading local literature to the use of paid informers or traitors.

**exfiltration**   The opposite of "infiltration," exfiltration refers to the smuggling of an agent or informer out of a country.

**firewall**   The term denotes an intentional separation between two or more agencies. Intended to protect sources through compartmentation, such a practice frequently stands in the way of coordinating counterintelligence activities.

**FUSAG**   An acronym for "First U.S. Army Group," a fictional or notional unit created to deceive the Germans into believing that forces were being marshalled for an invasion across the English Channel to land at Calais.

**GPU**   *Gosudarstvennoe Politicheskoe Upravlenie*, State Political Administration. Supplanted the Cheka as the secret police in the Soviet Union, 1922–1923. Quickly reorganized as *OGPU*.

**ground truth**   Information on the ground as distinct from aerial or satellite surveillance photographs.

**GRU**   *Glavnoe Razvedyvatelnoe Upravlenie*, the chief intelligence directorate or administration of the Soviet general staff, or military intelligence. Extremely secret, the organization was reputedly known only as "Military Department 44388." Both Richard Sorge and Alger Hiss reported to GRU.

**Ho Chi Minh Trail**   A series of paths and roads through the forested regions inside Laos, used by the North Vietnamese to transport arms, supplies, and personnel to the anti-government forces in South Vietnam.

**HUAC**   The House Committee on Un-American Activities. Incorrectly abbreviated as "HUAC" when "HCUA" or even "HCOUAA" would have been the correct acronym. Since it was difficult to pronounce either of those two versions, "HUAC" (pronounced hew-ack) caught on in the press and on radio and television. The committee succeeded in uncovering a few communist agents.

**human intelligence**   Human agents, including informants, as distinct from signals intelligence and technical intelligence. Abbreviated as humint.

**intelligence**   All the information about foreign powers that can be used in military or diplomatic planning.

**intelligence community**   In 2002, American analysts included 14 agencies in the term: Central Intelligence Agency (CIA), Department of the Treasury, Department of Energy, Department of State, Defense Intelligence Agency (DIA), Federal Bureau of Investigation (FBI), National Imagery and Mapping Agency (NIMA), National Reconnaissance Office (NRO), National Security Agency (NSA), U.S. Air Force Intelligence, U.S. Army Intelligence, U.S. Navy Intelligence, U.S. Marine Corps Intelligence, and U.S. Coast Guard Intelligence. Sometimes the term is used with less precision to include other agencies as well.

**Jedburghs**    Units of resistance troops supported by airdrops and a few military officers from SOE and from OSS during World War II. The Jedburghs were based on examples of guerrilla, irregular troops encountered by the British in Ireland and elsewhere.

**KGB**    *Komitet Gosudarstvennoe Bezopasnosti*, Committee of State Security. Replaced the MGB as the Soviet Union's secret police and espionage organization in the period 1954–1991. For the sake of convenience, earlier organizations performing the same role are sometimes called KGB.

**legend**    A legend is a life story made up to provide a false identity for an agent. Once the legend is created, corroborating documents and specific details can be fitted together to make the story credible.

*maquis* and *maquisard*    Terms used to refer to French resistance units during World War II. The words were derived from wild, brush-covered country on the island of Corsica.

**MGB**    *Ministerstvo Gosudarstvennoe Bezopasnosti*, Ministry of State Security (1946-1954). Replaced the NKGB and later was supplanted by the KGB as the Soviet Union's secret police and espionage organization.

**MI-5**    Also known as "Security Service," MI-5 is Britain's counterespionage or internal security bureau. It was first organized in 1909–1910 by Captain Vernon Kell as a Special Intelligence Bureau within Military Operations 5 or MO-5. In World War I, the agency was successful in rounding up all German spies in Britain.

**MI-6**    Also called the Secret Intelligence Service (SIS), MI-6 is Britain's overseas intelligence office, roughly equivalent to the CIA in the United States. MI-6 was first organized in 1912 as the Special Intelligence Section, and was built up by Commander Mansfield Cumming (known as "C").

**microdot**    A process invented by German intelligence early in World War II which involved reducing a photograph to a microscopic size by filming it through a reversed microscope lens. A page of data could be reduced to the size of a printed period.

**mole**    An agent who quietly pursues a career inside a government while spying for another government. The term was used to identify agents like the Cambridge Five, who spied for the Soviet Union. John Le Carre introduced the term "mole" in 1974 in the novel *Tinker, Tailor, Soldier, Spy*. Walter Pforzheimer, a retired CIA officer, discovered that the term had been used in a 1622 biography of King Henry VII to describe spies.

**NATO**    North Atlantic Treaty Organization. NATO and WTO made up the two "sides" in the cold war. Original NATO countries: Belgium, Canada, Denmark,

France, Greece, Iceland, Italy, Luxembourg, Netherlands, Norway, Portugal, Turkey, United Kingdom, and the United States of America. In 1955, the Federal Republic of Germany (West Germany) joined. Spain joined in 1982. After the end of the cold war, NATO began to admit nations formerly part of the Soviet bloc or WTO.

**neighbors**    The KGB and the GRU each referred to the other agency with the code-word "neighbors."

**NKGB**    *Norodnyi Komissariat Gosudarstvennoe Bezopasnosti*, People's Commissariat for State Security. Replaced the NKVD as the Soviet Union's secret police and espionage organization 1938–1943. Replaced by the MGB in 1946.

**NKVD**    *Norodnyi Komissariat Vnutrennikh Del* or People's Commissariat for Internal Affairs. Replaced the OGPU as the Soviet secret police and espionage organization 1934–1938. Replaced by NKGB.

**notional**    The term was created in Britain in World War II to refer to a fictional person or operation intended to deceive the enemy. The term later was expanded to include the creation of false organizations intended to lure subversive individuals into joining, and to include proprietaries, commercial companies created to serve an intelligence purpose.

**OGPU**    *Obedinennoe Gosudarstvennoe Politicheskoe Upravlenie*, Unified State Political Administration, 1922–1934. Soviet secret police and espionage organization. It was replaced by the NKVD.

**one-time pad**    A system of encryption in which the sender and receiver have a pad of paper with identical sets of random numbers printed on each sheet to be used when encoding and decoding messages.

**OSS**    Office of Strategic Services, the American intelligence and special operations agency, 1942–1945. Jokingly referred to as "Oh So Social," because of the members of high society recruited to work for the agency.

**partisans**    In Eastern Europe during World War II, most of the local resistance forces were known as partisans, representing irregular troops organized on a political or party basis.

**pixies**    The CIA and MI-6 cooperated in a program to send infiltrators into Albania in the late 1940s to develop resistance to the communist regime there and used the term "pixies" to describe the small units. All the pixies were apprehended or killed on arrival.

**plausible deniability**    A policy that began under CIA director Allen Dulles (1953–1961) and was discontinued under William Colby in the mid-1970s. According to this doctrine, there would be no paper trail of presidential authorization of an action.

**product**   Intelligence data comes from many sources, and after the data is analyzed, the result is known as product.

**proprietary companies** or **proprietaries**   The Central Intelligence Agency set up a number of companies to conduct operations overseas, the most well known of which was Air America, operating in Southeast Asia.

**recognition signal**   When one agent makes contact with another not previously met, the agents have recognition signals, such as a casual phrase or a carried item such as a package or pair of gloves. In Soviet tradecraft, recognition signals became quite elaborate.

**recruiter**   The Soviet Union employed specialists in recruiting agents in Britain, the United States, and elsewhere. The recruiter would identify potential agents, sound them out as to their willingness to provide information, and then turn them over to a control for development.

*rezident*   In Soviet terminology, a consular or embassy official, a correspondent for the Soviet Press agency, TASS, or a member of a trade mission whose position could be used for espionage purposes. The office of *rezidentura* was the post, while the *rezident* was the individual.

**rogue agency**   The charge in the 1970s that the CIA had become independent of control or "rogue," was given some believability by the doctrine of plausible deniability, which left no evidence or paper trail to the presidential authority behind particular actions.

**Room 40**   The British Naval Intelligence office was first located in Room 40 in the Admiralty Old Building, and was headed by Admiral Sir Reginald "Blinker" Hall. It was a section of the Room 40 cryptanalysts who deciphered the Zimmermann Note.

*ruse de guerre*   French expression used to apply to all sorts of deceptions or "ruses" practiced in war, including the use of false flags on naval or merchant ships and devices to deceive or confuse the enemy, such as false preparations for attack.

**sabotage**   Destruction of equipment or facilities. Derived from *sabot*, a type of wooden shoe. When thrown into factory equipment, it would destroy the works. The term was used by radical labor unionists early in the twentieth century and spread to more general acts of industrial and communications destruction.

**safe house**   An apartment or house that is available for temporary stays of agents or for meetings, usually in the target country and unknown to local counterintelligence.

**sanitized**   To protect the identity of a source and the method used to acquire information, the words or other details of a piece of intelligence are considerably changed. Such a document or data point is then said to be sanitized.

**SAS**   Special Air Service. The British maintained the SAS as a special operations military unit from World War II into the twenty-first century.

**SB**   *Sluzba Bezpieczentwa*, Polish Security Service.

**signals intelligence**   Intelligence received through the decoding of messages, including those sent in encrypted alphabetic, Morse code as well as voice messages. Some signals intelligence can be derived from analyzing the flow of information itself, without cracking the codes, in "traffic analysis," or by locating the geographic point of transmission through "direction finding."

**SIS**   See *MI-6*.

**sleeper cells**   Groups of terrorists who live in a country without committing any overt acts but who plan future sabotage activities. After the terrorist attacks of September 11, 2001, American intelligence agencies sought evidence of sleeper cells in the United States.

**SMERSH**   Soviet organization for tracking down spies. Assumed to derive from *smert shpionam*, meaning "death to spies," the term was probably an acronym derived from *spetsial'nie metodi razoblachenia shpinov*, meaning "special methods for exposing spies." The term was used in Ian Fleming's James Bond novels as well as in reality.

**SOE**   Special Operations Executive, the British agency engaged in World War II in providing aid, training, and arms to resistance forces in Nazi-occupied Europe. Disbanded at the end of the war.

**source**   A generic term to refer to a wide variety of ways of getting information, ranging from informants or agents through signals intelligence and other technical means of getting information.

**special operations**   When military operations need to be conducted covertly the work is best carried on by the military services rather than by an intelligence agency. Usually operating in small groups, "special ops" forces are often disliked by more traditional military officers as they tend to operate unconventionally and sometimes outside of normal channels of command. Special operations include clandestine training and support for resistance groups, as well as some commando and sabotage raids.

*stasi*   *Staatssicherheitsdienst–SSD*, East German State Security. This agency had the reputation as the most thorough and ruthless of the Eastern European internal secret police forces during the cold war.

**StB**   *Statni tajna Bezpecnost*, Czechoslovakian State Secret Security.

**subversive activities**   Political or sabotage activities intended to subvert a government.

**SVR** *Sluzhba Vneshnei Razvedki*, Foreign Intelligence Service (of Russia). This organization was the successor, since 1991, to the KGB as the espionage organization of Russia.

**talent scout** See *Recruiter.*

**Taliban** The government, made up of former religious school students, which took over Afghanistan in 1996. The term means "students" in Arabic.

**telemetry intelligence** Information gathered from weapons test radio signals sent by a foreign power for their own purposes of monitoring the performance of a missile or other weapons system. From such information, it was possible for the United States to learn some of the characteristics of long-range Soviet missiles, such as range and accuracy.

**The Pumpkin Papers** Whittaker Chambers had hidden some film of documents originally supplied by Alger Hiss in a pumpkin on his farm. The press soon dubbed the retrieved evidence The Pumpkin Papers.

**turned** When a secret agent was discovered, and then, through threats or rewards, converted to send false information to his original organization, he was said to be turned.

**UAVs** Unmanned Aerial Vehicles. Small drone aircraft, used in the Afghanistan campaign of 2001, to gather television images of ground action and sometimes to deliver ordnance to a target.

**Venona** The body of coded diplomatic messages from the Soviet Union's consular offices in the United States to Moscow, some 2,900 between 1940 and 1948. The batch of material was earlier known by other code names: Bride and Drug. Partially deciphered, the Venona messages assisted in tracking some spies. Publicly disclosed in the 1990s.

**walk-in** When a traitor volunteers to provide intelligence by walking in to an embassy or to a known intelligence office of a foreign power, that person is known as a walk-in.

**WTO** Warsaw Treaty Organization. Responding to the inclusion of West Germany in NATO in 1955, the Soviet Union formed the WTO, usually called the "Warsaw Pact." Joining the Soviet Union in the original WTO were Albania, Bulgaria, Czechoslovakia, German Democratic Republic (East Germany), Hungary, Poland, and Romania. In 1968, Albania withdrew. WTO disbanded in 1991.

# Appendix B

# Bibliography

Accoce, Pierre, and Pierre Quet. *A Man Called Lucy*. New York: Coward, McCann & Geoghegan, Inc., 1966.

Alcorn, Robert Hayden. *No Bugles for Spies: Tales of the OSS*. New York: David McKay, 1962.

Allen, Thomas B. and Norman Polmar. *Merchants of Treason*. New York: Dell, 1988.

Alvarez, David J. *Secret Messages: Codebreakers and American Diplomacy, 1930-1945*. Lawrence: University of Kansas Press, 2000.

Andrew, Christopher. *Her Majesty's Secret Service: The Making of the British Intelligence Community*. New York: Viking, 1986.

———. *For The President's Eyes Only: Secret Intelligence and the American Presidency from Washington to Bush*. New York: HarperCollins, 1995.

Andrew, Christopher and Vasili Mitrokhin. *The Sword and the Shield: The Mitrokhin Archive and the Secret History of the KGB*. New York: Basic Books, 1999.

Barron, John: *KGB: The Secret Work of Soviet Secret Agents*. New York: Bantam Books, 1974.

Bazna, Elyesa. *I Was Cicero.* Munich: Andre Duetsch, 1962; English translation Eric Bosbacher: New York: Dell, 1964.

Beesly, Patrick. *Room 40: British Naval Intelligence, 1914–1918.* New York: Harcourt-Brace, 1982.

Benson, Robert Louis and Michael Warner, eds. *Venona: Soviet Espionage and the American Response, 1937–1957.* Washington, D.C.: National Security Agency and Central Intelligence Agency.

Bernikow, Louise. *Abel.* New York: Ballantine, 1970.

Blitzer, Wolf. *Territory of Lies: The Exclusive Story of Jonathan Jay Pollard, The American Who Spied for Israel and How He Was Betrayed.* New York: Harper and Row, 1989.

Boyle, Andrew. *The Fourth Man.* New York: Dial Books, 1979.

Brown, Anthony Cave. *Bodyguard of Lies.* New York: Harper and Row, 1975.

Burleson, Clyde W. *The Jennifer Project.* Englewood Cliffs, New Jersey: Prentice Hall, 1977.

Burrows, William E. *Deep Black: The Startling Truth behind America's Top-Secret Spy Satellites.* New York: Berkley, 1986.

Calvocoressi, Peter. *Top Secret Ultra.* New York: Ballantine, 1980.

Carlisle, Rodney and Dominic J. Monetta. *Brandy: Our Man in Acapulco.* Denton, Texas: University of North Texas Press, 1999.

Casey, William J. *The Secret War Against Hitler.* Washington, D.C.: Regnery Publishing, 1988.

Collier, Basil. *Hidden Weapons: Allied Secret or Undercover Services in World War II.* London: Hamish Hamilton, 1982.

Deakin, F. W. and G. R. Storry. *The Case of Richard Sorge.* London: Chatto and Windus, 1960.

Donovan, James B. *Strangers on a Bridge: The Case of Colonel Abel.* New York: Atheneum, 1964.

Dorwart, Jeffery M. *The Office of Naval Intelligence: The Birth of America's First Intelligence Agency, 1865–1918.* Annapolis, Maryland: Naval Institute Press, 1979.

Drea, Edward J. *MacArthur's Ultra: Codebreaking and the War against Japan, 1942–1945.* Lawrence, Kansas: University of Kansas, 1992.

Dulles, Allen W. *Great True Spy Stories.* New York: Ballantine Books, 1968.

———. *The Craft of Intelligence.* New York: Harper and Row, 1965.

Dunlop, Richard. *Behind Japanese Lines: With the OSS in Burma.* New York: Rand McNally & Co., 1979.

———. *Donovan: America's Master Spy.* New York: Rand McNally & Co., 1982.

Early, Pete. *Family of Spies: Inside the John Walker Spy Ring.* New York: Bantam Books, 1988.

Fischer, Benjamin (ed.) *At Cold War's End: U.S. Intelligence on the Soviet Union and Eastern Europe, 1989-1991.* Washington: Central Intelligence Agency, 1999.

Gellman, Irwin F. *Secret Affairs: Franklin Roosevelt, Cordell Hull and Sumner Welles.* Baltimore, Maryland: Johns Hopkins University Press, 1995.

Gibney, Frank, ed. *The Penkovskiy Papers.* New York: Doubleday, 1965.

Grose, Peter. *Gentleman Spy: The Life of Allen Dulles.* New York: Houghton Mifflin, 1994.

Haines, Gerald K. and Robert E. Leggett, eds. *CIA's Analysis of the Soviet Union, 1947–1991, a Documentary Collection.* Center for the Study of Intelligence, CIA, 2001.

Harris, Ruth. "The 'Magic' Leak of 1941 and Japanese-American Relations," *Pacific Historical Review*, Vol 50, No. 1, February 1981, pgs. 77–96.

Haynes, John E. *Venona: Decoding Soviet Espionage in America.* New Haven, Conneticut.: Yale University Press, 2000.

Howe, Ellic. *The Black Game: British Subversive Operations Against the Germans During the Second World War.* London: Michael Joseph, 1982.

Jensen, Joan M. *Army Surveillance in America, 1775–1980.* New Haven, Connecticut: Yale University Press, 1991.

Kahn, David. *The Codebreakers.* New York: Signet, 1973.

———. *Hitler's Spies: German Military Intelligence in World War II.* New York: Macmillan, 1978.

Kane, Harnett T. *Spies for the Blue and Grey.* Garden City, NJ: Hanover House, 1954.

Kessler, Ronald. *The Spy in the Russian Club.* New York: Simon and Schuster, 1990.

Knott, Stephen F. *Secret and Sanctioned: Covert Operations and the American Presidency.* New York: Oxford University Press, 1996.

Landau, Henry. *The Enemy Within: The Inside Story of German Sabotage in America.* New York: Putnam, 1937.

Lewin, Ronald. *Ultra Goes to War: The First Account of World War II's Greatest Secret Based on Official Documents.* New York: McGraw Hill, 1978.

Lewis, Ronald. *The American Magic: Codes and Ciphers in the Defeat of Japan.* New York: Penguin, 1983.

Lewis, S. J. *Jedburgh Team Operations in Support of the 12th Army Group, August 1944.* Fort Leavenworth, Kansas: Combat Studies Institute, 1991.

Lindsey, Robert. *The Falcon and the Snowman: A True Story of Friendship and Espionage.* New York: Simon and Schuster, 1979.

———. *The Flight of the Falcon.* New York: Simon and Schuster, 1983.

Lockhart, Robin Bruce. *Reilly: Ace of Spies.* New York: Penguin, 1984.

Lowenthal, Mark. *Intelligence: From Secrets to Policy.* Washington: CQ Press, 2000.

Maas, Peter. *Killer Spy: The Inside Story of the FBI's Pursuit and Capture of Aldrich Ames, America's Deadliest Spy.* New York: Warner Books, 1995.

MacIntosh, Elizabeth. *Sisterhood of Spies: The Women of the OSS.* Thorndike, Maine: G.K.Hall, 2000.

Marchetti, Victor and John D. Marks. *The CIA and the Cult of Intelligence.* New York: Knopf, 1974.

Martin, David C. *Wilderness of Mirrors.* New York: Ballentine, 1981.

Masterman, J. C. *The Double-Cross System.* New Haven: Yale University Press, 1972.

Montagu, Ewen. *The Man Who Never Was.* New York: Lippincott, 1953 (reprinted: New York: Scholastic Book Services, 1967).

Morris, Boris. *My Ten Years as a Counterspy.* New York: Viking, 1959.

Moss, Norman. *Klaus Fuchs, A Biography: The Man Who Stole the Atom Bomb.* New York: St. Martins, 1987.

Murphy, David, et al. *Battleground Berlin: CIA vs. KGB in the Cold War.* New Haven, Conneticut.: Yale University Press, 1997.

Peebles, Curtis. *Dark Eagles: A History of Top Secret U.S. Aircraft Programs.* Novato, California: Presidio Press, 1995.

Penrose, Barrie and Simon Freeman. *Conspiracy of Silence: The Secret Life of Anthony Blunt.* New York: Vintage, 1986.

Persico, Joseph. *Piercing the Reich: The Penetration of Nazi Germany by American Secret Agents During WWII.* New York: Viking Press, 1979.

———. *Roosevelt's Secret War: FDR and World War II Espionage.* New York: Random House, 2001.

Petersen, Neal H., ed. *From Hitler's Doorstep: The Wartime Intelligence Reports of Allen Dulles, 1942–1945.* University Park, Pennsylvania: Pennsylvania State University Press, 1996.

Philby, Kim. *My Silent War.* New York: Ballantine Books, 1968.

Pincher, Chapman. *Too Secret, Too Long.* New York: St. Martins, 1984.

———. *Their Trade is Treachery.* London: Sidgwick and Jackson, 1981.

Powers, Francis Gary. *Operation Overflight*. New York: Holt, Rinehart and Winston, 1970.

Powers, Thomas. *The Man Who Kept the Secrets: Richard Helms and the CIA*. New York: Knopf, 1979.

———. *Heisenberg's War: The Secret Story of the German Bomb*. New York: Knopf, 1993.

Prados, John. *Combined Fleet Decoded: Secret History of American Intelligence and the Japanese Navy in World War II*. New York: Random House, 1995.

———. *Presidents' Secret Wars: CIA and Pentagon Covert Operations From World War II through Iranscam*. New York: William Morrow, 1986.

Prange, Gordon W. with Donald M. Goldstein and Katherine V. Dillon. *Target Tokyo: The Story of the Sorge Spy Ring*.

Radosh, Ronald and Joyce Milton. *The Rosenberg File: A Search for the Truth*. New York: Vintage, 1984.

Ranelagh, John. *The Agency: The Rise and Decline of the CIA*. New York: Simon and Schuster, 1986.

Read, Anthony and David Fisher. *Operation Lucy: Most Secret Spy Ring of the Second World War*. New York: Coward, McCann & Geoghegan, Inc., 1981.

Reilly, Sidney. *Britain's Master Spy: His Own Story*. New York: Dorset Press, 1985.

Robbins, Christopher. *Air America*. New York: Avon, 1985.

Sammon, Bill. *Fighting Back: The War on Terrorism from Inside the Bush White House*. Washington, D.C.: Regnery, 2002.

Shvets, Yuri B. *Washington Station: My Life as a KGB Spy in America*. New York: Simon and Schuster, 1995.

Smith, Arthur L. *Hitler's Gold: The Story of the Nazi War Loot*. Oxford: Berg Publishers, 1989.

Smith, Warner. *Covert Warrior: A Vietnam Memoir*. New York: Simon and Schuster Pocket Books, 1996.

Stevenson, William. *A Man Called Intrepid: The Secret War.* New York: Harcourt Brace Jovanovich, 1976.

Sudoplatov, Pavel and Anatoli Sudoplatov. *Special Tasks: The Memoirs of an Unwanted Witness, A Soviet Spymaster.* Boston, Massachusetts: Little Brown, 1994.

Sullivan, William C., with Bill Brown. *The Bureau. My Thirty Years in Hoover's FBI.* New York: W.W. Norton, 1979.

Suvarov, Viktor. *Inside the Aquarium: The Making of a Top Soviet Spy.* New York: Macmillan, 1986.

Talbert, Ray. *Negative Intelligence: The Army and the American Left, 1917–1941.* Jackson, Mississippi: University of Mississippi Press, 1991.

Tuchman, Barbara W. *The Zimmermann Telegram.* New York: Random House, 1966.

Turnbull, Malcolm. *The Spycatcher Trial.* Boston, Massachusetts: Salem House Publishers, 1988.

Varner, Roy and Wayne Collier. *A Matter of Risk: The Incredible Inside Story of the CIA's Hughes Glomar Explorer Mission to Raise a Russian Submarine.* New York: Ballantine, 1978.

Vise, David A. *The Bureau and the Mole.* New York: Grove Press, 2002.

Volkman, Ernest, and Blaine Baggett. *Secret Intelligence: The Inside Story of America's Espionage Empire.* New York: Berkley Books, 1991.

Warner, Michael. *Central Intelligence: Origin and Evolution.* Washington: Center for Intelligence, 2001.

Weinsten, Allen. *Perjury: The Hiss-Chambers Case.* New York: Random House, 1997.

Weinstein, Allen, and Alexander Vassiliev. *The Haunted Wood: Soviet Espionage in America—The Stalin Era.* New York: Random House, 1999.

West, Nigel. *The Circus: MI-5 Operations, 1945–1972.* Briarcliff Manor, NY: Stein and Day, 1983.

West, Rebecca. *The New Meaning of Treason.* New York: Viking, 1965.

Williams, Robert C. *Klaus Fuchs, Atom Spy*. Cambridge, Massachusetts: Harvard University Press, 1987.

Willoughby, Charles A. *Shanghai Conspiracy: The Sorge Spy Ring*. New York: Dutton, 1952.

Winterbotham, F. W. *The Ultra Secret*. New York: Harper and Row, 1974.

Wise, David. *Nightmover: How Aldrich Ames Sold the CIA to the KGB for $4.6 Million*. New York: HarperCollins, 1995.

Wohlstetter, Roberta. *Pearl Harbor: Warning and Decision*. Stanford, California: Stanford University Press, 1962.

Woodward, Bob. *Veil: The Secret Wars of the CIA, 1981–1987*. New York: Simon and Schuster, 1987.

Wright, Peter. *Spycatcher: The Candid Autobiography of a Senior Intelligence Officer*. New York: Viking, 1987.

Wynne, Greville. *Contact on Gorky Street*. New York: Atheneum, 1968.

Yardley, Herbert O. *The American Black Chamber*. New York: Ballantine Books, 1984.

# Index

# P-Q

# R